Frommer's

PORTABLE

Puerto Vallarta, Manzanillo & Guadalajara

4th Edition

by David Baird & Lynne Bairstow

Here's what critics say about Frommer's:

"Amazingly easy to use. Very portable, very complete."

—*Booklist*

"Detailed, accurate, and easy-to-read information for all price ranges."

—*Glamour Magazine*

Wiley Publishing, Inc.

Published by:

WILEY PUBLISHING, INC.
111 River St.
Hoboken, NJ 07030

ISBN 0-7645-3818-7
ISSN 1093-6998

Editor: Kendra L. Falkenstein
Production Editor: Blair J. Pottenger
Photo Editor: Richard Fox
Cartographer: John Decamillis
Production by Wiley Indianapolis Composition Services

For information on our other products and services or to obtain technical support, please contact our Customer Care Department within the U.S. at 800-762-2974, outside the U.S. at 317-572-3993 or fax 317-572-4002.

Wiley also publishes its books in a variety of electronic formats. Some content that appears in print may not be available in electronic formats.

Manufactured in the United States of America

5 4 3 2 1

Contents

Appendix 190

Index 199

List of Maps

About the Authors

David Baird is a writer, editor, and translator who doesn't much like writing about himself in the third person (too close to being an obituary). Texan by birth, Mexican by disposition, he has lived several years in different parts of Mexico following his interests, which include food, drink, and the afternoon siesta. Now based in Austin, Texas, he spends as much time in Mexico as possible. At home, his hobbies include painting, scraping, mowing, patching dry wall, and extemporaneous engineering.

For **Lynne Bairstow,** Mexico has become more home than her native United States. After living in Puerto Vallarta for most of the past 11 years, she's developed an appreciation and a true love of this country and its complex, colorful culture. Her travel articles on Mexico have appeared in the *New York Times,* the *San Francisco Chronicle,* the *Los Angeles Times, Frommer's Budget Travel* magazine, and *Alaska Airlines Magazine.* In 2000, Lynne was awarded the Pluma de Plata, a top honor granted by the Mexican government to foreign writers, for her work in the Frommer's guidebook to Puerto Vallarta.

An Invitation to the Reader

In researching this book, we discovered many wonderful places—hotels, restaurants, shops, and more. We're sure you'll find others. Please tell us about them, so we can share the information with your fellow travelers in upcoming editions. If you were disappointed with a recommendation, we'd love to know that, too. Please write to:

Frommer's Portable Puerto Vallarta, Manzanillo & Guadalajara, 4th Edition
Wiley Publishing, Inc. • 111 River St. • Hoboken, NJ 07030

An Additional Note

Please be advised that travel information is subject to change at any time—and this is especially true of prices. We therefore suggest that you write or call ahead for confirmation when making your travel plans. The authors, editors, and publisher cannot be held responsible for the experiences of readers while traveling. Your safety is important to us, however, so we encourage you to stay alert and be aware of your surroundings. Keep a close eye on cameras, purses, and wallets, all favorite targets of thieves and pickpockets.

Frommer's Star Ratings, Icons & Abbreviations

Every hotel, restaurant, and attraction listing in this guide has been ranked for quality, value, service, amenities, and special features using a **star-rating system.** In country, state, and regional guides, we also rate towns and regions to help you narrow down your choices and budget your time accordingly. Hotels and restaurants are rated on a scale of zero (recommended) to three stars (exceptional). Attractions, shopping, nightlife, towns, and regions are rated according to the following scale: zero stars (recommended), one star (highly recommended), two stars (very highly recommended), and three stars (must-see).

In addition to the star-rating system, we also use **seven feature icons** that point you to the great deals, in-the-know advice, and unique experiences that separate travelers from tourists. Throughout the book, look for:

Finds	Special finds—those places only insiders know about
Fun Fact	Fun facts—details that make travelers more informed and their trips more fun
Kids	Best bets for kids and advice for the whole family
Moments	Special moments—those experiences that memories are made of
Overrated	Places or experiences not worth your time or money
Tips	Insider tips—great ways to save time and money
Value	Great values—where to get the best deals

The following abbreviations are used for credit cards:

AE	American Express	DISC	Discover	V	Visa
DC	Diners Club	MC	MasterCard		

Frommers.com

Now that you have the guidebook to a great trip, visit our website at **www.frommers.com** for travel information on more than 3,000 destinations. With features updated regularly, we give you instant access to the most current trip-planning information available. At Frommers.com, you'll also find the best prices on airfares, accommodations, and car rentals—and you can even book travel online through our travel booking partners. At Frommers.com, you'll also find the following:

- Online updates to our most popular guidebooks
- Vacation sweepstakes and contest giveaways
- Newsletter highlighting the hottest travel trends
- Online travel message boards with featured travel discussions

1

Planning Your Trip to Mid-Pacific Mexico

Along the Pacific coast of Mexico, palm-studded jungles sweep down to meet the deep blue of the Pacific Ocean, providing spectacular backdrops for three modern resort cities, as well as smaller coastal villages. This lovely stretch of coastline, which extends from Puerto Vallarta down to Manzanillo, is known as the Mexican Riviera. Modern hotels, easy air access, and a growing array of activities and adventure tourism attractions have transformed this region of Mexico into one of the country's premier resort areas.

A little advance planning can make the difference between a good trip and a great trip. When should you go? What's the best way to get there? How much should you plan on spending? What festivals or special events will be taking place during your visit? What safety or health precautions are advised? We'll answer these and other questions for you in this chapter.

In addition to these basics, I highly recommend taking a little time to learn a little about the culture and traditions of Mexico. (For instance, try reading some literature by Mexican authors such as Octavio Paz's *Labyrinth of Solitude* or Carlos Fuentes). It can make the difference between simply "getting away" and truly adding understanding to the experience.

1 The Region in Brief

Puerto Vallarta, with its traditional Mexican architecture and gold-sand beaches bordered by jungle-covered mountains, is currently the second most visited resort in Mexico (trailing only Cancún). Vallarta (as the locals refer to it) maintains a small-town charm despite sophisticated hotels, great restaurants, a thriving arts community, an active nightlife, and a growing variety of ecotourism attractions. **Mazatlán** may be the greatest resort value in Mexico, luring visitors with its exceptional fishing, historic downtown, and new championship golf facilities. **Manzanillo** is surprisingly relaxed, even

Mexico's Mid-Pacific Coast

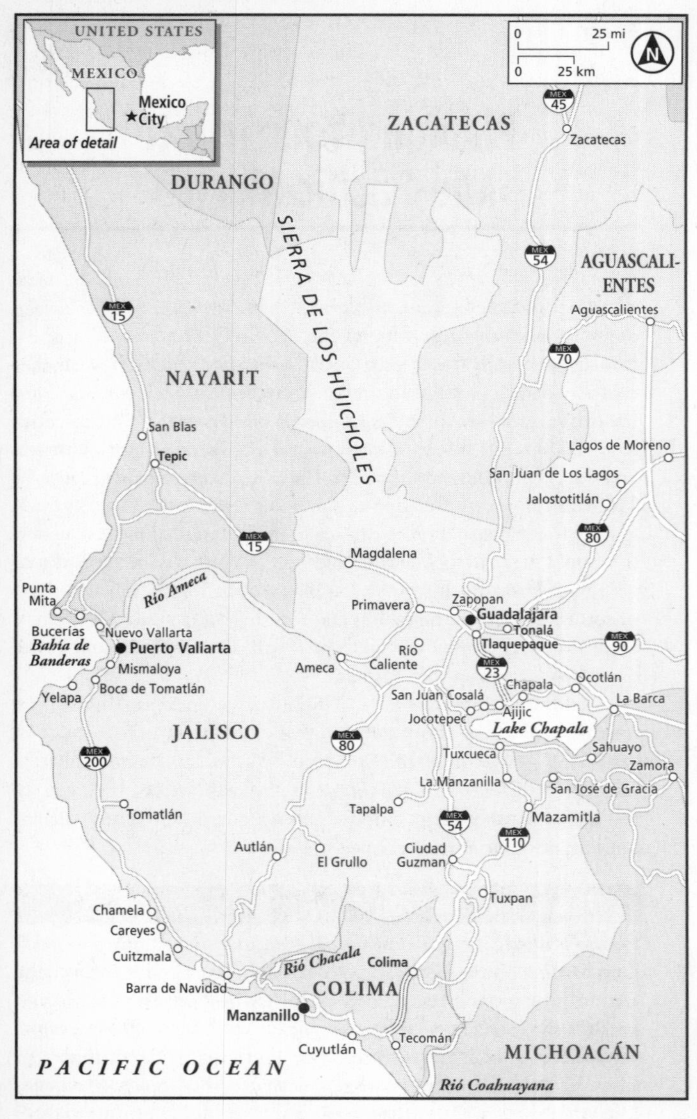

though it's one of Mexico's most active commercial ports; it also offers great fishing and golf. And along the **Costa Alegre,** between Puerto Vallarta and Manzanillo, pristine coves are home to unique luxury and value-priced resorts that cater to travelers seeking seclusion and privacy. Just north of Puerto Vallarta is **Punta Mita,** home of the first Four Seasons resort in Latin America and a Jack Nicklaus golf course. With four more luxury resorts—including one by Rosewood—and two more golf courses on tap, it is emerging as Mexico's most exclusive luxury address.

If you're looking for a more "authentic" Mexican experience, head inland over the mountains to **Guadalajara,** Mexico's second-largest city and the birthplace of many of the country's traditions.

International airports at all three cities make getting to each easier; Guadalajara and Puerto Vallarta have the most frequent connections. Distances in the region are easily managed by car; most drives between major points take from 45 minutes to 6 hours on roads that are in generally good condition.

If you decide to visit this region, you have several choices about how to allot your time. Most people pick one coastal resort and stay there for the duration of their vacations, but, if you wish, you can easily enjoy more than one resort during your time in Mexico.

Barra de Navidad, for example, is so close to Manzanillo that it's easy to combine several days there with a stay in Manzanillo. From Puerto Vallarta, Bucerías, Yelapa, San Sebastian, and San Blas all offer a change of pace and scenery. Hotelito Desconocido and Las Alamandas are both closer to Puerto Vallarta, with the remainder of the luxury coastal resorts between Manzanillo and Puerto Vallarta, nearer to Manzanillo. There are more frequent flights, however, to and from Puerto Vallarta, and many people find that Puerto Vallarta provides the best access to the coastal area.

2 Visitor Information

SOURCES OF INFORMATION

The **Mexico Hot Line** (**© 800/44-MEXICO**) is an excellent source for general information and for answers to the most commonly asked questions. They also fulfill requests for brochures on the country. More information about Mexico is available from the official **Mexican Tourism Board**'s website: **www.visitmexico.com**.

The **U.S. State Department** (**© 202/647-5225** for travel information and Overseas Citizens Services) offers a Consular Information Sheet on Mexico, with a compilation of safety, medical, driving, and general travel information gleaned from reports by official U.S. State Department offices in Mexico. You can also request the Consular Information Sheet by fax (© 202/647-3000). The State Department is also on the Internet; check out http://travel.state.gov/mexico.html for the Consular Information Sheet on Mexico and http://travel.state.gov/travel_warnings.html for other Consular Information sheets and travel warnings. Another source for information is the State Department's "Background Notes" series home page at www.state.gov/r/pa/ei/bgn.

The **Centers for Disease Control Hotline** (© **800/311-3435** or 404/639-3534) is another source for medical information affecting travelers to Mexico and elsewhere. The center's website, www.cdc.gov, provides lengthy information on health issues for specific countries. The new **CDC Travelers' Health** toll-free hotline number is © **877/FYI-TRIP.** The toll-free fax number for requesting information is © 888/232-3299, though any information available by fax is also available on the website, www.cdc.gov/travel. Here, you'll also find links to health resources for people traveling with children or with special needs, as well as tips on safe food and water. The U.S. State Department offers medical information for Americans traveling abroad at http://travel.state.gov/medical.html. This site provides general information and a list of air ambulance services.

MEXICO TOURISM BOARD OFFICES

The **Mexico Tourism Board** has several offices in major North American cities, in addition to their main office in Mexico City (© **55/5203-1103**).

United States: Chicago, IL (© **312/606-9252**); Houston, TX (© **713/772-2581,** ext. 105); Los Angeles, CA (© **213/351-2069**); Miami, FL (© **305/718-4095**); New York, NY (© **212/821-0304**); and the Mexican Embassy Tourism Delegate, 1911 Pennsylvania Ave., Washington, DC 20005 (© **202/728-1750**).

Canada: Montréal, QC (© **514/871-1052**); Toronto, ON (© **416/925-0704**); Vancouver, BC (© **604/669-2845**). The embassy office is at 1500-45 O'Connor St., Ottawa, ON, K1P 1A4 (© **613/233-8988**).

3 Entry Requirements & Customs

ENTRY REQUIREMENTS

All travelers to Mexico are required to present **proof of citizenship,** such as an original birth certificate with a raised seal, a valid

Destination Mid-Pacific Mexico: Red Alert Checklist

- Did you check to see if there any health concerns in the area you'll be travelling to? Check the **Centers for Disease Control** (✆ **800/311-3435**; www.cdc.gov/travel) for the most up-to-date information.
- If you purchased traveler's checks, have you recorded the check numbers, and stored the documentation separately from the checks?
- Did you stop the newspaper and mail delivery, and leave a set of keys with someone reliable?
- Did you pack your camera and an extra set of camera batteries, and purchase enough film?
- Do you have a safe, accessible place to store money?
- Did you bring emergency drug prescriptions and extra glasses and/or contact lenses?
- Did you find out your daily ATM withdrawal limit?
- Do you have your credit card pin numbers? Is there a daily withdrawal limit on credit card cash advances?
- If you have an e-ticket, do you have documentation?
- Did you leave a copy of your itinerary with someone at home?
- Did you check to see if any travel advisories have been issued by the **U.S. State Department (http://travel.state.gov/travel_warnings.html)** regarding your destination?
- Do you have the address and phone number of your country's embassy with you?

passport, or naturalization papers. Those using a birth certificate should also have current photo identification such as a driver's license or official ID. Those whose last name on the birth certificate is different from their current name (women using a married name, for example) should also bring a photo identification card *and* legal proof of the name change, such as the *original* marriage license or certificate. This proof of citizenship may also be requested when you want to reenter either the U.S. or Mexico. Note that photocopies are *not* acceptable. When reentering the U.S., you must prove both your citizenship and your identification, so always take a picture ID, such as a driver's license or, better yet, a valid passport. Birth certificates alone will enable you to enter Mexico but will not enable you to reenter the U.S.

Note: Although the U.S. State Department endorses these entry requirements outlined, some readers have reported problems trying to enter Mexico using only a birth certificate. To ensure against any needless delay at immigration, make sure you follow the requirements to the letter—the birth certificate must be the *original* version with the raised seal. Or, avoid any potential problem by carrying your U.S. passport.

You must also carry a **Mexican Tourist Permit (FMT),** which is issued free of charge by Mexican border officials after proof of citizenship is accepted. (These forms are also provided by the airlines.) The FMT is more important than a passport in Mexico, so guard it carefully. If you lose it, you may not be permitted to leave the country until you can replace it—a bureaucratic hassle that can take anywhere from a few hours to a week. (If you do lose your tourist permit, get a police report from local authorities indicating that your documents were stolen; having one *might* lessen the hassle of exiting the country without all your identification.) You should also contact the nearest consular office to report the stolen papers so that they can issue a reentry document.

A tourist permit can be issued for up to 180 days, although your stay south of the border may be shorter than that. Sometimes officials don't ask—they just stamp a time limit, so be sure to say "6 months" (or at least twice as long as you intend to stay). If you decide to extend your stay, you may request that additional time be added to your FMT at an official immigration office in Mexico.

Note that children under age 18 traveling without parents or with only one parent must have a notarized letter from the absent parent or parents authorizing the travel.

LOST DOCUMENTS

To replace a lost passport, contact your embassy or nearest consular agent (see "Fast Facts: Mexico," later in this chapter). You must establish a record of your citizenship and also fill out a form requesting another Mexican Tourist Permit (assuming it, too, was lost). Without the tourist permit, you can't leave the country, and without an affidavit affirming your passport request and citizenship, you may have problems at Customs when you try to get back home, so it's important to clear everything up before trying to leave. Mexican Customs may, however, accept the police report of the loss of the tourist permit and allow you to leave.

Tips **Passport Savvy**

Allow plenty of time before your trip to apply for a passport; processing normally takes 3 weeks but can take longer during busy periods (especially spring). And keep in mind that if you need a passport in a hurry, you'll pay a higher processing fee. When traveling, safeguard your passport in an inconspicuous, inaccessible place like a money belt and keep a copy of the critical pages with your passport number in a separate place. If you lose your passport, visit the nearest consulate of your native country as soon as possible for a replacement.

CUSTOMS

WHAT YOU CAN BRING INTO MEXICO

When you enter Mexico, Customs officials will be tolerant as long as you have no illegal drugs or firearms. You're allowed to bring in two cartons of cigarettes, or 50 cigars, plus a kilogram (2.2 lb.) of smoking tobacco; the liquor allowance is two 1-liter bottles of anything, wine or hard liquor; you are also allowed 12 rolls of film. A laptop computer, camera equipment, and sporting equipment (golf clubs, scuba gear, a bicycle) that could feasibly be used during your stay are also allowed. The underlying guideline is that they will disallow anything that they feel you will be attempting to resell in Mexico.

WHAT YOU CAN TAKE HOME FROM MEXICO

Returning **U.S. citizens** who have been away for at least 48 hours are allowed to bring back, once every 30 days, $800 worth of merchandise duty-free. You'll be charged a flat rate of 4% duty on the next $1,000 worth of purchases. Be sure to have your receipts handy. On mailed gifts, the duty-free limit is $200. With some exceptions, you cannot bring fresh fruits and vegetables into the United States. For specifics on what you can bring back, download the invaluable free pamphlet *Know Before You Go* online at www.customs.gov. (Click on "Traveler Information," then "Know Before You Go.") Or contact the **U.S. Customs Service,** 1300 Pennsylvania Ave., NW, Washington, DC 20229 (© **877/287-8867**) and request the pamphlet.

For a clear summary of **Canadian** rules, write for the booklet *I Declare,* issued by the **Canada Customs and Revenue Agency** (© **800/461-9999** in Canada, or 204/983-3500; www.ccra-adrc.gc.ca). Canada allows its citizens a C$750 exemption, and you're allowed to bring back duty-free one carton of cigarettes, one can of tobacco, 40 imperial ounces of liquor, and 50 cigars. In addition, you're allowed to mail gifts to Canada valued at less than C$60 each day, provided they're unsolicited and don't contain alcohol or tobacco (write on the package "Unsolicited gift, under $60 value"). All valuables should be declared on the Y-38 form before departure from Canada, including serial numbers of valuables you already own, such as expensive foreign cameras. ***Note:*** The C$750 exemption can only be used once a year and only after an absence of 7 days.

U.K. citizens returning from **a non-EU country** have a customs allowance of: 200 cigarettes; 50 cigars; 250 grams of smoking tobacco; 2 liters of still table wine; 1 liter of spirits or strong liqueurs (over 22% volume); 2 liters of fortified wine, sparkling wine, or other liqueurs; 60cc (ml) of perfume; 250cc (ml) of toilet water; and £145 worth of all other goods, including gifts and souvenirs. Individuals under 17 cannot have the tobacco or alcohol allowance. For more information, contact **HM Customs & Excise** at ✆ **0845/010-9000** (from outside the U.K., 020/8929-0152), or consult their website at www.hmce.gov.uk.

The duty-free allowance in **Australia** is A$400 or, for those under 18, A$200. Citizens can bring in 250 cigarettes or 250 grams of loose tobacco, and 1,125 milliliters of alcohol. If you're returning with valuables you already own, such as foreign-made cameras, you should file form B263. For more information, call the **Australian Customs Service** at ✆ **1300/363-263,** or log on to www.customs.gov.au.

The duty-free allowance for **New Zealand** is NZ$700. Citizens over 17 can bring in 200 cigarettes, 50 cigars, or 250 grams of tobacco (or a mixture of all three if their combined weight doesn't exceed 250g); plus 4.5 liters of wine and beer, or 1.125 liters of liquor. New Zealand currency does not carry import or export restrictions. Fill out a certificate of export, listing the valuables you are taking out of the country; that way, you can bring them back without paying duty. Most questions are answered in a free pamphlet available at New Zealand consulates and Customs offices: *New Zealand Customs Guide for Travellers, Notice no. 4.* For more information, contact **New Zealand Customs,** The Customhouse, 17–21 Whitmore St., Box 2218, Wellington (✆ **04/473-6099** or 0800/428-786; www.customs.govt.nz).

GOING THROUGH CUSTOMS

Mexican Customs inspection has been streamlined. At most points of entry, tourists are requested to press a button in front of what looks like a traffic signal, which alternates on touch between red and green signals. Green light and you go through without inspection; red light and your luggage or car may be inspected briefly or thoroughly. If you have an unusual amount of luggage or an oversized piece, you may be subject to inspection despite the traffic signal routine.

4 Money

CASH/CURRENCY

The currency in Mexico is the Mexican **peso.** Paper currency comes in denominations of 20, 50, 100, 200, and 500 pesos. Coins come in denominations of 1, 2, 5, 10, and 20 pesos, and 50 centavos (100 centavos equal 1 peso). The current exchange rate for the U.S. dollar is around 10 pesos; at that rate, an item that costs 10 pesos would be equivalent to US$1.

Getting change continues to be a problem in Mexico. Small-denomination bills and coins are hard to come by, so start collecting them early in your trip and continue as you travel. Shopkeepers everywhere seem always to be out of change and small bills; that's doubly true in a market.

Tips A Few Words About Prices

The peso's value continues to fluctuate—at press time, it was roughly 10 pesos to the dollar. Prices in this book *(which are always given in U.S. dollars)* have been converted to U.S. dollars at 10 pesos to the dollar. Most hotels in Mexico—with the exception of places that receive little foreign tourism—quote prices in U.S. dollars. Thus, currency fluctuations are unlikely to affect the prices charged by most hotels.

Mexico has a **value-added tax** of 15% (*Impuesto al Valor Agregado,* or IVA, pronounced "ee-bah") on most everything, including restaurant meals, bus tickets, and souvenirs. Hotels charge the usual 15% IVA, plus a locally administered bed tax of 2% (in many but not all areas), for a total of 17%. IVA will not necessarily be included in the prices quoted by hotels and restaurants. You may find that upper-end properties (three stars and above) quote prices without IVA included, while lesser-price hotels include IVA in their quotes. Always ask to see a printed price sheet, and always ask if the tax is included.

EXCHANGING MONEY

It's a good idea to exchange at least some money—just enough to cover airport incidentals and transportation to your hotel—before you leave home, so you can avoid lines at airport ATMs (automated teller machines). You can exchange money at your local American Express or Thomas Cook office or your bank. If you're far away from a bank with currency-exchange services, **American Express** offers travelers checks and foreign currency, though with a $15 order fee and additional shipping costs, at www.americanexpress.com or **© 800/807-6233.**

The rate of exchange fluctuates a tiny bit daily, so you probably are better off not exchanging too much of your currency at once. Don't forget, however, to have enough pesos to carry you over a weekend or Mexican holiday, when banks are closed. In general, avoid carrying the U.S. $100 bill. It is the most commonly counterfeited bill in Mexico, and therefore, the most difficult to exchange, especially in smaller towns. Because small bills and coins in pesos are hard to come by in Mexico, the U.S. $1 bill is very useful for tipping.

Exchange houses *(casas de cambio)* are generally more convenient than banks because they have more locations and longer hours; the rate of exchange may be the same as a bank or only slightly lower. ***Note:*** Before leaving a bank or exchange-house window, always count your change in front of the teller before the next client steps up.

Large airports have currency-exchange counters that often stay open whenever flights are arriving or departing. Though convenient, these generally do not offer the most favorable rates.

A hotel's exchange desk commonly pays less favorable rates than banks; however, when the currency is in a state of flux, higher-priced hotels are known to pay higher than bank rates, in their effort to attract dollars. ***The bottom line:*** It pays to shop around, but in almost all cases, you'll receive a better exchange by changing money first, then paying for goods or services in pesos, rather than by paying dollars directly to an establishment.

BANKS

Banks in Mexico are rapidly expanding and improving services. New hours tend to be from 9am until 5 or 6pm, with many open for at least a half day on Saturday, and some even offering limited hours on Sunday. The exchange of dollars, which used to be limited until noon, can now be accommodated anytime during business

Money Matters

Note: The universal currency sign ($) is used to indicate pesos in Mexico. The use of this symbol in this book, however, denotes U.S. currency. Many establishments dealing with tourists, especially in coastal resort areas, quote prices in dollars. To avoid confusion, they use the abbreviations "Dlls." for dollars and "M.N." (moneda nacional, or national currency) for pesos. All dollar equivalencies in this book were based on an exchange rate of 10 pesos per dollar.

hours in the larger resorts and cities. Some, but not all, banks charge a service fee of about 1% to exchange traveler's checks. However, most purchases can be paid for directly with traveler's checks at the stated exchange rate of the establishment. Don't even bother with personal checks drawn on a U.S. bank—although theoretically they may be cashed, it's not without weeks of delay, and the bank will wait for your check to clear before giving you your money.

ATMS

Travelers to Mexico can also access money from ATMs, now available in most major cities and resort areas in Mexico. Most machines offer Spanish/English menus and dispense pesos, but some offer the option of withdrawing dollars. The **Cirrus** (**© 800/424-7787;** www.mastercard.com) and **PLUS** (**© 800/843-7587;** www.visa.com) networks span the globe; look at the back of your bank card to see which network you're on, then call or check online for ATM locations at your destination. Be sure you know your personal identification number (PIN) before you leave home and be sure to find out your daily withdrawal limit before you depart. Also keep in mind that many banks impose a fee every time a card is used at a different bank's ATM, and that fee can be higher for international transactions (up to $5 or more) than for domestic ones (where they're rarely more than $1.50). On top of this, the bank from which you withdraw cash may charge its own fee. However, the exchange rate is generally more favorable than one found at a currency house. To compare banks' ATM fees within the U.S., use www.bankrate.com. For international withdrawal fees, ask your bank.

You can also get cash advances on your credit card at an ATM. Keep in mind that credit card companies try to protect themselves from theft by limiting the funds someone can withdraw outside

Tips Small Change

When you change money, ask for some small bills or loose change. Petty cash will come in handy for tipping and public transportation. Consider keeping the change separate from your larger bills, so that it's readily accessible and you'll be less of a target for theft.

their home country, so call your credit card company before you leave home.

TRAVELER'S CHECKS

Traveler's checks are something of an anachronism from the days before the ATM made cash accessible at any time. Traveler's checks used to be the only sound alternative to traveling with dangerously large amounts of cash. They were as reliable as currency, but, unlike cash, could be replaced if lost or stolen.

These days, traveler's checks are less necessary because most cities have 24-hour ATMs that allow you to withdraw small amounts of cash as needed. However, keep in mind that you will likely be charged an ATM withdrawal fee if the bank is not your own, so if you're withdrawing money every day, you might be better off with traveler's checks—provided that you don't mind showing identification every time you want to cash one.

Traveler's checks are readily accepted nearly everywhere, but they can be difficult to cash on a weekend or holiday or in an out-of-the-way place. Their best value is their easy replacement in case of theft. Frequently in Mexico, a bank or establishment will provide a better rate for traveler's checks than for cash dollars.

If you choose to carry traveler's checks, be sure to keep a record of their serial numbers separate from your checks in the event that they are stolen or lost. You'll get a refund faster if you know the numbers.

CREDIT CARDS

Credit cards are a safe way to carry money; they provide a convenient record of all your expenses, and they generally offer good exchange rates (credit-card charges will be billed in pesos, then later converted into dollars by the bank issuing the credit card). You can also withdraw cash advances from your credit cards at banks or ATMs, provided you know your PIN. If you've forgotten yours, or didn't even know you had one, call the number on the back of your credit card and ask the bank to send it to you. It usually takes 5 to 7 business days, though some banks will provide the number over the phone if you tell them your mother's maiden name or some other personal information. Your credit card company will likely charge a commission (1% or 2%) on every foreign purchase you make, but don't sweat this small stuff; for most purchases, you'll still get the best deal with credit cards when you factor in things like ATM fees and higher traveler's check exchange rates.

You'll be able to charge most hotel, restaurant, and store purchases, as well as almost all airline tickets, on your credit card in Mexico, though you generally can't charge gasoline purchases. Visa, MasterCard, and American Express are the most accepted cards.

THEFT

Almost every credit-card company has an emergency toll-free number that you can call if your wallet or purse is stolen. They may be able to wire you a cash advance off your credit card immediately, and in many places, they can deliver an emergency credit card in a day or two. The issuing bank's toll-free number is usually on the back of the credit card—though of course that doesn't help you much if the card is stolen. The **toll-free information directory** will provide the number if you dial ✆ **800/555-1212.** From within Mexico, dial ✆ **001-880-555-1212**—this will not be a toll-free call, but it does provide you with access to this toll-free number. **Citicorp Visa**'s U.S. emergency number is ✆ **800/336-8472. American Express** cardholders and traveler's check holders should call ✆ **800/221-7282** for all money emergencies. **MasterCard** holders should call ✆ **800/307-7309.**

Tips **Dear Visa: I'm Off to Mexico!**

Some credit card companies recommend that you notify them of any impending trip abroad so that they don't become suspicious when the card is used numerous times in a foreign destination and block your charges. Even if you don't call your credit card company in advance, you can always call the card's toll-free emergency number if a charge is refused—a good reason to carry the phone number with you. But perhaps the most important lesson here is to carry more than one card with you on your trip; a card might not work for any number of reasons, so having a backup is the smart way to go.

If you choose to carry traveler's checks, be sure to keep a record of their serial numbers separate from your checks in the event that they are stolen or lost. You'll get a refund faster if you know the numbers.

Odds are that if your wallet is gone, the police won't be able to recover it for you. However, after you realize that it's gone and you cancel your credit cards, it is still worth informing them. Your credit card company or insurer may require a police report number. If you do lose your wallet, before panicking, retrace your steps—you'll be surprised at how many honest people are in Mexico and it is likely that you'll find someone trying to find you to return your wallet.

5 When to Go

TRAVEL SEASONS

Mexico has two principal travel seasons: high and low. High season begins around December 20 and continues through Easter, although in some places high season can begin as early as mid-November. Low season begins the day after Easter and continues through mid-December; during low season, prices may drop 20% to 50%. In beach destinations, the prices may also increase during the months of July and August, the traditional national summer vacation period. Prices in inland cities, such as Guadalajara, seldom fluctuate from high to low season, but may rise dramatically during Easter and Christmas weeks.

THE CLIMATE

From Puerto Vallarta south to Huatulco, Mexico offers one of the world's most perfect winter climates—dry and balmy with temperatures ranging from the 80s during the day to the 60s at night. From Puerto Vallarta south, you can swim year-round.

High mountains shield Pacific beaches from *nortes* (northers—freezing blasts out of Canada via the Texas Panhandle). The states of Jalisco and Colima, like most of Mexico, have the most rain May through September; the rainiest month is September. Tropical showers generally begin around 4 or 5pm and last a few hours. Though these rains can come on suddenly and be quite strong, they usually end just as fast and cool off the air for the evening.

HOLIDAYS & SPECIAL EVENTS

On national holidays, banks, stores, and businesses are closed; hotels fill up quickly; and transportation is crowded. Also note that Mexican governmental offices—including immigration—are all closed.

January

New Year's Day (Año Nuevo). National holiday. Parades, religious observances, parties, and fireworks welcome in the New Year everywhere. In traditional indigenous communities, new tribal leaders are inaugurated with colorful ceremonies rooted in the pre-Hispanic past. January 1.

Three Kings Day. Commemorates the Three Kings' bringing of gifts to the Christ Child. On this day, children receive gifts, much like the traditional gift-giving that accompanies Christmas in the United States. Friends and families gather to share the *Rosca de Reyes,* a special cake. Inside the cake there is a small doll representing the Christ Child; whoever receives the doll in his or her piece must host a tamales-and-atole party the next month. January 6.

February

Candlemas. Music, dances, processions, food, and other festivities lead up to a blessing of seed and candles, a ritual that mixes pre-Hispanic and European traditions marking the end of winter. All those who attended the Three Kings' Celebration reunite to share atole and tamales at a party hosted by the recipient of the doll found in the Rosca. February 2.

Carnaval. Carnaval takes place the 3 days preceding Ash Wednesday and the beginning of Lent. It is celebrated with special gusto in Mazatlán. Here, the celebration resembles New Orleans's Mardi Gras, with a festive atmosphere and parades. Transportation and hotels are packed, so it's best to make reservations 6 months in advance and arrive a couple of days ahead of the beginning of celebrations. In 2004, the dates are from February 20 to 22.

Ash Wednesday. The start of Lent and time of abstinence. It's a day of reverence nationwide, but some towns honor it with folk dancing and fairs. In 2004, the date is February 25.

March

Benito Juárez's Birthday. National holiday. March 21.

April

Holy Week. Celebrates the last week in the life of Christ, from Palm Sunday to Easter Sunday, with somber religious processions almost nightly, spoofings of Judas, and reenactments of specific biblical events, plus food and craft fairs. Businesses close during this week of Mexican national vacations.

If you plan on traveling to or around Mexico during Holy Week, make your reservations early. Airline seats on flights into and out of the country are often reserved months in advance. Buses to almost anywhere in Mexico will be full, so try arriving on the Wednesday or Thursday before Good Friday. Easter Sunday is quiet. In 2004, April 5 to 10 is Holy Week, Easter Sunday is April 11, and the week following is a traditional vacation period.

May

Labor Day. Workers' parades countrywide and everything closes. May 1.

Holy Cross Day (Día de la Santa Cruz). Workers place a cross on top of unfinished buildings and celebrate with food, bands, folk dancing, and fireworks around the work site. May 3.

Cinco de Mayo. A national holiday that celebrates the defeat of the French at the Battle of Puebla. May 5.

June

National Ceramics Fair and Fiesta, Tlaquepaque, Jalisco. This pottery center on the outskirts of Guadalajara offers craft demonstrations and competitions as well as mariachis, dancers, and colorful parades. June 14.

Día de San Pedro (St. Peter and St. Paul's Day). Celebrated wherever St. Peter is the patron saint, and honors anyone named Pedro or Peter. It's especially festive at San Pedro Tlaquepaque, near Guadalajara, with numerous mariachi bands, folk dancers, and parades with floats. In Mexcatitlan, Nayarit, shrimpers hold a regatta to celebrate the season opening. June 29.

September

Mariachi Festival, Guadalajara, Jalisco. Public mariachi concerts, including visiting mariachi groups from around the world (even Japan!). Workshops and lectures are given on the history, culture, and music of the mariachi in Mexico. Plans for an extension of this festival in Puerto Vallarta are being worked out—call ✆ **800-44-MEXICO** to confirm dates and schedule of performances. September 1 to 15.

Independence Day. Celebrates Mexico's independence from Spain. A day of parades, picnics, and family reunions throughout the country. At 11pm on September 15, the president of Mexico gives the famous independence grito (shout) from the National Palace in Mexico City, which is duplicated by every presidente municipal (mayor) in every town plaza in Mexico. Both Guadalajara and Puerto Vallarta have great parties in the town plaza on the nights of September 15 and 16.

October

Fiestas de Octubre (October Festivals), Guadalajara. This "most Mexican of cities" celebrates for a whole month with its mariachi music trademark. A bountiful display of popular culture and fine arts, and a spectacular spread of traditional foods, Mexican beers, and wines all add to the celebration. All month.

November

Day of the Dead. What's commonly called the Day of the Dead is actually 2 days, All Saints' Day—honoring saints and deceased children—and All Souls' Day, honoring deceased adults. Relatives gather at cemeteries countrywide, carrying candles and food, and often spend the night beside the graves of loved ones. Weeks before, bakers begin producing bread shaped like mummies or round loaves decorated with bread "bones." Decorated sugar skulls emblazoned with glittery names are sold everywhere. Many days ahead, homes and churches erect special altars laden with Day of the Dead bread, fruit, flowers, candles, and favorite foods and photographs of saints and of the deceased. During those 2 nights, children, dressed in costumes and masks, carry mock coffins and pumpkin lanterns through the streets, expecting people to drop money in them. November 1 to 2.

Fiesta del Mar, Puerto Vallarta. A weeks-long calendar of activities including art festivals, sports competitions, the Governor's Cup golf tournament, and an outstanding Gourmet Dining festival, with featured guest chefs from around the world working with local chefs in select restaurants. Among the sporting events are sailing regattas, windsurfing exhibitions, and beach volleyball competitions. November 10 to 30.

Revolution Day. Commemorates the start of the Mexican Revolution in 1910 with parades, speeches, rodeos, and patriotic events. November 20.

December

Feast of the Virgin of Guadalupe. Throughout the country, the patroness of Mexico is honored with religious processions, street fairs, dancing, fireworks, and masses. It is one of Mexico's most moving and beautiful displays of traditional culture. The Virgin of Guadalupe appeared to a young man, Juan Diego, in December 1531, on a hill near Mexico City. He convinced the bishop that he had seen the apparition by revealing his cloak, upon which the Virgin was emblazoned. It's customary for children to dress up as Juan Diego, wearing mustaches and red bandannas. December 12.

In Puerto Vallarta, the celebration begins on December 1 and extends through December 12, with traditional processions to the church for a brief misa (mass) and blessing. In the final days, the processions and festivities take place around the clock, with many of the processions featuring floats, mariachis, Aztec dancers, and fireworks. The central plaza is filled with street vendors and a festive atmosphere, and a major fireworks exhibition takes place on December 12 at 11pm.

Christmas Posadas. On each of the 9 nights before Christmas, it's customary to reenact the Holy Family's search for an inn, with door-to-door candlelit processions in cities and villages nationwide. Most business and community organizations host them in place of the northern tradition of a Christmas party. December 15 to 24.

Christmas. Mexicans extend this celebration, often beginning 2 weeks before Christmas, all the way through New Year's. Many businesses close, and resorts and hotels fill up. December 24 and 25.

New Year's Eve. As in the rest of the world, New Year's Eve in Vallarta is celebrated with parties, fireworks, and plenty of noise. December 31.

6 Travel Insurance

Check your existing insurance policies and credit card coverage before you buy travel insurance. You may already be covered for lost luggage, cancelled tickets, or medical expenses. The cost of travel insurance varies widely, depending on the cost and length of your trip, your age, health, and the type of trip you're taking.

If you'll be driving in Mexico, see "By Car," under "Getting There," and "Getting Around," later in this chapter, for information on collision and damage and personal accident insurance.

Even the most careful of us can still experience a traveler's nightmare: You discover you've lost your wallet, your passport, your airline ticket, or your tourist permit. Always keep a photocopy of these documents in your luggage—it makes replacing them easier. To be reimbursed for insured items once you return, you'll need to report the loss to the Mexican police and get a written report. If you don't speak Spanish, take along someone who does. If you lose official documents, you'll need to contact both Mexican and U.S. officials in Mexico before you leave the country.

TRIP-CANCELLATION INSURANCE Trip-cancellation insurance helps you get your money back if you have to back out of a trip, if you have to go home early, or if your travel supplier goes bankrupt. Allowed reasons for cancellation can range from sickness to natural disasters to the State Department declaring your destination unsafe for travel. In this unstable world, trip-cancellation insurance is a good buy if you're getting tickets well in advance—who knows what the state of the world, or of your airline, will be in 9 months? Keep in mind that in the aftermath of the September 11, 2001, terrorist attacks, insurers no longer cover some airlines, cruise lines, and tour operators. ***The bottom line:*** Always, always check the fine print before you sign; more and more policies have built-in exclusions and restrictions that may leave you out in the cold if something goes awry.

Insurance policy details vary, so read the fine print—and especially make sure that your airline or cruise line is on the list of carriers covered in case of bankruptcy. For information, contact one of the following insurers: **Access America** (✆ 866/807-3982; www.accessamerica.com); **Travel Guard International** (✆ 800/826-4919; www.travelguard.com); **Travel Insured International** (✆ 800/243-3174; www.travelinsured.com); and **Travelex Insurance Services** (✆ 888/457-4602; www.travelex-insurance.com).

MEDICAL INSURANCE Most health insurance policies cover you if you get sick away from home—but check, particularly if you're insured by an HMO. With the exception of certain HMOs and Medicare/Medicaid, your medical insurance should cover medical treatment—even hospital care—overseas. However, most out-of-country hospitals make you pay your bills up front, and send you a refund after you've returned home and filed the necessary paperwork. And in a worst-case scenario, there's the high cost of emergency evacuation. If you require additional medical insurance, try **MEDEX International** (✆ **800/527-0218** or 410/453-6300; www.medexassist.com) or **Travel Assistance International** (✆ **800/821-2828;** www.travelassistance.com; for general information on services, call the company's Worldwide Assistance Services, Inc., at ✆ **800/777-8710**).

LOST-LUGGAGE INSURANCE On international flights (including U.S. portions of international trips), baggage is limited to approximately $9.07 per pound, up to approximately $635 per checked bag. If you plan to check items more valuable than the standard liability, see if your valuables are covered by your homeowner's policy, get baggage insurance as part of your comprehensive travel-insurance package, or buy Travel Guard's "BagTrak" product. Don't buy insurance at the airport, as it's usually overpriced. Be sure to take any valuables or irreplaceable items with you in your carry-on luggage, as many valuables (including books, money, and electronics) aren't covered by airline policies.

If your luggage is lost, immediately file a lost-luggage claim at the airport, detailing the luggage contents. For most airlines, you must report delayed, damaged, or lost baggage within 4 hours of arrival. The airlines are required to deliver luggage, once found, directly to your house or destination free of charge.

7 Health & Safety

STAYING HEALTHY

BUG OFF Mosquitoes and gnats are prevalent along the coast. Insect repellent *(repelente contra insectos)* is a must, and it's not always available in Mexico. If you'll be in these areas and are prone to bites, bring a repellent along that contains the active ingredient DEET. Avon's "Skin So Soft" also works well. If you're sensitive to bites, pick up some antihistamine cream from a drugstore at home.

Most readers won't ever see a scorpion *(alacrán)*. But if you're stung, go immediately to a doctor.

MORE SERIOUS DISEASES You shouldn't be overly concerned about tropical diseases if you stay on the normal tourist routes and don't eat street food. However, both dengue fever and cholera have appeared in Mexico in recent years. Talk to your doctor, or a tropical-disease medical specialist, about any precautions you should take. You can also get medical bulletins from the U.S. State Department and the Centers for Disease Control (see "Sources of Information," earlier in this chapter). You can protect yourself by taking some simple precautions. Watch what you eat and drink; don't swim in stagnant water (ponds, slow-moving rivers, or wells); and avoid mosquito bites by covering up, using repellent, and sleeping under mosquito netting (which you'll find in smaller hotels, inns, and villas that don't have air conditioning). The most dangerous areas seem to be on Mexico's west coast, away from the big resorts (which are relatively safe).

EMERGENCY CARE Puerto Vallarta has a modern, U.S.-standards health care facility that offers insured care while in Mexico. **Ameri-Med,** Plaza Neptuno, in Marina Vallarta (© **800/815-1921** or 322/221-0023; fax 322/221-0026; www.amerimed-hospitals.com), provides complete, 24-hour, emergency health care adhering to U.S. medical standards. Facilities include CAT scan, radiology,

Tips What to Do If You Get Sick

It's called "travelers' diarrhea" or *turista,* the Spanish word for "tourist": the persistent diarrhea, often accompanied by fever, nausea, and vomiting, that used to attack many travelers to Mexico. Some in the United States call this "Montezuma's revenge," but you won't hear it referred to this way in Mexico. Widespread improvements in infrastructure, sanitation, and education have practically eliminated this ailment, especially in well-developed resort areas. In resort areas, and generally throughout Mexico, only purified ice is used.

Doctors say it's not caused by just one thing, but by a combination of consuming different foods and water, upsetting your schedule, lack of sleep, and the stresses of travel. A good high-potency (or "therapeutic") vitamin supplement, and even extra vitamin C is a help; yogurt is good for healthy digestion. If you do happen to come down with this ailment, nothing beats Pepto Bismol, readily available in Mexico.

Because dehydration can quickly become life threatening, the Public Health Service emphasizes the importance of **replacing fluids and electrolytes** (potassium, sodium, and the like) during a bout of diarrhea. Do this by drinking Pedialyte, a rehydration solution available at most Mexican pharmacies, glasses of natural fruit juice (high in potassium) with a pinch of salt added, or a glass of boiled pure water with a quarter teaspoon of sodium bicarbonate (baking soda) added.

ultrasound, and emergency air-evacuation services. Prices are in line with the standard of care, meaning that it's more costly than other medical facilities in Mexico.

For extreme medical emergencies, there's a service from the United States that will fly people to American hospitals: **Global Lifeline** (© **888/554-9729** or 01-800/305-9400 in Mexico) is a 24-hour air ambulance. There are several companies that offer air evac service; for a list refer to the U.S. State Department website at http://travel.state.gov/medical.html.

Over-the-Counter Drugs

Antibiotics and other drugs that you'd need a prescription to buy in the States are sold over-the-counter in Mexican pharmacies. Mexican pharmacies also have common over-the-counter cold, sinus, and allergy remedies, although not the broad selection we're accustomed to finding easily in the States.

GETTING SICK AWAY FROM HOME In most cases, your existing health plan will provide the coverage you need. But double-check; you may want to buy **travel medical insurance** instead. (See the section on insurance, above.) Bring your insurance ID card with you when you travel.

If you suffer from a chronic illness, consult your doctor before your departure. For conditions like epilepsy, diabetes, or heart problems, wear a **Medic Alert Identification Tag** (✆ **800/825-3785;** www.medicalert.org), which will immediately alert doctors to your condition and give them access to your records through Medic Alert's 24-hour hotline.

Pack **prescription medications** in your carry-on luggage, and carry prescription medications in their original containers, with pharmacy labels—otherwise they won't make it through airport security. Also bring along copies of your prescriptions in case you lose your pills or run out. Don't forget an extra pair of contact lenses or prescription glasses. You should also carry the generic name of prescription medicines, in case a local pharmacist is unfamiliar with the brand name.

Contact the **International Association for Medical Assistance to Travelers (IAMAT)** (✆ **716/754-4883** or 416/652-0137; www.iamat.org) for tips on travel and health concerns in the countries you're visiting, and lists of local, English-speaking doctors. The United States **Centers for Disease Control and Prevention** (✆ **800/311-3435;** www.cdc.gov) provides up-to-date information on necessary vaccines and health hazards by region or country. Any foreign consulate can provide a list of area doctors who speak English. If you get sick, consider asking your hotel concierge to recommend a local doctor—even his or her own. You can also try the emergency room at a local hospital; many have walk-in clinics for emergency cases that are not life-threatening. You may not get immediate attention, but you won't pay the high price of an emergency room visit.

STAYING SAFE

I have lived and traveled in Mexico for over 9 years, have never had any serious trouble, and rarely feel suspicious of anyone or any situation. You will probably feel physically safer in most Mexican cities and villages than in any comparable place at home. See "Crime, Bribes & Scams," below, and "Sources of Information," earlier, for more information and how to access the latest U.S. State Department advisories.

CRIME, BRIBES & SCAMS

CRIME

Crime in Mexico received much attention in the North American press a few years ago, but either the reality has improved or the coverage has diminished. The most severe crime problems were concentrated in Mexico City, located far away from the Mexican Riviera; however, the city of Guadalajara has experienced an increase in street crime.

Precautions are necessary, but travelers should be realistic. When traveling anyplace in the world, common sense is essential. The crime rate is on the whole much lower in Mexico than in most parts of the United States, and the nature of crimes in general is less violent—most crime is motivated by robbery, or by jealousy. Random, violent crimes or serial crimes are essentially unheard of in Mexico. You are much more likely to meet kind and helpful Mexicans than you are to encounter those set on thievery and deceit. A good rule of thumb is that you can generally trust people whom you approach for help, assistance, or directions—but be wary of anyone who approaches you offering the same. The more insistent they are, the more cautious you should be.

BRIBES & SCAMS

As is the case around the world, there are the occasional bribes and scams, targeted at people believed to be naive in the ways of the place—for example, obvious tourists. For years Mexico was known as a place where bribes—called *propinas* (tips) or *mordidas* ("bites")—were expected; however, the country is rapidly changing. Offering a bribe today, especially to a police officer, is frequently considered an insult, and it can land you in deeper trouble.

If you believe a bribe is being requested, here are a few tips on dealing with the situation. Even if you speak Spanish, don't utter a word of it to Mexican officials. That way you'll appear innocent, all the while understanding every word.

When you are crossing the border, should the man who inspects your car ask for a tip, you can ignore this request—but understand that the official may suddenly decide that a complete search of your belongings is in order. If faced with a situation where you feel you're being asked for a propina, how much should you offer? Usually $3 to $5 or the equivalent in pesos will do the trick. To report irregularities with Customs officials, call ✆ **01/800-0-014800** in Mexico. Your call will go to the office of the **Comptroller and Administrative Development Secretariat (SECODAM);** however, be forewarned that most personnel do not speak English. Be sure you have some basic information—such as the name of the person who requested a bribe or acted in a rude manner, as well as the place, time, and day of the event.

Whatever you do, avoid impoliteness; under no circumstances should you insult a Latin American official. Mexico is ruled by extreme politeness, even in the face of adversity. In Mexico, gringos have a reputation for being loud and demanding. By adopting the local custom of excessive courtesy, you'll have greater success in negotiations of any kind. Stand your ground, but do it politely.

As you travel in Mexico, you may encounter several types of scams, which are typical throughout the world. One involves some sort of a distraction or feigned commotion. While your attention is diverted, a pickpocket makes a grab for your wallet. In another common scam, an unaccompanied child pretends to be lost and frightened and takes your hand for safety. Meanwhile the child, or an accomplice, manages to plunder your pockets. A third involves confusing currency. A shoeshine boy, street musician, guide, or other individual might offer you a service for a price that seems reasonable—in pesos. When it comes time to pay, they tell you the price is in dollars, not pesos, and become very hostile if payment is not made. Be very clear on the price and currency when services are involved.

8 Specialized Travel Resources

FAMILY TRAVEL

If you have enough trouble getting your kids out of the house in the morning, dragging them thousands of miles away may seem like an insurmountable challenge. But family travel can be immensely rewarding, giving you new ways of seeing the world through smaller pairs of eyes.

I can't think of a better place today to introduce children to the exciting adventure of exploring a different culture.

Hotels in Mexico can often arrange for a babysitter. Some hotels in the moderate-to-luxury range even have small playgrounds and pools for children and hire caretakers with special activity programs during the day. Few budget hotels offer these amenities.

Before leaving home, you should check with your doctor to get advice on medications to take along with you. Disposable diapers cost about the same in Mexico but are of poorer quality. You can get Huggies Supreme and Pampers identical to the ones sold in the United States, but at a higher price. Gerber's baby foods are sold in many stores. Dry cereals, powdered formulas, baby bottles, and purified water are all easily available in midsize and large cities and resorts.

Cribs, however, may present a problem. Only the largest and most luxurious hotels provide cribs. However, rollaway beds to accommodate children staying in the room with parents are often available. Child seats or high chairs at restaurants are common, and most restaurants will go out of their way to accommodate your child.

You might want to consider bringing your own car seat if you're planning on renting a car; these are not readily available for rent in Mexico.

You can find good family-oriented vacation advice on the Internet from sites like the **Family Travel Network** (www.familytravel network.com); **Traveling Internationally with Your Kids** (www. travelwithyourkids.com), a comprehensive site offering sound advice for long-distance and international travel with children; and **Family Travel Files** (www.thefamilytravelfiles.com), which offers an online magazine and a directory of off-the-beaten-path tours and tour operators for families. In addition, the book ***How to Take Great Trips with Your Kids*** (The Harvard Common Press) is full of good general advice that can apply to travel anywhere.

GAY & LESBIAN TRAVELERS

Mexico is a conservative country, with deeply rooted Catholic religious traditions. As such, public displays of same-sex affection are rare and still considered shocking for men, especially outside of urban or resort areas. Women in Mexico frequently walk hand in hand, but anything more would cross the boundary of acceptability. However, gay and lesbian travelers are generally treated with respect and should not experience any harassment, assuming the appropriate regard is given to local culture and customs.

Puerto Vallarta is perhaps the most welcoming and accepting destination in Mexico, with a selection of accommodations and nightlife oriented especially toward gay and lesbian travelers. **Susan Weisman** (✆ **322/223-4424;** bayside@pvnet.com.mx; www.baysidepuertovallarta.com) has a travel service that rents gay-friendly condos, villas, and hotels for individuals and large groups. Her services are customized to individual needs, and she can offer airport pickups and in-villa cooks.

Arco Iris is a gay-owned, full-service travel agency and tour operator (✆ **800/795-5549;** www.arcoiristours.com) specializing in Mexico packages and special group travel, including to Puerto Vallarta.

The International Gay & Lesbian Travel Association (IGLTA) (✆ **800/448-8550** or 954/776-2626; www.iglta.org) is the trade association for the gay and lesbian travel industry, and offers an online directory of gay- and lesbian-friendly travel businesses; go to their website and click on "Members."

Many agencies offer tours and travel itineraries specifically for gay and lesbian travelers. **Above and Beyond Tours** (✆ **800/397-2681;** www.abovebeyondtours.com) is the exclusive gay and lesbian tour operator for United Airlines. **Now, Voyager** (✆ **800/255-6951;** www.nowvoyager.com) is a well-known San Francisco–based gay-owned and -operated travel service. **Olivia Cruises & Resorts** (✆ **800/631-6277** or 510/655-0364; www.olivia.com) charters entire resorts and ships for exclusive lesbian vacations and offers smaller group experiences for both gay and lesbian travelers.

The following travel guides are available at most travel bookstores and gay and lesbian bookstores, or you can order them from **Giovanni's Room** bookstore, 1145 Pine St., Philadelphia, PA 19107 (✆ **215/923-2960;** www.giovannisroom.com): ***Out and About*** (✆ **800/929-2268** or 415-644-8044; www.outandabout.com), which offers guidebooks and a newsletter 10 times a year packed with solid information on the global gay and lesbian scene; ***Spartacus International Gay Guide*** and ***Odysseus,*** both good, annual English-language guidebooks focused on gay men; the ***Damron*** guides, with separate, annual books for gay men and lesbians; and ***Gay Travel A to Z: The World of Gay & Lesbian Travel Options at Your Fingertips*** by Marianne Ferrari (Ferrari Publications; Box 35575, Phoenix, AZ 85069), a very good gay and lesbian guidebook series.

TRAVELERS WITH DISABILITIES

Most disabilities shouldn't stop anyone from traveling. There are more options and resources out there than ever before. Nevertheless, Mexico may seem like one giant obstacle course to travelers in wheelchairs or on crutches. At airports, you may encounter steep stairs before finding a well-hidden elevator or escalator—if one exists. Few airports offer the luxury of boarding an airplane from the waiting room. You either descend stairs to a bus that ferries you to the waiting plane that's boarded by climbing stairs, or you walk across the airport tarmac to your plane and ascend the stairs. Deplaning presents the same problem in reverse. However, airlines will often arrange wheelchair assistance for passengers to the baggage area. Porters are generally available to help with luggage at airports and large bus stations, once you've cleared baggage claim.

Few restrooms are equipped for travelers with disabilities, or when one is available, access to it may be via a narrow passage that won't accommodate a wheelchair or someone on crutches. Many deluxe hotels (the most expensive) now have rooms with baths for people with disabilities. Those traveling on a budget should stick with one-story hotels or those with elevators. Even so, there will probably still be obstacles somewhere. Stairs without handrails abound in Mexico, and escalators (there aren't many in the country) are often out of operation. Generally speaking, no matter where you are, someone will lend a hand, although you may have to ask for it.

One exception is Puerto Vallarta, which has recently renovated the majority of their downtown sidewalks and plazas with ramps that accommodate wheelchair access. A local disabled citizen is to credit with this impressive task—hopefully setting the stage for greater accessibility in other towns and resorts in Mexico.

Organizations that offer assistance to disabled travelers include the **Moss Rehab Hospital** (www.mossresourcenet.org), which provides a library of accessible-travel resources online; the **Society for Accessible Travel and Hospitality** (© **212/447-7284;** www.sath.org; annual membership fees: $45 adults, $30 seniors and students), which offers a wealth of travel resources for all types of disabilities and informed recommendations on destinations, access guides, travel agents, tour operators, vehicle rentals, and companion services; and the **American Foundation for the Blind** (© **800/232-5463;** www.afb.org), which provides information on traveling with Seeing Eye dogs.

For more information specifically targeted to travelers with disabilities, the community website **iCan** (www.icanonline.net/channels/travel/index.cfm) has destination guides and several regular columns on accessible travel. Also check out the quarterly magazine **Emerging Horizons** ($14.95 per year, $19.95 outside the U.S.; www.emerginghorizons.com); **Twin Peaks Press** (✆ **360/694-2462;** http://disabilitybookshop.virtualave.net/blist84.htm), offering travel-related books for travelers with special needs; and ***Open World Magazine,*** published by the Society for Accessible Travel and Hospitality (see above; subscription: $18 per year, $35 outside the U.S.).

SENIOR TRAVEL

Mexico is a popular country for retirees. For decades, North Americans have been living indefinitely in Mexico by returning to the border and recrossing with a new tourist permit every 6 months. Mexican immigration officials have caught on, and now limit the maximum time in the country to 6 months within any year. This is to encourage even partial residents to comply with the proper documentation.

Some of the most popular places for long-term stays are Guadalajara, Lake Chapala, Ajijic, and Puerto Vallarta—all in the state of Jalisco; and to a lesser extent Manzanillo, in Colima.

AIM, Apdo. Postal 31–70, 45050 Guadalajara, Jalisco, Mexico, is a well-written, candid, and very informative newsletter on retirement in Mexico. Subscriptions cost $18 to the United States and $21 to Canada. Back issues are three for $5.

Sanborn Tours, 2015 S. 10th St., Post Office Drawer 519, McAllen, TX 78505-0519 (✆ **800/395-8482**), offers a "Retire in Mexico" Guadalajara orientation tour. American Express, Discover, MasterCard, and Visa are accepted.

Mention the fact that you're a senior citizen when you make your travel reservations. Although all of the major U.S. airlines except America West have cancelled their senior discount and coupon book programs, many hotels still offer discounts for seniors. In most cities, people over the age of 60 qualify for reduced admission to theaters, museums, and other attractions, as well as discounted fares on public transportation.

Members of **AARP** (formerly known as the American Association of Retired Persons), 601 E St. NW, Washington, DC 20049 (✆ **800/424-3410** or 202/434-2277; www.aarp.org), get discounts on hotels, airfares, and car rentals. AARP offers members a wide range of benefits, including *AARP: The Magazine* and a monthly newsletter. Anyone over 50 can join.

Recommended publications offering travel resources and discounts for seniors include: the quarterly magazine ***Travel 50 & Beyond*** (www.travel50andbeyond.com); ***Travel Unlimited: Uncommon Adventures for the Mature Traveler*** (Avalon); ***101 Tips for Mature Travelers,*** available from Grand Circle Travel (✆ **800/221-2610** or 617/350-7500; www.gct.com); ***The 50+ Traveler's Guidebook*** (St. Martin's Press); and ***Unbelievably Good Deals and Great Adventures That You Absolutely Can't Get Unless You're Over 50*** (McGraw Hill).

SINGLE TRAVELERS

Mexico may be an old favorite for romantic honeymoons, but it's also a great place to travel on your own without really being or feeling alone. Although offering an identical room rate regardless of single or double occupancy is slowly becoming a trend in Mexico, many of the hotels mentioned in this book still offer singles at lower rates.

Mexicans are very friendly, and it's easy to meet other foreigners. But if you don't like the idea of traveling alone, then try **Travel Companion Exchange (TCE)** (✆ **631/454-0880;** www.travelcompanions.com), one of the nation's oldest roommate finders for single travelers. Register with them and find a travel mate who will split the cost of the room with you and be around as little, or as often, as you like during the day.

For more information, check out Eleanor Berman's ***Traveling Solo: Advice and Ideas for More Than 250 Great Vacations*** (Globe Pequot), a guide with advice on traveling alone, whether on your own or on a group tour. (It's been updated for 2003.) Or turn to the **Travel Alone and Love It** website (www.travelaloneandloveit.com), designed by former flight attendant Sharon Wingler, the author of the book of the same name. Her site is full of tips for single travelers.

WOMEN TRAVELERS

As a female traveling alone, I can tell you firsthand that I feel safer traveling in Mexico than in the United States. But I still use the same common-sense precautions I use traveling anywhere else in the world, and I am alert to what's going on around me.

Mexicans in general, and men in particular, are nosy about single travelers, especially women. If a taxi driver or anyone else with whom you don't want to become friendly asks about your marital status, family, and so on, my advice is to make up a set of answers (regardless of the truth): "I'm married, traveling with friends, and I have three children."

Saying you are single and traveling alone may send out the wrong message about availability. Movies and television shows exported from the United States have created an image of sexually aggressive North American women. If bothered by someone, don't try to be polite—just leave or head into a public place.

Check out the travel guide ***Safety and Security for Women Who Travel*** by Sheila Swan Laufer and Peter Laufer (Travelers' Tales, Inc.), offering common-sense advice and tips on safe travel.

9 Planning Your Trip Online

SURFING FOR AIRFARES

The "big three" online travel agencies, **Expedia.com, Travelocity.com,** and **Orbitz.com** sell most of the air tickets bought on the Internet. (Canadian travelers should try expedia.ca and Travelocity.ca; U.K. residents can go for expedia.co.uk and opodo.co.uk.) Each has different business deals with the airlines and may offer different fares on the same flights, so it's wise to shop around. Expedia and Travelocity will also send you **e-mail notification** when a cheap fare becomes available to your favorite destination. Of the smaller travel agency websites, **SideStep** (www.sidestep.com) has gotten the best reviews from Frommer's authors. It's a browser add-on that purports to "search 140 sites at once," but in reality only beats competitors' fares as often as other sites do.

Also remember to check **airline websites,** whose fares are often misreported or simply missing from travel agency websites. Even with major airlines, you can often shave a few bucks from a fare by booking directly through the airline and avoiding a travel agency's transaction fee. But you'll get these discounts only by **booking online:** Most airlines now offer online-only fares that even their phone agents know nothing about. For the websites of airlines that fly to and from your destination, go to "Getting There," later in this chapter.

Great **last-minute deals** are available through free weekly e-mail services provided directly by the airlines. Most of these are announced on Tuesday or Wednesday and must be purchased online. Most are only valid for travel that weekend, but some can be booked weeks or months in advance. Sign up for weekly e-mail alerts at airline websites or check mega-sites that compile comprehensive lists of last-minute specials, such as **Smarter Living**

Airline Websites

Below are the websites for the major airlines that service Mexico. These sites offer schedules and booking, and most of the airlines have E-saver alerts for weekend deals and late-breaking bargains.

- **Aeromexico.** www.aeromexico.com
- **Alaska Airlines.** www.alaskaair.com
- **American Airlines.** www.aa.com
- **America West.** www.americawest.com
- **Continental Airlines.** www.continental.com
- **Delta.** www.delta.com
- **Mexicana.** www.mexicana.com
- **Northwest Airlines.** www.nwa.com
- **United Airlines.** www.ual.com
- **US Airways.** www.usairways.com

(smarterliving.com). For last-minute trips, **site59.com** in the U.S. and **lastminute.com** in Europe often have better deals than the major-label sites.

If you're willing to give up some control over your flight details, use an **opaque fare service** like **Priceline** (www.priceline.com; www.priceline.co.uk for Europeans) or **Hotwire** (www.hotwire.com). Both offer rock-bottom prices in exchange for travel on a "mystery airline" at a mysterious time of day, often with a mysterious change of planes en route. The mystery airlines are all major, well-known carriers, but your chances of getting a 6am or 11pm flight are pretty high. Hotwire tells you flight prices before you buy; Priceline usually has better deals than Hotwire, but you have to play their "name our price" game. If you're new at this, the helpful folks at **BiddingForTravel** (www.biddingfortravel.com) do a good job of demystifying Priceline's prices. Priceline and Hotwire are great for flights within North America and between the U.S. and Europe. But for flights to other parts of the world, consolidators will almost always beat their fares.

For much more about airfares and savvy air-travel tips and advice, pick up a copy of *Frommer's Fly Safe, Fly Smart* (Wiley Publishing, Inc.).

SURFING FOR HOTELS

Shopping online for hotels is much easier in the U.S., Canada, and certain parts of Europe than it is in the rest of the world. Also, many

Tips Sleeping in Style

Mexico lends itself beautifully to the concept of small, private hotels set in idyllic settings. These may vary in style from grandiose to a return to the basics of palm-thatched bungalows. **Mexico Boutique Hotels** (www.MexicoBoutiqueHotels.com) is a new company that specializes in smaller places to stay with a high level of personal attention and service. Most options have fewer than 50 rooms, and the type of accommodations can consist of entire villas, casitas, bungalows, or a combination of these. The Yucatán is especially noted for the luxury haciendas found throughout the peninsula.

smaller hotels and B&Bs—especially outside the U.S.—don't show up on websites at all. Of the "big three" sites, **Expedia** may be the best choice, thanks to its long list of special deals. **Travelocity** runs a close second. Hotel specialist sites **hotels.com** and **hoteldiscounts.com** are also reliable. An excellent free program, **TravelAxe** (www.travelaxe.net), can help you search multiple hotel sites at once, even ones you may never have heard of.

Priceline and Hotwire are even better for hotels than for airfares; with both, you're allowed to pick the neighborhood and quality level of your hotel before offering up your money. Priceline's hotel product even covers Europe and Asia, though it's much better at getting five-star lodging for three-star prices than at finding anything at the bottom of the scale. ***Note:*** Hotwire overrates its hotels by one star—what Hotwire calls a four-star is a three-star anywhere else.

SURFING FOR RENTAL CARS

For booking rental cars online, the best deals are usually found at rental-car company websites, although all the major online travel agencies also offer rental-car reservations services. Priceline and Hotwire work well for rental cars, too; the only "mystery" is which major rental company you get, and for most travelers the difference between Hertz, Avis, and Budget is negligible.

10 The 21st-Century Traveler

INTERNET ACCESS AWAY FROM HOME

Travelers have any number of ways to check their e-mail and access the Internet on the road. Of course, using your own laptop—or even a PDA (personal digital assistant) or electronic organizer with

Frommers.com: The Complete Travel Resource

For an excellent travel-planning resource, we highly recommend **Frommers.com** (www.frommers.com). We're a little biased, of course, but we guarantee that you'll find the travel tips, reviews, monthly vacation giveaways, and online-booking capabilities thoroughly indispensable. Among the special features are our popular **Message Boards,** where Frommer's readers post queries and share advice (sometimes even our authors show up to answer questions); **Frommers.com Newsletter,** for the latest travel bargains and insider travel secrets; and **Frommer's Destinations Section,** where you'll get expert travel tips, hotel and dining recommendations, and advice on the sights to see for more than 3,000 destinations around the globe. When your research is done, the **Online Reservations System** (www.frommers.com/book_a_trip) takes you to Frommer's preferred online partners for booking your vacation at affordable prices.

a modem—gives you the most flexibility. But even if you don't have a computer, you can still access your e-mail and even your office computer from cybercafes.

WITHOUT YOUR OWN COMPUTER

It's hard nowadays to find a city that *doesn't* have a few cybercafes. Although there's no definitive directory for cybercafes—these are independent businesses, after all—three places to start looking are at **www.cybercaptive.com**, **www.netcafeguide.com**, and **www.cybercafe.com**.

Aside from formal cybercafes, most **youth hostels** nowadays have at least one computer you can get to the Internet on. And most **public libraries** around the world offer Internet access free or for a small charge. Avoid **hotel business centers,** which often charge exorbitant rates.

Most major airports now have **Internet kiosks** scattered throughout their gates. These kiosks, which you'll also see in shopping malls, hotel lobbies, and tourist information offices around the world, give you basic Web access for a per-minute fee that's usually higher than cybercafe prices. The kiosks' clunkiness and high price means they should be avoided whenever possible.

To retrieve your e-mail, ask your **Internet Service Provider (ISP)** if it has a Web-based interface tied to your existing e-mail account. If your ISP doesn't have such an interface, you can use the free **mail2web** service (www.mail2web.com) to view (but not reply to) your home e-mail. For more flexibility, you may want to open a free, Web-based e-mail account with **Yahoo! Mail** (http://mail.yahoo.com). (Microsoft's Hotmail is another popular option, but Hotmail has severe spam problems.) Your home ISP may be able to forward your e-mail to the Web-based account automatically.

If you need to access files on your office computer, look into a service called **GoToMyPC** (www.gotomypc.com). The service provides a Web-based interface for you to access and manipulate a distant PC from anywhere—even a cybercafe—provided your "target" PC is on and has an always-on connection to the Internet (such as with Road Runner cable). The service offers top-quality security, but if you're worried about hackers, use your own laptop rather than a cybercafe to access the GoToMyPC system.

WITH YOUR OWN COMPUTER

Major ISPs have **local access numbers** around the world, allowing you to go online by simply placing a local call. Check your ISP's website or call its toll-free number and ask how you can use your current account away from home, and how much it will cost.

If you're traveling outside the reach of your ISP, the **iPass** network has dial-up numbers in most of the world's countries. You'll have to sign up with an iPass provider, who will then tell you how to set up your computer for your destination(s). For a list of iPass providers, go to www.ipass.com and click on "Reseller Locator." Under "Select a Country" pick the country that you're coming from, and under "Who is this service for?" pick "Individual." One solid provider is **i2roam** (www.i2roam.com; ✆ **866/811-6209** or 920/235-0475).

Wherever you go, bring a **connection kit** of the right power and phone adapters, a spare phone cord, and a spare Ethernet network cable.

Most business-class hotels throughout the world offer dataports for laptop modems, and some hotels now offer high-speed Internet access using an Ethernet network cable. **Call your hotel in advance** to find out what the options are and to find out if you need to bring your own cables.

Community-minded individuals have also set up **free wireless networks** in major cities around the world. These networks are spotty, but you get what you (don't) pay for. Each network has a home page explaining how to set up your computer for their particular system; start your explorations at www.personaltelco.net/index.cgi/WirelessCommunities.

USING A CELLPHONE OUTSIDE THE U.S.

The three letters that define much of the world's **wireless capabilities** are GSM (Global System for Mobiles), a big, seamless network that makes for easy cross-border cellphone use throughout dozens of countries worldwide. In the U.S., T-Mobile, AT&T Wireless, and Cingular use this quasi-universal system; in Canada, Microcell and some Rogers customers use GSM, and all Europeans and most Australians use GSM.

If your cellphone is on a GSM system, and you have a world-capable phone such as many (but not all) Sony Ericsson, Motorola, or Samsung models, you can make and receive calls across civilized areas on much of the globe, from Andorra to Uganda. Just call your wireless operator and ask for "international roaming" to be activated on your account. Unfortunately, per-minute charges can be high—usually $1 to $1.50 in Western Europe and up to $5 in places like Russia and Indonesia.

World-phone owners can bring down their per-minute charges with a bit of trickery. Call up your cellular operator and say you'll be going abroad for several months and want to "unlock" your phone to use it with a local provider. Usually, they'll oblige. Then, in your destination country, pick up a cheap, prepaid phone chip at a mobile phone store and slip it into your phone. (Show your phone to the salesperson, as not all phones work on all networks.) You'll get a local phone number in your destination country—and much, much lower calling rates.

Otherwise, **renting** a phone is a good idea. (Even worldphone owners will have to rent new phones if they're traveling to non-GSM regions.) While you can rent a phone from any number of overseas sites, including kiosks at airports and at car-rental agencies, we suggest renting the phone before you leave home. That way you can give loved ones your new number, make sure the phone works, and take the phone wherever you go—especially helpful when you rent overseas, where phone-rental agencies bill in local currency and may not let you take the phone to another country.

Online Traveler's Toolbox

Veteran travelers usually carry some essential items to make their trips easier. Following is a selection of online tools to bookmark and use.

- **Visa ATM Locator** (www.visa.com), for locations of PLUS ATMs worldwide, or **MasterCard ATM Locator** (www.mastercard.com), for locations of Cirrus ATMs worldwide.
- **Foreign Languages for Travelers** (www.travlang.com). Learn basic terms in more than 70 languages and click on any underlined phrase to hear what it sounds like.
- **Intellicast** (www.intellicast.com) and **Weather.com** (www.weather.com). Gives weather forecasts for cities around the world.
- **Mapquest** (www.mapquest.com). This best of the mapping sites lets you choose a specific address or destination, and in seconds, it will return a map and detailed directions.
- **Universal Currency Converter** (www.xe.com/ucc). See what your dollar or pound is worth in more than 100 other countries.
- **Cybercafes.com** (www.cybercafes.com). Locate Internet cafes at hundreds of locations around the globe.
- **Travel Warnings** (http://travel.state.gov/travel_warnings.html, www.fco.gov.uk/travel, www.voyage.gc.ca, www.dfat.gov.au/consular/advice). These sites report on places where health concerns or unrest might threaten American, British, Canadian, and Australian travelers. Generally, U.S. warnings are the most paranoid; Australian warnings are the most relaxed.

Phone rental isn't cheap. You'll usually pay $40 to $50 per week, plus airtime fees of at least a dollar a minute. The bottom line: Shop around.

Two good wireless rental companies are **InTouch USA** (✆ **800/872-7626;** www.intouchglobal.com) and **RoadPost** (✆ **888/290-1606** or 905/272-5665; www.roadpost.com). Give them your itinerary, and they'll tell you what wireless products you need. InTouch will also, for free, advise you on whether your existing phone will work overseas; simply call © **703/222-7161** between 9am and 4pm EST, or go to http://intouchglobal.com/travel.htm.

For trips of more than a few weeks spent in one country, **buying a phone** becomes economically attractive, as many nations have cheap, no-questions-asked prepaid phone systems. Stop by a local cellphone shop and get the cheapest package; you'll probably pay less than $100 for a phone and a starter calling card. Local calls may be as low as 10¢ per minute, and in many countries incoming calls are free.

True wilderness adventurers, or those heading to less-developed countries, should consider renting a **satellite phone** (see above). Per-minute call charges can be even cheaper than roaming charges with a regular cellphone, but the phone itself is more expensive (up to $150 a week), and depending on the service you choose, people calling you may incur high long-distance charges.

11 Getting There

BY PLANE

The airline situation in Mexico is changing rapidly, with many new regional carriers offering scheduled service to areas previously not served. In addition to regularly scheduled service, charter service direct from U.S. cities to resorts is making Mexico more accessible: Now more than ever it has become much easier to fly to destinations without having to go through Mexico City.

THE MAJOR INTERNATIONAL AIRLINES The main airlines operating direct or nonstop flights from the United States to points in Mexico include **Aerocalifornia** (© 800/237-6225), **Aeromexico** (© 800/237-6639), **Alaska Airlines** (© 800/426-0333), **American** (© 800/433-7300), **America West** (© 800/235-9292), **Continental** (© 800/231-0856), **Lacsa** (© 800/225-2272), **Mexicana** (© 800/531-7921), **Northwest** (© 800/225-2525), **United** (© 800/241-6522), and **US Airways** (© 800/428-4322).

The main departure points in North America for international airlines are Atlanta, Chicago, Dallas/Fort Worth, Denver, Houston, Los Angeles, Miami, New Orleans, New York, Orlando, Philadelphia, Raleigh/Durham, San Antonio, San Francisco, Seattle, Toronto, Tucson, and Washington, D.C.

GETTING THROUGH THE AIRPORT

With the federalization of airport security, security procedures at U.S. airports are more stable and consistent than ever. Generally, you'll be fine if you arrive at the airport **1 hour** before a domestic flight and **2 hours** before an international flight; if you show up late, tell an airline employee and she'll probably whisk you to the front of the line.

Bring a **current, government-issued photo ID** such as a driver's license or passport, and if you've got an e-ticket, print out the **official confirmation page;** you'll need to show your confirmation at the security checkpoint, and your ID at the ticket counter or the gate. (Children under 18 do not need photo IDs for domestic flights, but the adults checking in with them need them.)

Security lines are getting shorter than they were during 2001 and 2002, but some doozies remain. If you have trouble standing for long periods of time, tell an airline employee; the airline will provide a wheelchair. Speed up security by **not wearing metal objects** such as big belt buckles or clanky earrings. If you've got metallic body parts, a note from your doctor can prevent a long chat with the security screeners. Keep in mind that only **ticketed passengers** are allowed past security, except for folks escorting disabled passengers or children.

Federalization has stabilized **what you can carry on** and **what you can't.** The general rule is that sharp things are out, nail clippers are okay, and food and beverages must be passed through the X-ray machine—but that security screeners can't make you drink from your coffee cup. Bring food in your carry-on rather than checking it, as explosive-detection machines used on checked luggage have been known to mistake food (especially chocolate, for some reason) for bombs. Travelers in the U.S. are allowed one carry-on bag, plus a "personal item" such as a purse, briefcase, or laptop bag. Carry-on hoarders can stuff all sorts of things into a laptop bag; as long as it has a laptop in it, it's still considered a personal item. The Transportation Security Administration (TSA) has issued a list of restricted items; check its website (www.tsa.gov/public/index.jsp) for details.

In 2003, the TSA will be phasing out **gate check-in** at all U.S. airports. Passengers with e-tickets and without checked bags can still beat the ticket-counter lines by using **electronic kiosks** or even **online check-in.** Ask your airline which alternatives are available, and if you're using a kiosk, bring the credit card you used to book the ticket. If you're checking bags, you will still be able to use most airlines' kiosks; again call your airline for up-to-date information. **Curbside check-in** is also a good way to avoid lines, although a few airlines still ban curbside check-in entirely; call before you go.

At press time, the TSA is also recommending that you **not lock your checked luggage** so screeners can search it by hand if necessary. The agency says to use plastic "zip ties" instead, which can be bought at hardware stores and can be easily cut off.

FLYING FOR LESS: TIPS FOR GETTING THE BEST AIRFARE

Passengers sharing the same airplane cabin rarely pay the same fare. Travelers who need to purchase tickets at the last minute, change their itinerary at a moment's notice, or fly one-way often get stuck paying the premium rate. Here are some ways to keep your airfare costs down.

- Passengers who can book their ticket **long in advance,** who can **stay over Saturday night,** or who **fly midweek** or **at less-trafficked hours** will pay a fraction of the full fare. If your schedule is flexible, say so, and ask if you can secure a cheaper fare by changing your flight plans.
- You can also save on airfares by keeping an eye out in local newspapers for **promotional specials** or **fare wars,** when airlines lower prices on their most popular routes. You rarely see fare wars offered for peak travel times, but if you can travel in the off-months, you may snag a bargain.
- Search **the Internet** for cheap fares (see "Planning Your Trip Online").
- **Consolidators,** also known as bucket shops, are great sources for international tickets, although they usually can't beat the Internet on fares within North America. Start by looking in Sunday newspaper travel sections; U.S. travelers should focus on the *New York Times, Los Angeles Times,* and *Miami Herald.* For less-developed destinations, small travel agencies who cater to immigrant communities in large cities often have the best deals. ***Beware:*** Bucket shop tickets are usually nonrefundable or rigged with stiff cancellation penalties, often as high as 50% to 75% of the ticket price, and some put you on charter airlines with questionable safety records. Several reliable consolidators are worldwide and available on the Net. **STA Travel** is now the world's leader in student travel, thanks to their purchase of Council Travel. It also offers good fares for travelers of all ages. **Flights.com** (✆ **800/TRAV-800;** www.flights.com) started in Europe and has excellent fares worldwide, but particularly to that continent. It also has "local" websites in 12 countries. **FlyCheap** (✆ **800/FLY-CHEAP;** www.flycheap.com) is

owned by package-holiday megalith MyTravel and so has especially good access to fares for sunny destinations. **Air Tickets Direct** (✆ **800/778-3447;** www.airticketsdirect.com) is based in Montreal and leverages the currently weak Canadian dollar for low fares.

- Join **frequent-flier clubs.** Accrue enough miles, and you'll be rewarded with free flights and elite status. It's free, and you'll get the best choice of seats, faster response to phone inquiries, and prompter service if your luggage is stolen, if your flight is canceled or delayed, or if you want to change your seat. You don't need to fly to build frequent-flier miles—**frequent-flier credit cards** can provide thousands of miles for doing your everyday shopping.
- For many more tips about air travel, including a rundown of the major frequent-flier credit cards, pick up a copy of *Frommer's Fly Safe, Fly Smart* (Wiley Publishing, Inc.).

BY CAR

Driving is not the cheapest way to get to Mexico, but it is the best way to see the country. Even so, you may think twice about taking your own car south of the border once you've pondered the bureaucratic requirements that affect foreign drivers here. One option would be to rent a car, for touring around a specific region, once you arrive in Mexico. Rental cars in Mexico are now generally new, clean, and very well maintained. Although pricier than in the United States, discounts are often available for rentals of a week or longer, especially when arrangements are made in advance from the United States. (See "Car Rentals," under "Getting Around," later in this chapter, for more details.)

If, after reading the section that follows, you have any additional questions or you want to confirm the current rules, call your nearest Mexican consulate, or the Mexican Government Tourist Office. Although travel insurance companies are generally helpful, they may not have the most accurate information available. To check on road conditions or to get help with any travel emergency while in Mexico, call ✆ **01-800/903-9200** or 55/5250-0151 in Mexico City. Both numbers are staffed by English-speaking operators, however they are unlikely to be able to send immediate assistance. Toll-roads do have emergency phones in place every half a kilometer.

In addition, check with the U.S. State Department (see "Sources of Information," earlier in this chapter) for their warnings about dangerous driving areas.

CAR DOCUMENTS

You must carry your temporary car-importation permit, tourist permit (see "Entry Requirements," earlier in this chapter), and, if you purchased it, your proof of Mexican car insurance (see "Mexican Auto Insurance," below) in the car at all times. The temporary car-importation permit papers will be issued for 6 months to a year, while the tourist permit is usually issued for 30 days. It's a good idea to overestimate the time you'll spend in Mexico, so that if something unforeseen happens and you have to (or want to) stay longer, you'll avoid the hassle of getting your papers extended. Whatever you do, don't overstay either permit. Doing so invites heavy fines and/or confiscation of your vehicle, which will not be returned. Remember also that 6 months does not necessarily work out to be 180 days—be sure to return before the expiration date.

To drive your car into Mexico, you'll need a **temporary car-importation permit,** which is granted after you provide a strictly required list of documents (see below). The permit can be obtained through Banco del Ejército (Banjercito) officials, who have a desk, booth, or office at the Mexican Customs (Aduana) building after you cross the border into Mexico. Insurance companies such as AAA and Sanborn's used to be able to issue this permit, however no longer can.

The following requirements for border crossing were accurate at press time:

- A **valid driver's license,** issued outside of Mexico.
- **Current, original car registration and a copy of the original car title.** If the registration or title is in more than one name and not all the named people are traveling with you, a notarized letter from the absent person(s) authorizing use of the vehicle for the trip is required; have it ready just in case. In addition, the car registration and your credit card (see below) must be in the same name.
- A **valid international major credit card.** With a credit card, you are only required to pay a $16 car-importation fee. The credit card must be in the same name as the car registration. If you do not have a major credit card (Visa, MasterCard, American Express, or Diners Club) you will have to post a bond or make a deposit equal to the value of the vehicle. Check cards are not accepted.
- **Original immigration documentation.** This will either be your tourist permit (FMT) or the original immigration booklet, FM2 or FM3, if you hold this more permanent status.

- A **signed declaration promising to return to your country of origin** with the vehicle. This form (Carta Promesa de Retorno) is provided by AAA or Sanborn's before you go or by Banjercito officials at the border. There's no charge. The form does not stipulate that you must return through the same border entry you came through on your way south.
- **Temporary Importation Application.** Upon signing this form, you are stating that you are only temporarily importing the car for your personal use, and will not be selling the vehicle. This is to help regulate the entry and restrict the resale of unauthorized cars and trucks. Vehicles in the U.S. are much less expensive, and for years were brought into Mexico for resale.

If you receive your documentation at the border, Mexican officials will make two copies of everything and charge you for the copies. For up-to-the-minute information, a great source is the Customs office in Nuevo Laredo (Módulo de Importación Temporal de Automóviles, Aduana Nuevo Laredo; © **52-867/712-2071**).

Important reminder: Someone else may drive the car, but the person (or relative of the person) whose name appears on the car-importation permit must always be in the car at the same time. (If stopped by police, a nonregistered family member driving without the registered driver must be prepared to prove familial relationship to the registered driver—no joke.) Violation of this rule makes the car subject to impoundment and the driver subject to imprisonment and/or a fine. You can only drive a car with foreign license plates if you have an international (non-Mexican) driver's license.

MEXICAN AUTO INSURANCE

Liability auto insurance is legally required in Mexico. U.S. insurance is invalid in Mexico; to be insured in Mexico, you must purchase Mexican insurance. Any party involved in an accident who has no insurance may be sent to jail and his or her car impounded until all claims are settled. This is true even if you just drive across the border to spend the day. U.S. companies that broker Mexican insurance are commonly found at the border crossing, and several will quote daily rates.

Car insurance can also be purchased through **Sanborn's Mexico Insurance,** P.O. Box 52840, 2009 S. 10th, McAllen, TX 78505-2840 (© **956/686-3601;** fax 956/686-0732 or 800/222-0158; www.sanbornsinsurance.com). The company has offices at all of the border crossings in the United States. Its policies cost the same as the competition's do, but you get legal coverage (attorney and bail bonds if needed) and a detailed mile-by-mile guide for your proposed route. Most of Sanborn's border offices are open Monday through Friday, and a few are staffed on Saturday and Sunday. AAA auto club also sells insurance.

RETURNING TO THE U.S. WITH YOUR CAR

The car papers you obtained when you entered Mexico must be returned when you cross back with your car or at some point within 180 days. (You can cross as many times as you wish within the 180 days.) If the documents aren't returned, heavy fines are imposed ($250 for each 15 days late) and your car may be impounded and confiscated or you may be jailed if you return to Mexico. You can only return the car documents to a Banjercito official on duty at the Mexican Customs (Aduana) building before you cross back into the United States. Some border cities have Banjercito officials on duty 24 hours a day, but others do not; some also do not have Sunday hours. On the U.S. side, customs agents may or may not inspect your car from stem to stern.

BY SHIP

Numerous cruise lines serve Mexico's Central Pacific coast, known as the Mexican Riviera. Ships from California cruise down to the Baja Peninsula (including specialized whale-watching trips) and ports of call along the Pacific Coast.

If you don't mind taking off at the last minute, several cruise-tour specialists arrange substantial discounts on unsold cabins. One such company is **The Cruise Line,** 150 NW 168 St., North Miami Beach, Miami, FL 33169 (© **800/777-0707** or 305/521-2200).

12 Packages for the Independent Traveler

Say the word "package tour" and many people automatically feel as though they're being forced to choose: money or lifestyle. This isn't necessarily the case. Most Mexican packages let you have both your independence and your in-the-black bank-account balance. Package tours are not the same thing as escorted tours. They are simply a way of buying your airfare, accommodations, and other pieces of your trip (usually airport transfers, and sometimes meals and activities) at the same time.

For popular destinations like Mexico's beach resorts, they're often the smart way to go because they can save you a ton of money. In many cases, a package that includes airfare, hotel, and transportation to and from the airport will cost you less than just the hotel alone if you booked it yourself. That's because packages are sold in bulk to tour operators, who resell them to the public.

You can buy a package at any time of the year, but the best deals usually coincide with low season—from May to early December—when room rates and airfares plunge. But packages vary widely. Some offer a better class of hotels than others. Some offer the same hotels for lower prices. Some offer flights on scheduled airlines while others book charters. In some packages, your choices of accommodations and travel days may be limited. Each destination usually has some packagers that are better than the rest because they buy in even bigger bulk. Not only can that mean better prices, but it can also mean more choices—a packager that just dabbles in Mexico may have only a half-dozen or so hotels for you to choose from.

WARNINGS

- **Read the fine print.** Make sure you know exactly what's included in the price you're being quoted, and what's not.
- **Don't compare Mayas and Aztecs.** When you're looking over different packagers, compare the deals that they're offering on similar properties. Most packagers can offer bigger savings on some hotels than others.
- **Know what you're getting yourself into**—and if you can get yourself out of it. Before you commit to a package, make sure you know how much flexibility you have.
- **Use your best judgment.** Stay away from fly-by-nights and shady packagers. Go with a reputable firm with a proven track record. This is where your travel agent can come in handy.

WHERE TO BROWSE

- For one-stop shopping on the Web, go to **www.vacation packager.com**, an extensive search engine that'll link you up with more than 30 packagers offering Mexican beach vacations—and even let you custom design your own package.
- At **www.2travel.com** you'll find a page with links to a number of the big-name Mexico packagers, including several of the ones listed here.
- For last minute air-only or package bargains, check out Vacation Hotline, **www.vacationhotline.net**. Once you find your "deal," you'll need to call them to make final booking arrangements, but they offer packages from both the popular Apple and Funjet vacation wholesalers.

RECOMMENDED PACKAGERS

- **Aeromexico Vacations** (✆ **800/245-8585;** www.aeromexico.com): Year-round packages for Puerto Vallarta, including connections to Guadalajara, with a large selection of hotels in these destinations in a variety of price ranges.
- **Alaska Airlines Vacations** (✆ **800/468-2248;** www.alaskair.com) sells packages to Puerto Vallarta from Los Angeles, San Diego, San Jose, San Francisco, Seattle, Vancouver, Anchorage, and Fairbanks.
- **American Airlines Vacations** (✆ **800/321-2121;** www. americanair.com): American has year-round deals for Puerto Vallarta. You don't have to fly with American if you can get a better deal on another airline; land-only packages include hotel, airport transfers, and hotel room tax. American's hubs to Mexico are Dallas/Fort Worth, Chicago, and Miami, so you're likely to get the best prices—and the most direct flights—if you live near those cities.
- **America West Vacations** (✆ **800/356-6611;** www. americawest.com) has deals to Manzanillo and Puerto Vallarta, mostly from its Phoenix gateway.
- **Apple Vacations** (✆ **800/365-2775**): Apple offers inclusive packages with the largest choice of hotels: 6 in Manzanillo and 31 in Puerto Vallarta. Apple perks include baggage handling and the services of an Apple representative at the major hotels.
- **Classic Custom Vacations** (✆ **800/221-3949** and 800/344-5687; www.classiccustomvacations.com) is a newer company that specializes in package vacations to Mexico's finest luxury resorts. They combine discounted first class and economy airfares on American, Continental, Mexicana, Alaska, America West, and Delta Airlines with stays at the most exclusive hotels in Guadalajara, Puerto Vallarta, Mazatlán, Costa Alegre, and Manzanillo. In many cases, these packages also include meals, private airport transfers, and upgrades.
- **Continental Vacations** (✆ **800/634-5555;** and 888/989-9255; www.continental.com): With Continental, you've got to buy air from the carrier if you want to book a room. The airline has year-round packages available to Puerto Vallarta, and the best deals are from Houston; Newark, New Jersey; and Cleveland.
- **Funjet Vacations** (bookable through travel agents or online at **www.funjet.com**): One of the largest vacation packagers in the United States, Funjet has packages to Mexico's resorts,

including Puerto Vallarta. You can choose a charter or fly on American, Continental, Aeromexico, Alaska Airlines, or TWA.

- **Mexicana Vacations** (or MexSeaSun Vacations) (✆ **800/531-9321;** www.mexicana.com) offers getaways to Puerto Vallarta from Los Angeles, Chicago, and Denver.
- **Pleasant Mexico Holidays** (✆ **800/448-3333;** www.pleasant holidays.com) is another of the largest vacation packagers in the United States, with hotels in the most popular destinations including Mazatlán and Puerto Vallarta.

13 Special-Interest Trips

The diverse geography of the Mexican Riviera and its wealth of eco- and adventure-tour options has made it a natural favorite of travelers looking for more active vacations.

Excellent golf courses are located in Guadalajara, Puerto Vallarta, Punta Mita, and along the coastline down to Manzanillo. Tennis, water-skiing, surfing, biking, and horseback riding are all sports visitors can enjoy in this region. Scuba diving is excellent along the Pacific Coast at Puerto Vallarta and Manzanillo, where a wide array of sea life can be observed, including dolphins, sea turtles, and giant mantas.

ORGANIZATIONS & TOUR OPERATORS

There's an active association in Mexico of eco- and adventure-tour operators called **AMTAVE** (Asociación Mexicana de Turismo de Aventura y Ecoturismo, A.C.). They publish an annual catalog of participating firms and their offerings, all of which must meet certain criteria for security, and for quality and training of the guides, as well as for sustainability of natural and cultural environments. For more information, contact AMTAVE (✆ **800/509-7678;** www.amtave.com.mx).

Bike Mex Adventures, calle Guerrero s/n, 48300 Puerto Vallarta, Jalisco (✆ **322/223-1680;** www.bikemex.com), offers day or overnight mountain-biking excursions in the Sierra Madre foothills near Puerto Vallarta. One overnight trip travels to the old mountain mining towns of Mascota, Talpa de Allende, and San Sebastian. This excellent trip is a combination of van transport and biking between towns, with stays in old haciendas.

Culinary Adventures, 6023 Reid Dr. NW, Gig Harbor, WA 98335 (✆ **253/851-7676;** fax 253/851-9532), offers a short but special list of cooking tours of particular regions of Mexico known for excellent cuisine, and featuring well-known cooks. The owner,

Marilyn Tausend, is the co-author of *Mexico the Beautiful Cookbook,* and *Cocinas de la Familia (Family Kitchens).*

One World Workforce, P.O. Box 3188, La Mesa, CA 91944 (✆ **800/451-9564**), has weeklong "hands-on conservation trips" that offer working volunteers a chance to help with sea-turtle conservation along the Majahuas beach 60 miles south of Puerto Vallarta during the summer and fall.

Open Air Expeditions, calle Guerrero 339, Col. Centro, Apdo. Postal 105-B, Puerto Vallarta, Jal. C.P. 48300 (✆ **322/222-3310;** fax 322/223-2407; www.vivamexico.com), offers true eco-adventures guided by experts trained as marine biologists, oceanographers, or geologists. Their specialty is whale-watching tours (December through May); they have documented the returning whale population in an annual photo-ID study for the past 5 years. Other offerings include tours to sea turtle preservation camps, hiking, sea kayaking, and bird watching. All are in small groups, with minimal environmental impact and great sensitivity to the natural surroundings.

Trek America, P.O. Box 189, Rockaway, NJ 07866 (✆ **800/221-0596** or 973/983-1144; fax 973/983-8551), organizes lengthy, active trips that combine trekking, hiking, van transportation, and camping in the Yucatán, Chiapas, Oaxaca, the Copper Canyon, and Mexico's Pacific coast, and touching on Mexico City and Guadalajara.

Vallarta Adventures, Edif. Marina Golf Local 13c, Marina Vallarta, Puerto Vallarta, Jal., C.P. 48354 (✆ **322/297-1212,** or 322/221-0657; www.vallarta-adventures.com), Puerto Vallarta's premier adventure tour company, offers expeditions by boat to the Marietas Islands nature preserve, by land to the foothills of the Sierra Madre, and by air to the remote mining village of San Sebastian and the town of Tequila. They also have two adjacent dolphin-swim facilities, with an emphasis on education and interactive communication, a canopy tour which takes you swinging from treetop to treetop, and a day spa at the private cove of Caletas, the former home of film great John Huston. All adventures are top quality, led by enthusiastic guides who mix adventure with spirited fun.

14 Getting Around

An important note: If your travel schedule depends on an important connection, say a plane trip between points or a ferry or bus connection, use the telephone numbers in this book or other information resources mentioned here to find out if the connection you are depending on is still available. Although we've done our best to provide accurate information, transportation schedules can and do change.

BY PLANE

To fly from point to point within Mexico, you'll rely on Mexican airlines. Mexico has two privately owned large national carriers: **Mexicana** (✆ **800/366-5400**) and **Aeromexico** (✆ **800/021-4000**), in addition to several up-and-coming regional carriers. Mexicana and Aeromexico both offer extensive connections to the United States as well as within Mexico.

Several of the new regional carriers are operated by or can be booked through Mexicana or Aeromexico. Regional carriers are **Aerocaribe** (see Mexicana); **Aerolitoral** (see Aeromexico); and **Aero Mar** (see Mexicana). The regional carriers are expensive, but they go to difficult-to-reach places. In each applicable section of this book, we mention regional carriers with all pertinent telephone numbers.

Because major airlines can book some regional carriers, read your ticket carefully to see if your connecting flight is on one of these smaller carriers—they may leave from a different airport or check in at a different counter, especially true in the Guadalajara airport.

AIRPORT TAXES Mexico charges an airport tax on all departures. Passengers leaving the country on an international departure pay $18.00—in dollars or the peso equivalent. It has become a common practice to include this departure tax in your ticket price, but double-check to make sure. Taxes on each domestic departure you make within Mexico cost around $12.50, unless you're on a connecting flight and have already paid at the start of the flight; you shouldn't be charged again if you have to change planes for a connecting flight. These taxes are usually included in the price of your ticket.

Starting in May 1999, Mexico began charging an additional $18 "tourism tax," the proceeds of which go into a tourism promotional fund. This may or may not be included in your ticket price, so be sure to set aside this amount in either dollars or pesos to pay at the airport upon departure.

RECONFIRMING FLIGHTS Although airlines in Mexico say it's not necessary to reconfirm a flight, it's still a good practice. To avoid getting bumped on popular, possibly overbooked flights, check in for an international flight an hour and a half in advance of travel.

BY CAR

Most Mexican roads are not up to U.S. standards of smoothness, hardness, width of curve, grade of hill, or safety marking. Driving at night is dangerous: The roads aren't very good and are rarely lit; the carts, pedestrians, bicycles, and even many trucks usually have no lights; and you can hit potholes, animals, rocks, dead ends, or bridges with no warning.

The "spirited" style of Mexican driving sometimes requires super vision and reflexes. Be prepared for different behavior, as when a truck driver flips on his left-turn signal when there's not a crossroad for miles. He's probably telling you the road's clear ahead for you to pass—after all, he's in a better position to see than you are. Another custom that's very important to respect is how to make a left turn. Never turn left by stopping in the middle of a highway with your left signal on. Instead, pull off the highway onto the right shoulder, wait for traffic to clear, then proceed across the road.

GASOLINE There's one government-owned brand of gas and one gasoline station name throughout the country—Pemex (Petroleras Mexicanas). There are two types of gas in Mexico: magna, an 87-octane unleaded gas; and the newer premium 93-octane. In Mexico, fuel and oil are sold by the liter, which is slightly more than a quart (40 liters equals about 10½ gal.). ***Important note:*** No credit cards are accepted for gas purchases. There is a new trend toward franchise Pemex stations, many of which have bathroom facilities and convenience stores—a great improvement over the old Pemex stations.

TOLL ROADS Mexico charges among the highest tolls in the world for its network of new toll roads. As a result, they are little used. Generally speaking, using the toll roads will cut your travel time between destinations. Older toll-free roads are generally in good condition but travel times are usually longer, because they tend to be mountainous and clotted with slow-moving trucks.

BREAKDOWNS Your best guide to repair shops is the Yellow Pages. For specific makes and shops that repair cars, look under "Automoviles y Camiones: Talleres de Reparación y Servicio"; auto-parts stores are listed under "Refacciones y Accesorios para Automoviles." To find a mechanic on the road, look for a sign that says TALLER MECÁNICO.

Places called *Vulcanizadora* or *Llantera* repair flat tires, and it is common to find them open 24 hours a day on the most traveled highways. Even if the place looks empty, chances are you will find someone who can help you fix a flat.

If your car breaks down on the road, help might already be on the way. Radio-equipped, green repair trucks operated by uniformed English-speaking officers patrol the major highways during daylight hours to aid motorists in trouble. These "Green Angels" will perform minor repairs and adjustments for free, but you pay for parts and materials.

MINOR ACCIDENTS When possible, many Mexicans drive away from minor accidents to avoid hassles with police, or try to make an immediate settlement to avoid involving the police. If the police arrive while the involved persons are still at the scene, everyone may be locked in jail until blame is assessed. In any case, you have to settle up immediately, which may take days of red tape. Foreigners who don't speak fluent Spanish are at a distinct disadvantage when trying to explain their side of the event. Three steps may help the foreigner who doesn't wish to do as the Mexicans do: If you're in your own car, notify your Mexican insurance company, whose job it is to intervene on your behalf. If you're in a rental car, notify the rental company immediately and ask how to contact the nearest adjuster. (You did buy insurance with the rental, right?) Finally, if all else fails, ask to contact the nearest Green Angel, who may be able to explain to officials that you are covered by insurance.

See also "Mexican Auto Insurance" under "Getting There," earlier in this chapter.

CAR RENTALS

You'll get the best price on Mexican rental cars if you reserve a car a week in advance in the United States. U.S. car-rental firms include **Avis** (© **800/331-1212** in the U.S.; 800/TRY-AVIS in Canada), **Budget** (© **800/527-0700** in the U.S. and Canada), **Hertz** (© **800/654-3131** in the U.S. and Canada), and **National** (© **800/CAR-RENT** in the U.S. and Canada). For European travelers, **Kemwel Holiday Auto** (© **800/678-0678**) and **Auto Europe** (© **800/223-5555**) can arrange Mexican rentals, sometimes through other agencies. These and some local firms have offices in Mexico City and most other large Mexican cities. You'll find rental desks at airports, all major hotels, and many travel agencies.

Cars are easy to rent if you have a major credit card, are 25 or over, and have a valid driver's license and passport with you. Without a credit card you must leave a cash deposit, usually a big one. Rent-here/leave-there arrangements are usually simple to make but more costly.

Car-rental costs are high in Mexico, because cars are more expensive here. The condition of rental cars has improved greatly over the years, however, and clean, comfortable, new cars are the norm. At press time, the basic cost of a 1-day rental of a Volkswagen Beetle, with unlimited mileage (but before 17% tax and $15 daily insurance), was $40 in Puerto Vallarta. Renting by the week gives you a lower daily rate. Avis was offering a basic 7-day weekly rate for a VW Beetle (before tax or insurance) of $220 in Puerto Vallarta. Prices may be considerably higher if you rent around a major holiday.

Car-rental companies usually write up a credit-card charge in U.S. dollars.

DEDUCTIBLES Be careful—these vary greatly in Mexico; some are as high as $2,500, which comes out of your pocket immediately in case of car damage. Hertz's deductible is $1,000 on a VW Beetle; Avis's is $500 for the same car.

INSURANCE Insurance is offered in two parts: Collision and damage insurance covers your car and others if the accident is your fault, and personal accident insurance covers you and anyone in your car. Read the fine print on the back of your rental agreement and note that insurance may be invalid if you have an accident while driving on an unpaved road.

DAMAGE Always inspect your car carefully and note every damaged or missing item, no matter how minute, on your rental agreement, or you may be charged.

TROUBLE NUMBER It's advisable to carefully note the rental company's trouble number, as well as the direct number of the agency where you rented the car.

BY TAXI

Taxis are the preferred way to get around almost all of the resort areas of Mexico, and also within Guadalajara. Short trips within towns are generally charged by preset zones, and are quite reasonable compared with U.S. rates. For longer trips or excursions to nearby cities, taxis can generally be hired for around $10 to $15 per hour, or for a negotiated daily rate. Even drops to different destinations, say between Puerto Vallarta and Barra de Navidad, can be arranged. A negotiated one-way price is usually much less than the cost of a rental car for a day, and service is much faster than traveling by bus. For anyone who is uncomfortable driving in Mexico, this is a convenient, comfortable route. An added bonus is that you have a Spanish-speaking person with you in case you run into any car or road trouble. Many taxi drivers speak at least some English. Your hotel can assist you with the arrangements.

Tips **Know Spanish for the Bus Ride**

There's little English spoken at bus stations, so come prepared with your destination written down, then double-check the departure.

BY BUS

Mexican buses are frequent, readily accessible, and can get you to almost anywhere you want to go. They're often the only way to get from large cities to other nearby cities and small villages. Don't hesitate to ask questions if you're confused about anything.

Dozens of Mexican companies operate large, air-conditioned buses between most cities. Travel class is generally labeled first (primera), second (segunda), and deluxe, which is referred to by a variety of names. The deluxe buses often have fewer seats than regular buses, show video movies en route, are air-conditioned, and have few stops; some also have complimentary refreshments. Many run express from the origin to the final destination, and they are well worth the few dollars more that you'll pay. In rural areas, buses are often of the school-bus variety, with lots of local color.

Whenever possible, it's best to buy your reserved-seat ticket, often via a computerized system, a day in advance for many long-distance routes and especially before holidays. Schedules are fairly dependable, so be at the terminal on time for departure. Current information must be obtained from local bus stations.

15 Tips on Accommodations

SAVING ON YOUR HOTEL ROOM

The **rack rate** is the maximum rate that a hotel charges for a room. Hardly anybody pays this price, however. To lower the cost of your room:

- **Ask about special rates or other discounts.** Always ask whether a room less expensive than the first one quoted is available, or whether any special rates apply to you. You may qualify for corporate, student, military, senior, or other discounts. Mention membership in AAA, AARP, frequent-flier programs, or trade unions, which may entitle you to special deals as well. Find out the hotel policy on children—do kids stay free in the room or is there a special rate?

- **Dial direct.** When booking a room in a chain hotel, you'll often get a better deal by calling the individual hotel's reservation desk than by calling the chain's main number.
- **Book online.** Many hotels offer Internet-only discounts, or supply rooms to Priceline, Hotwire, or Expedia at rates much lower than the ones you can get through the hotel itself.
- **Remember the law of supply and demand.** Resort hotels are most crowded and therefore most expensive on weekends, so discounts are usually available for midweek stays. Business hotels in downtown locations are busiest during the week, so you can expect big discounts over the weekend. Many hotels have high-season and low-season prices, and booking the day after "high season" ends can mean big discounts.
- **Look into group or long-stay discounts.** If you come as part of a large group, you should be able to negotiate a bargain rate, because the hotel can then guarantee occupancy in a number of rooms. Likewise, if you're planning a long stay (at least 5 days), you might qualify for a discount. As a general rule, expect 1 night free after a 7-night stay.
- **Avoid excess charges and hidden costs.** When you book a room, ask whether the hotel charges for parking. Use your own cellphone, pay phones, or prepaid phone cards instead of dialing direct from hotel phones, which usually have exorbitant rates. And don't be tempted by the room's minibar offerings: Most hotels charge through the nose for water, soda, and snacks. Finally, ask about local taxes and service charges, which can increase the cost of a room by 15% or more. If a hotel insists upon tacking on a surprise "energy surcharge" that wasn't mentioned at check-in or a "resort fee" for amenities you didn't use, you can often make a case for getting it removed.
- Consider the pros and cons of **all-inclusive** resorts and hotels. The term "all-inclusive" means different things at different hotels. Many all-inclusive hotels will include three meals daily, sports equipment, spa entry, and other amenities; others may include all or most drinks. In general, you'll save money going the "all-inclusive" way—as long as you use the facilities provided. The down side is that your choices are limited and you're stuck eating and playing in one place for the duration of your vacation.
- **Book an efficiency.** A room with a kitchenette allows you to shop for groceries and cook your own meals. This is a big money saver, especially for families on long stays.

LANDING THE BEST ROOM

Somebody has to get the best room in the house. It might as well be you. You can start by joining the hotel's frequent-guest program, which may make you eligible for upgrades. A hotel-branded credit card usually gives its owner "silver" or "gold" status in frequent-guest programs for free. Always ask about a corner room. They're often larger and quieter, with more windows and light, and they often cost the same as standard rooms. When you make your reservation, ask if the hotel is renovating; if it is, request a room away from the construction. Ask about nonsmoking rooms, rooms with views, rooms with twin, queen-size, or king-size beds. If you're a light sleeper, request a quiet room away from vending machines, elevators, restaurants, bars, and discos. Ask for one of the rooms that have been most recently renovated or redecorated.

If you aren't happy with your room when you arrive, say so. If another room is available, most lodgings will be willing to accommodate you.

In resort areas, particularly in warm climates, ask the following questions before you book a room:

- What's the view like? Cost-conscious travelers may be willing to pay less for a back room facing the parking lot, especially if they don't plan to spend much time in their room.
- Does the room have air-conditioning or ceiling fans? Do the windows open? If they do, and the nighttime entertainment takes place alfresco, you may want to find out when show time is over.
- What's included in the price? Your room may be moderately priced, but if you're charged for beach chairs, towels, sports equipment, and other amenities, you could end up spending more than you bargained for.
- How far is the room from the beach and other amenities? If it's far, is there transportation to and from the beach?

FAST FACTS: Mexico

Abbreviations Dept. (apartments); Apdo. (post office box); av. (avenida; avenue); c/ (calle; street); calz. (calzada; boulevard). "C" on faucets stands for caliente (hot), and "F" stands for fría (cold). PB (planta baja) means ground floor, and most buildings count the next floor up as the first floor (1).

Business Hours In general, businesses in larger cities are open between 9am and 7pm; in smaller towns many close between 2 and 4pm. Most are closed on Sunday. Bank hours are Monday through Friday from 9 or 9:30am to 5 or 6pm. Increasingly, banks are offering Saturday hours for at least a half-day.

Cameras/Film Film costs about the same as in the United States.

Customs See "Entry Requirements & Customs," earlier in this chapter.

Doctors/Dentists Every embassy and consulate can recommend local doctors and dentists with good training and modern equipment; some of the doctors and dentists even speak English. Hotels with a large foreign clientele can often recommend English-speaking doctors. Almost all first-class hotels in Mexico have a doctor on call.

Drug Laws To be blunt, don't use or possess illegal drugs in Mexico. Mexican officials have no tolerance for drug users, and jail is their solution, with very little hope of getting out until the sentence (usually a long one) is completed or heavy fines or bribes are paid. Remember—in Mexico the legal system assumes you are guilty until proven innocent. (***Important note:*** It isn't uncommon to be befriended by a fellow user, only to be turned in by that "friend"—he's collected a bounty for turning you in.) Bring prescription drugs in their original containers. If possible, pack a copy of the original prescription with the generic name of the drug.

U.S. Customs officials are also on the lookout for diet drugs that are sold in Mexico but are illegal in the U.S. If you buy antibiotics over the counter (which you can do in Mexico)—say, for a sinus infection—and still have some left, you probably won't be hassled by U.S. Customs.

Drugstores Drugstores (farmacias) will sell you just about anything you want, with a prescription or without one. Most drugstores are open Monday through Saturday from 8am to 8pm. There are generally one or two 24-hour pharmacies in each major resort area. If you are in a smaller town and need to buy medicines after normal hours, ask for the *farmacia de turno;* pharmacies take turns staying open during off-hours.

Electricity The electrical system in Mexico is 110 volts A/C (60 cycles), as in the United States and Canada. However, in reality it may cycle more slowly and overheat your appliances. To compensate, select a medium or low speed for hair dryers. Many older hotels still have electrical outlets for flat two-prong plugs; you'll need an adapter for any modern electrical apparatus that has an enlarged end on one prong or that has three prongs. Many first-class and deluxe hotels have the three-holed outlets (*trifásicos* in Spanish). Those that don't may have loan adapters, but to be sure, it's always better to carry your own.

Embassies/Consulates They provide valuable lists of doctors and lawyers, as well as regulations concerning marriages in Mexico. Contrary to popular belief, your embassy cannot get you out of a Mexican jail, provide postal or banking services, or fly you home when you run out of money. Consular officers can provide you with advice on most matters and problems, however. Most countries have a representative embassy in Mexico City, and many have consular offices or representatives in the provinces.

The Embassy of the **United States** in Mexico City is next to the Hotel María Isabel Sheraton at Paseo de la Reforma 305, at the corner of Río Danubio (✆ **55/5080-2000,** 55/5209-9100, or 55/5511-9980). Hours are 10am to 2pm Monday through Friday. There is a U.S. Consulate General in Guadalajara, Progreso 175 (✆ **33/3825-2700**), and a consular agency in Puerto Vallarta (✆ **322/222-0069**). For the services tourists are most likely to require, the consulates are open from 8:30am to noon Monday to Friday.

The Embassy of **Australia** in Mexico City is at Rubén Darío 55, Col. Polanco (✆ **55/5531-5225;** fax 55/5531-9552). It's open Monday to Thursday from 8:30am to 2pm and 3 to 5pm, and Friday from 8:30am to 2pm.

The Embassy of **Canada** in Mexico City is at Schiller 529, in Polanco (✆ **55/5724-7900**); it's open Monday through Friday from 9am to 1pm and 2 to 5pm (at other times the name of a duty officer is posted on the embassy door). Additionally, Canada has consular services in Guadalajara (✆ **33/3615-6215**) and in Puerto Vallarta at Zaragoza 160, 1st floor (✆ **322/222-5398**).

The Embassy of the **United Kingdom** in Mexico City is in Río Lerma 71, Col. Cuahutemoc (✆ **55/5207-2089;** www.embajadabritanica.com.mx); it's open Monday through Friday from 8:30am to 3:30pm. There's also a UK consular office in Guadalajara (✆ **33/3761-6405**).

The Embassy of **Ireland** in Mexico City is at Cerrada Blvd. Avila Camacho 76, 3rd floor, Col. Lomas de Chapultepec (✆ **55/5520-5803**). It's open Monday to Friday from 9am to 5pm.

The **South African** Embassy is at Andres Bello 10, 9th floor, Col. Polanco (✆ **55/5282-9260**). It's open Monday to Friday from 8am to 3:30pm.

The Embassy of **New Zealand** in Mexico City is at José Luis Lagrange 103, 10th floor, Col. Los Morales Polanco (✆ **55/5283-9460;** kiwimexico@compuserve.com.mx); it's open Monday through Thursday from 9am to 2pm and 3 to 5pm, and Friday from 9am to 2pm.

Emergencies The 24-hour Tourist Help Line in Mexico City is ✆ **800/903-9200** or 55/5250-0151. A tourist legal assistance office (Procuraduría del Turista) is located in Mexico City (✆ **55/5625-8153** or 55/5625-8154). Though the phones are frequently busy, they do offer 24-hour service, and there is always an English-speaking person available.

Internet Access In large cities and resort areas, a growing number of hotels offer Internet access. You'll also find at least one cybercafe. Note that many ISPs will automatically cut off your Internet connection after a specified period of time (say, 10 min.), because telephone lines are at a premium. Some Telmex offices also have free access Internet kiosks in their reception areas.

Legal Aid International Legal Defense Counsel, 111 S. 15th St., 24th Floor, Packard Building, Philadelphia, PA 19102 (✆ **215/977-9982**), is a law firm specializing in legal difficulties of Americans abroad. See also "Embassies/Consulates" and "Emergencies," above.

Liquor Laws The legal drinking age in Mexico is 18; however, it is extremely rare that anyone will be asked for ID or denied purchase. Grocery stores sell everything from beer and wine to national and imported liquors. Authorities are beginning to target drunk drivers more aggressively. It's a good idea to drive defensively.

Mail Postage for a postcard or letter is 59¢; it may arrive anywhere between 1 and 6 weeks later. A registered letter costs $1.90. To send a package can be quite expensive—the Mexican Postal service charges $8.00 per kilo (2.20 lbs.)—and unreliable; it takes between 2 and 6 weeks, if it arrives at all.

Packages are frequently lost within the Mexican postal system, although the situation has improved in recent years. The recommended way to send a package or important mail continues to be through Federal Express, DHL, UPS, or any other reputable international mail service.

Newspapers/Magazines In Puerto Vallarta, the English-language *Vallarta Today* is published daily, and the *Tribune* is published weekly. Newspaper kiosks also carry a selection of English-language magazines.

Police In Mexico City, police are to be suspected as frequently as they are to be trusted; however, you'll find many who are quite honest and helpful. In the rest of the country, especially in the tourist areas, the majority are very protective of international visitors. Several cities, including Puerto Vallarta, have gone as far as to set up a special corps of English-speaking Tourist Police to assist with directions, guidance, and more.

Taxes There's a 15% IVA tax on goods and services in most of Mexico, and it's supposed to be included in the posted price. There is an exit tax of around $18 imposed on every foreigner leaving the country, usually included in the price of airline tickets.

Telephone/Fax Mexico's telephone system is slowly but surely catching up with modern times. All telephone numbers have 10 digits. Every city and town that has telephone access has a 2-digit (Mexico City, Monterrey, and Guadalajara) or 3-digit (everywhere else) area code. In Mexico City, Monterrey, and Guadalajara, local numbers have 8 digits; elsewhere, local numbers have 7 digits. To place a local call, you do not need to dial the area code. Many fax numbers are also regular telephone numbers; ask whomever answers for the fax tone (*"me da tono de fax, por favor"*). Cellular phones are very popular for small businesses in resort areas and smaller communities. To call a cellular number inside the same area code, dial 044 and then the number. To dial the cellular phone from anywhere else in Mexico, first dial 01, and then the 3-digit area code and the 7-digit number. To dial it from the U.S., dial 011-52, plus the 3-digit area code and the 7-digit number.

The **country code** for Mexico is **52.**

To call Mexico: If you're calling Mexico from the United States:

1. Dial the international access code: 011
2. Dial the country code: 52

3. Dial the 2- or 3-digit area code, then the 8- or 7-digit number. For example, if you wanted to call the U.S. consulate in Acapulco from the U.S., the whole number would be 011-52-744-469-0556. If you wanted to dial the U.S. embassy in Mexico City, the whole number would be 011-52-55-5209-9100.

To make international calls: To make international calls from Mexico, first dial 00, then the country code (U.S. or Canada 1, U.K. 44, Ireland 353, Australia 61, New Zealand 64). Next, dial the area code and number. For example, to call the British Embassy in Washington, you would dial 00-1-202-588-7800.

For directory assistance: Dial ✆ **040** if you're looking for a number inside Mexico. ***Note:*** Listings usually appear under the owner's name, not the name of the business, and your chances of finding an English-speaking operator are slim to none.

For operator assistance: If you need operator assistance in making a call, dial 090 to make an international call, and 020 to call a number in Mexico.

Toll-free numbers: Numbers beginning with 800 within Mexico are toll-free, but calling a U.S. toll-free number from Mexico costs the same as an overseas call. To call an 800 number in the U.S., dial 001-880 and the last 7 digits of the toll-free number. To call an 888 number in the U.S., dial 001-881 and the last 7 digits of the toll-free number.

Time Zone Central standard time prevails throughout most of Mid-Pacific Mexico, but the state of Nayarit, including Nuevo Vallarta, is on Mountain Standard Time. Mexico observes daylight savings time.

Tipping Most service employees in Mexico count on tips for the majority of their income—especially true for bellboys and waiters. Bellboys should receive the equivalent of 50¢ to $1 U.S. per bag; waiters generally receive 10% to 20% depending on the level of service. In Mexico, it is not customary to tip taxi drivers, unless they are hired by the hour, or provide touring or other special services.

Toilets Public toilets are not common in Mexico, but an increasing number are available, especially at fast-food restaurants and Pemex gas stations. These facilities and restaurant and club restrooms commonly have attendants, who expect a small tip (about 50¢).

Useful Phone Numbers **Tourist Help Line,** available 24 hours (✆ **800/903-9200** toll-free inside Mexico). **Mexico Hotline** (✆ **800/44-MEXICO**). **U.S. Dept. of State Travel Advisory,** staffed 24 hours (✆ **202/647-5225**). **U.S. Passport Agency** (✆ **202/647-0518**). **U.S. Centers for Disease Control International Traveler's Hotline** (✆ **404/332-4559**).

Water Most hotels have decanters or bottles of purified water in the rooms, and the better hotels have either purified water from regular taps or special taps marked agua purificada. Some hotels will charge for in-room bottled water. Virtually any hotel, restaurant, or bar will bring you purified water if you specifically request it, but you'll usually be charged for it. Bottled purified water is sold widely at drugstores and grocery stores (popular brands include Santa Maria, Ciel, Agua Pura, Pureza, and Bonafit). Evian and other imported brands are widely available.

2

Settling into Puerto Vallarta

No matter how extensively I travel in Mexico, Puerto Vallarta remains my favorite part of this colorful country, for its unrivaled combination of simple pleasures and sophisticated charms. No other place in Mexico offers both the best of the country's natural beauty and an authentic dose of its vibrant culture.

Vallarta was never the "sleepy little fishing village" that many proclaim. It began life as a port for processing silver brought down from mines in the Sierra Madre—then was forever transformed by a movie director and two star-crossed lovers. In 1963, John Huston brought stars Ava Gardner and Richard Burton here to film the Tennessee Williams play *Night of the Iguana.* Burton's new love, Elizabeth Taylor, came along to ensure the romance remained in full bloom—even though both were married to others at the time. Titillated, the international paparazzi arrived, and when they weren't shooting photos of the famous couple—or of Gardner water-skiing back to Vallarta's Los Muertos pier from the set in Mismaloya, surrounded by a bevy of beach boys—they photographed the beauty of Puerto Vallarta.

Luxury hotels and shopping centers have sprung up north and south of the original town, allowing Vallarta to grow into a city of 250,000 without sacrificing its considerable charms. It boasts the services and infrastructure of a modern city as well as the authenticity of a colonial Mexican village.

Cool breezes flow down from the mountains along the Río Cuale, which runs through the center of town. Fanciful public sculptures grace the main waterfront street, or *malecón,* which is bordered by lively restaurants, shops, and bars. The *malecón* is a magnet for both residents and visitors who stroll the broad walkway to take in an ocean breeze, a multihued sunset, or a moonlit, perfect wave.

1 Puerto Vallarta Essentials

885km (553 miles) NW of Mexico City; 339km (212 miles) W of Guadalajara; 285km (178 miles) NW of Manzanillo; 447km (278 miles) SE of Mazatlán; 239km (149 miles) SW of Tepic

Puerto Vallarta: Hotel Zone & Beaches

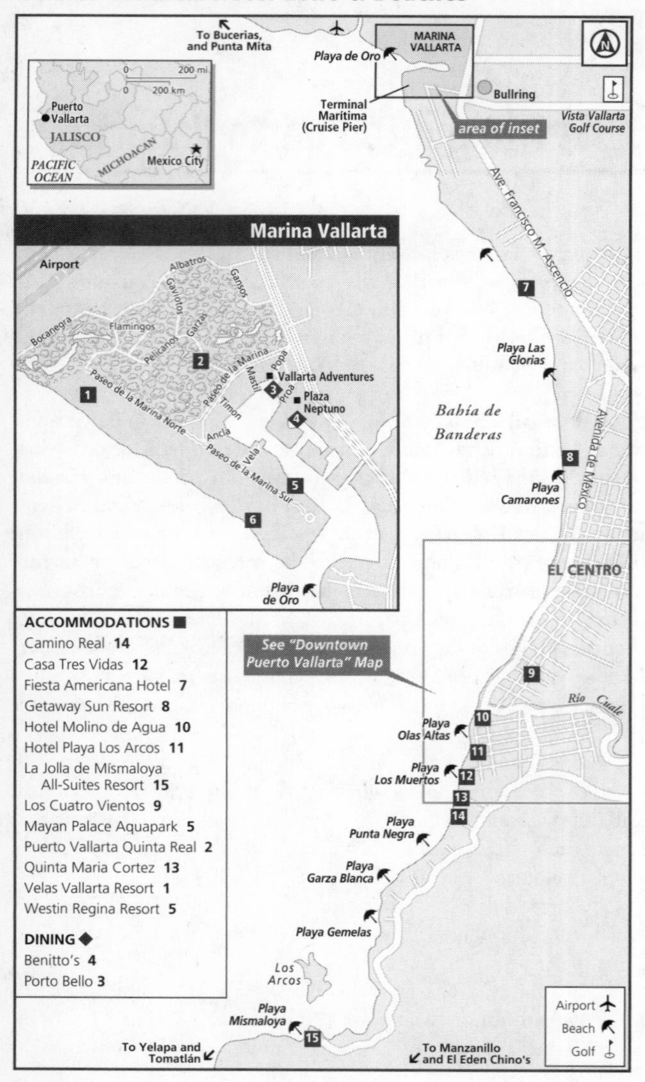

GETTING THERE & DEPARTING

BY PLANE For a list of international carriers serving Mexico, see chapter 1. Local numbers of some international carriers serving

Puerto Vallarta are **Alaska Airlines** (✆ **322/221-1350** or 322/221-1353), **American Airlines** (✆ **322/221-1799** or 322/221-1927), **America West** (✆ **322/221-1333,** or 001-880/235-9292 inside Mexico), and **Continental** (✆ **322/221-1025** or 322/221-2212).

Aeromexico (✆ **322/224-2777** or 322/221-1055) flies from Los Angeles, Aguascalientes, Guadalajara, La Paz, León, Mexico City, Morelia, and Tijuana. **Mexicana** (✆ **322/224-8900** or 322/221-1266) has direct or nonstop flights from Chicago, Los Angeles, Guadalajara, Mazatlán, and Mexico City.

BY CAR The coastal **Highway 200** is the only choice from Mazatlán (6 hr. north) or Manzanillo (3½-4 hr. south). Highway 15 from Guadalajara to Tepic takes 6 hours; to save as much as 2 hours, take Highway 15A from Chapalilla to Compostela, bypassing Tepic, then continue south on Highway 200 to Puerto Vallarta.

BY BUS The bus station, **Central Camionera de Puerto Vallarta,** is just north of the airport, approximately 11km (7 miles) from downtown. It offers overnight guarded parking and baggage storage. Most major first-class bus lines operate from here, with transportation to points throughout Mexico, including Mazatlán, Tepic, Manzanillo, Guadalajara, and Mexico City. Taxis into town cost approximately $7.50 and are readily available; public buses operate from 7am to 11pm and regularly stop in front of the arrivals hall.

ORIENTATION

ARRIVING BY PLANE The airport is close to the north end of town near the Marina Vallarta, about 10km (6 miles) from downtown. **Transportes Terrestres** minivans and **Aeromovil** taxis make the trip. They use a zone pricing system, with fares clearly posted at the ticket booths. Fares start at $10 for a ride to Marina Vallarta and go up to $30 for the south shore hotels. Federally licensed airport taxis exclusively provide transportation from the airport, and their fares are more than three times as high as city (yellow) taxi fares. A trip to downtown Puerto Vallarta costs $20, whereas a return trip using a city taxi costs only $5. Only airport cabs may pick up passengers leaving the airport. However, if you don't have too much baggage, you can cross the highway using the new overpass, and there you'll find yellow cabs lined up.

VISITOR INFORMATION The **Municipal Tourism Office,** Juárez and Independencia (✆ **322/223-2500,** ext. 230), is in a corner of the white Presidencia Municipal building (city hall) on the northwest end of the main square. In addition to offering a listing of current events and promotional brochures for local activities and services, the employees can also assist with specific questions—there's usually an English speaker on staff. This is also the office of the tourist police. It's open Monday through Friday from 9am to 8pm. During low season it may close for lunch between 1 and 3pm or 2 and 4pm.

The **State Tourism Office,** Plaza Marina L 144, 2nd floor (✆ **322/221-2676,** 322/221-2677, or 322/221-2678), also offers brochures and can assist with specific questions about Puerto Vallarta and other points in the state of Jalisco, including Guadalajara, Costa Alegre, the town of Tequila, and the program that promotes stays in authentic rural haciendas. It's open Monday through Friday from 9am to 5pm.

CITY LAYOUT The seaside promenade, the *malecón,* is a common reference point for giving directions. It's next to **Paseo Díaz Ordaz** and runs north-south through the central downtown area. From the waterfront, the town stretches back into the hills a half-dozen blocks. The areas bordering the **Río Cuale** are the oldest parts of town—the original Puerto Vallarta. The area immediately south of the river, called **Olas Altas** after its main street (and sometimes Los Muertos after the beach of the same name), is home to a growing selection of sidewalk cafes, fine restaurants, espresso bars, and hip nightclubs. In the center of town, nearly everything is within walking distance both north and south of the river. **Bridges** on Insurgentes (northbound traffic) and Ignacio Vallarta (southbound traffic) link the two sections of downtown.

AREA LAYOUT Beyond downtown, Puerto Vallarta has grown along the beach to the north and south. Linking downtown to the airport is **Avenida Francisco Medina Ascencio.** Along this main thoroughfare are many luxury hotels (in an area called the **Zona Hotelera,** or Hotel Zone), plus several shopping centers with casual restaurants.

Marina Vallarta, a resort city within a city, is at the northern edge of the Hotel Zone not far from the airport. It boasts modern luxury hotels, condominiums, and homes, a huge marina with 450 yacht slips, a golf course, restaurants and bars, a water park, and several shopping plazas. Because it was originally a swamp, the beaches are the least desirable in the area, with darker sand and seasonal inflows of cobblestones. The Marina Vallarta peninsula faces the bay and looks south to the town of Puerto Vallarta.

Nuevo Vallarta is a planned resort north of the airport, across the Ameca River in the state of Nayarit (about 13km/8 miles north of downtown). It also has hotels, condominiums, and a yacht marina, with a limited selection of restaurants and shopping, although the new Paradise Plaza mall is bringing in new options. Most hotels there are all-inclusive, with some of the finest beaches in the bay, but guests usually travel into Puerto Vallarta (about a $13 cab ride) for anything other than poolside or beach action. Regularly scheduled public bus service costs about $1.50 and runs until 10pm.

Bucerías, a small beachfront village of cobblestone streets, villas, and small hotels, is farther north along Banderas Bay, 30km (19 miles) beyond the airport. Past Bucerías, following the curved coastline of Banderas Bay, is **Punta Mita.** Once a rustic fishing village, it is in the process of development as a luxury destination. In the works are a total of five exclusive luxury boutique resorts, private villas, and three golf courses. The site of an ancient celestial observatory, it is an exquisite setting, with white sand beaches and clear waters.

In the other direction from downtown is the southern coastal highway, home to more luxury hotels. Immediately south of town lies the exclusive residential and rental district of **Conchas Chinas.** Ten kilometers (6 miles) south, on **Playa Mismaloya** (where *Night of the Iguana* was filmed), lies the Jolla de Mismaloya resort, emerging as the west coast's premier dive resort. There's no road on the southern shoreline of Banderas Bay, but three small coastal villages are popular attractions for visitors to Puerto Vallarta: **Las Animas, Quimixto,** and **Yelapa,** all accessible only by boat. The tiny, pristine cove of **Caletas,** site of John Huston's former home, is a popular day- or nighttime excursion (contact **Vallarta Adventures; © 866/256-2739** toll-free in the U.S. or 322/297-1212, ext. 3; for more information on this trip).

GETTING AROUND

BY TAXI Taxis are plentiful and relatively inexpensive in Puerto Vallarta. Most trips from downtown to the northern Hotel Zone and Marina Vallarta cost $3.50 to $7; to or from Marina Vallarta to Mismaloya Beach (to the south) costs $10. Rates are charged by zone and are generally posted in the lobbies of hotels. Taxis can also be hired by the hour or day for longer trips. Rates run $12 to $15 per hour, with discounts available for full-day rates—consider this as an alternative to renting a car.

Tips **Steer Clear of the Rambo Bus!**

Buses in Vallarta tend to be rather aggressive, and some even sport names—including "Terminator," "Rambo," and "Tornado." Don't tempt fate by assuming these buses will stop for pedestrians. Although Vallarta has an extremely low crime rate, bus accidents are frequent—and frequently fatal.

BY CAR Rental cars are available at the airport and through travel agencies, but unless you're planning a distant side trip, don't bother. Car rentals are expensive, averaging $66 per day, and parking around town is difficult. If you see a sign for a $10 jeep rental or $20 car rental, be aware that these are lures to get people to attend timeshare presentations. Unless you are interested in a timeshare, stopping to inquire will be a waste of your time.

BY BUS City buses, easy to navigate and inexpensive, will serve just about all your transportation needs. They run from the airport through the Hotel Zone along Morelos Street (1 block inland from the *malecón*), across the Río Cuale, and inland on Vallarta, looping back through the downtown hotel and restaurant districts on Insurgentes and several other downtown streets. To get to the northern hotel strip from old Puerto Vallarta, take the ZONA HOTELES, IXTAPA, or LAS JUNTAS bus. These buses may also post the names of hotels they pass, such as Krystal, Fiesta Americana, Sheraton, and others. Buses marked MARINA VALLARTA travel inside this area, stopping at the major hotels there.

Other buses operate every 10 to 15 minutes south to either Mismaloya Beach or Boca de Tomatlán (a sign in the front window indicates the destination) from Constitución and Basilio Badillo, a few blocks south of the river.

Buses run generally from 6am to 11pm, and it's rare to wait more than a few minutes for one. The fare is about 40¢.

BY BOAT The cruise ship pier *(muelle),* also called Terminal Marítima, is where **excursion boats** to Yelapa, Las Animas, Quimixto, and the Marietas Islands depart. It's north of town near the airport, an inexpensive taxi or bus ride from town. Just take any bus marked IXTAPA, LAS JUNTAS, PITILLAL, or AURORA and tell the driver to let you off at the Terminal Marítima. ***Note:*** Odd though it may seem, you must pay a $1 fee (this is a federal tax) to gain access to the pier—and your departing excursion boat.

Tips Don't Let Taxi Drivers Steer You Wrong

Beware of restaurant recommendations offered by taxi drivers—many receive a commission from restaurants where they discharge passengers. Be especially wary if a driver tries to talk you out of a restaurant you've already selected.

Water taxis to Yelapa, Las Animas, and Quimixto leave at 10:30 and 11am from the pier at Los Muertos Beach (south of downtown), on Rodolfo Rodríguez next to the Hotel Marsol. Another water taxi departs at 11am from the beachfront pier at the northern edge of the *malecón.* A round-trip ticket to Yelapa (the farthest point) costs $25. Return trips usually depart between 3 and 4pm, but confirm the pickup time with your water taxi captain. Other water taxis depart from Boca de Tomatlán, about 30 minutes south of town by public bus. These water taxis are the better option if you want more flexible departure and return times from the southern beaches. Generally, they leave on the hour for the southern shore destinations, or more frequently if there is traffic. Price is about $12 round-trip, with rates now clearly posted on a sign on the beach. A private water taxi costs $35 to $55 (depending on your destination) and allows you to choose your own return time. They'll take up to eight people for that price, so often people band together at the beach to hire one.

FAST FACTS: Puerto Vallarta

American Express The local office is at Morelos 660, at the corner of Abasolo (© **01-800/504-0400** in Mexico, or 322/223-2955). It's open Monday through Friday from 9am to 6pm, Saturday from 9am to 1pm. It offers excellent, efficient travel agency services in addition to money exchange and traveler's checks.

Area Code The telephone area code is **322.**

Climate It's warm all year, with tropical temperatures; however, evenings and early mornings in the winter can turn quite cool. Summers are sunny, with an increase in humidity during the rainy season, between May and October. Rains come almost every afternoon in June and July, and are usually brief but strong—just enough to cool off the air for evening activities. In September, heat and humidity are least comfortable and rains heaviest.

Consumer Assistance Tourists with complaints about taxis, stores, abusive timeshare presentations, or other matters should contact **PROFECO,** the consumer protection office (✆ **322/225-0000** or 322/225-0018). The office is open Monday through Friday from 8:30am to 3:30pm and may not have fluent English-speaking staff.

Currency Exchange Banks are found throughout downtown and in the other prime shopping areas. Most banks are open Monday through Friday from 9am to 5pm, with shorter hours on Saturday. ATMs are common throughout Vallarta, including the central plaza downtown. They are becoming the most favorable way to exchange currency, with bank rates plus 24-hour convenience. Money exchange houses *(casas de cambio),* located throughout town, offer longer hours than the banks with only slightly lower exchange rates.

Embassies/Consulates The consulates are in a building on the southern border of the central plaza (you'll see the U.S. and Canadian flags). The **U.S. Consular Agency** office (✆ **322/222-0069;** fax 322/223-0074, 24 hr. a day for emergencies) is open Monday through Friday from 10am to 2pm. The **Canadian Consulate** (✆ **322/222-5398** or 322/223-0858; 24-hr. emergency line 01-800/706-2900) is open Monday through Friday from 9am to 4pm.

Emergencies **Police** emergency, ✆ **060;** local police, ✆ **322/221-2587** or 322/221-2588; intensive care **ambulance,** ✆ **322/225-0386** (*Note:* English-speaking assistance is not always available at this number); **Red Cross,** ✆ **322/222-1533; Global Life Ambulance Service** (provides both ground and air ambulance service), ✆ **322/226-1010,** ext. 304.

Hospitals The following offer U.S.-standards service and are available 24 hours: **Ameri-Med Urgent Care,** Avenida Francisco Medina Ascencio at Plaza Neptuno, Local D-1, Marina Vallarta (✆ **322/221-0023;** fax 322/221-0026; www.amerimed-hospitals.com); and **San Javier Marina Hospital,** Av. Francisco Medina Ascencio 2760, Zona Hotelera (✆ **322/226-1010**).

Internet Access Puerto Vallarta is probably the most wired destination in Mexico. **The Net House,** Ignacio L. Vallarta 232

(✆ **322/222-6953;** info@vallartacafes.com), two blocks past the southbound bridge, has 15 computers with fast connections and English keyboards. It's open daily from 8am to 2am and charges $3.50 per hour. **Café.com** (✆ **322/222-0092**), Olas Altas 250, at the corner of Basilio Badillo, charges $2 for 30 minutes. It offers complete computer services, a full bar, and food service. It's open daily from 8am to 2am. Some hotels have lobby e-mail kiosks, but they're more expensive than the Net cafes.

Newspapers & Magazines ***Vallarta Today,*** a daily English-language newspaper (✆ **322/225-3303** or 322/224-2829), is a good source for local information and upcoming events. The bilingual quarterly city magazine ***Vallarta Lifestyles*** (✆ **322/221-0106**) is also very popular but provides listings only of services that advertise. Both are for sale at area newsstands and hotel gift shops. The weekly English-language ***P.V. Tribune*** (✆ **322/223-0585**) is distributed free throughout town and offers a more objective local viewpoint.

Pharmacies **CMQ Farmacia,** Basilio Badillo 365 (✆ **322/222-1330**), is open 24 hours and delivers between 5 and 11pm, free to hotels, with a minimum purchase of $10. **Farmacias Guadalajara,** Emiliano Zapata 232 (✆ **322/224-1811**), is also open 24 hours.

Post Office The *correo* is at Mina 188 (✆ **322/222-1888**). It's open Monday through Friday from 8am to 7pm, Saturday from 9am to 1pm. A second location, on Colombia St., behind Hidalgo park, is open the same hours.

Safety Puerto Vallarta enjoys a very low crime rate. Public transportation is safe to use, and Tourist Police (dressed in white safari uniforms with white hats) are available to answer questions, give directions, and offer assistance. Most encounters with the police are linked to using or purchasing drugs—so don't (see chapter 1). ***Note:*** The tourist police conduct random personal searches for drugs. Although there is some question about their right to do this, the best course of action if they want to frisk you is to comply—objecting will likely result in a free tour of the local jail. However, you are within your rights to request the name of the officer. Report any unusual incidents to the local consular office.

2 Where To Stay

Beyond a varied selection of hotels, Puerto Vallarta has many other types of accommodations. Oceanfront or marina-view condominiums and elegant private villas can offer families and small groups a better value and more ample space than a hotel. For more information on short-term rentals, check out **www.virtualvallarta.com**. Prices start at $99 a night for non-beachfront condos and go to $1,000 for penthouse condos or private villas. One full-service travel agency that specializes in villa rentals is **Holland's** (✆ **415/841-1194** or 618/236-2787; www.PuertoVallartaVillas.com). Susan Weisman's **Bayside Properties,** Francisco Rodríguez 160, corner of Olas Altas (✆ **322/223-4424;** www.puertovallarta bayside.com), rents gay-friendly condos, villas, and hotels for individuals and large groups. She can arrange airport pickup and in-villa cooks.

This section lists hotels in directional order, moving south along Banderas Bay from the airport.

MARINA VALLARTA

Marina Vallarta is the most modern and deluxe area of hotel development in Puerto Vallarta. Located immediately south of the airport and just north of the cruise-ship terminal, it's a planned development whose centerpiece is a 450-slip modern marina.

The hotels reviewed below are on the beachfront of the peninsula. The beaches here are much less attractive than beaches in other parts of the bay; the sand is darker, firmly packed, and, during certain times of the year, quite rocky. These hotels compensate with oversize pool areas and exotic landscaping. This area suits families and those looking for lots of centralized activity. Marina Vallarta is also home to an 18-hole **golf course** designed by Joe Finger. Also here, across from the Mayan Palace Resort, is the **Mayan Palace Aquapark** (✆ **322/226-6000,** ext. 824), with water slides and tubes, pools, an inner-tube canal, and snack-bar facilities. It's open to the public daily from 11am to 6pm and costs $7 for adults, $5 for kids.

In addition to the hotels reviewed below, another reliable choice is the **Puerto Vallarta Quinta Real,** on the golf course at Pelicanos 311 (✆ **322/221-0800;** fax 322/221-0801). The elegant, boutique-style hotel has extra-large rooms, an on-site spa, and a lovely pool. High-season rates average $250.

Because of traffic more than distance, a taxi from the Marina to downtown takes 20 to 30 minutes.

Velas Vallarta Grand Suite Resort ★★★ Kids The beachfront Velas Vallarta is an excellent choice for families. Each suite offers a full-size, fully equipped kitchen, ample living and dining areas, separate bedroom or bedrooms, and a large balcony with seating. The apartments—recently upgraded with new furnishings—are tastefully decorated, with light wood furnishings, cool terrazzo floors, bright fabrics, and marble tub/shower combinations. This property is part hotel, part full-ownership condominiums, which means each suite is the size of a residential unit. The suites all have partial ocean views; they face a central area where three freeform swimming pools, complete with bridges and waterfalls, meander through tropical gardens. A full range of services means you'll never need to leave the place if you don't want to. The Marina Vallarta Golf Club is across the street, and special packages are available for Velas guests.

Paseo de la Marina 485, Marina Vallarta, Puerto Vallarta, Jal., 48354. ✆ **800/659-8477** in the U.S. and Canada, or 322/221-0091. Fax 322/221-0755. www.velas vallarta.com. 361 units. High season $258 double, $410–$760 suite; low season $211 double, $351–$700 suite. AE, DC, MC, V. Free indoor parking. **Amenities:** 2 restaurants; poolside snack bar; lobby bar; 3 pools; golf privileges at Marina Vallarta Golf Club; 3 lighted tennis courts; fitness center with spa and massage; beach with watersports equipment rental; bicycle rentals; activities program for children and adults; concierge; travel agency; car rental; minimarket; deli; salon; room service; laundry. *In room:* A/C, TV, dataport, full kitchen with coffeemaker, hair dryer, iron, safe.

Westin Regina Resort ★★★ Stunning architecture and vibrant colors are the hallmark of this award-winning property, considered Puerto Vallarta's finest. Although the grounds are large—over 21 acres with 258m (850 ft.) of beachfront—the warm service and gracious hospitality create the feeling of an intimate resort. Hundreds of tall palms surround the spectacular central freeform pool. Frequently you'll find hammocks strung between the palms closest to the beach, where there's a wooden playground for kids. Rooms are contemporary in style, with oversize wood furnishings, tile floors, original art, and tub/shower combinations. Balconies have panoramic views. Eight junior suites and some double rooms have Jacuzzis, and the five grand suites and presidential suite are two-level, with ample living areas. Two floors of rooms make up the Royal Beach Club, with VIP services, including private concierge. The fitness center is one of the most modern, well-equipped facilities in Vallarta.

Paseo de la Marina Sur 205, Marina Vallarta, Puerto Vallarta, Jal., 48321. ✆ **800/228-3000** in the U.S., or 322/221-1100. Fax 322/221-1121. www.westinpv.com. 280 units. High season $258–$295 double, $585–$802 suite; low season $217–$234 double, $480–$600 suite. AE, DC, MC, V. Free parking. **Amenities:** 2 restaurants; 2 poolside bars; lobby bar; oceanside pool; golf privileges at Marina Vallarta Golf Club; 3 lighted grass tennis courts; full-service, state-of-the-art health club with treadmills, Stairmasters, resistance equipment, sauna, steam room, solarium, whirlpool, massage, and salon; Kids' Club; travel agency; car rental; shopping arcade; 24-hr. room service; laundry. *In room:* A/C, TV, dataport, minibar, coffeemaker, hair dryer, iron, safe-deposit box.

THE HOTEL ZONE

The main street running between the airport and town is Avenida Francisco Medina Ascencio, commonly referred to as Avenida de las Palmas. The hotels here offer excellent, wide beachfronts with generally tranquil waters for swimming. From here it's a quick taxi or bus ride to downtown.

Fiesta Americana Puerto Vallarta ★ The Fiesta Americana's towering, three-story, thatched *palapa* lobby is a landmark in the Hotel Zone, and the hotel is known for its excellent beach and friendly service. An abundance of plants, splashing fountains, constant breezes, and comfortable seating areas in the lobby create a casual South Seas ambience. The nine-story terra-cotta-colored building embraces a large plaza with a pool facing the beach. Marble-trimmed rooms in neutral tones with pastel accents contain carved headboards and comfortable rattan and wicker furniture. All have private balconies with ocean and pool views.

Av. Francisco Medina Ascencio Km 2.5, Puerto Vallarta, Jal., 48300. ✆ **322/224-2010.** Fax 322/224-2108. www.fiestaamericana.com. 291 units. High season $232 double; low season $148 double. Year-round $256–$819 suite. AE, DC, MC, V. Limited free parking. **Amenities:** 3 restaurants; lobby bar with live music nightly; large pool with activities and children's activities in high season; travel agency; salon; room service; laundry. *In room:* A/C, TV, minibar, hair dryer, safe.

Getaway Sun Resort ★ *Value* This all-inclusive hotel caters to adults only and has an outstanding location just minutes from town on a wide, beautiful stretch of beach. It's also an exceptional value, with all meals, beverages, activities, and entertainment included in the price of your room. The buffets are varied, and you have the option of an a la carte restaurant.

Three types of rooms are available. The four-story Coral tower has the best rooms (double superior), with tile floors, small balconies with ocean or mountain views, and bathrooms with showers and tubs. The 11-story Arcos tower houses deluxe and standard rooms. Deluxe rooms are the most spacious, with private balconies and ocean views. Standard rooms are the least expensive and are smaller, do not have balconies, and have showers without tubs. These rooms offer mountain views only, through small, curtained windows, but are a great value, especially because you probably won't spend too much time in your room.

The hotel is next door to the Sheraton Buganvilias, which is larger and offers family activities and a disco, but doesn't have as nice a beach.

Av. Francisco Medina Ascencio Km 1.5, Puerto Vallarta, Jal., 48310. ✆ **322/226-3600.** Fax 322/223-3601. www.sunresorts.com. 291 units. High season $200 standard double, $300 superior double, $362 deluxe double; low season $174 standard double, $186 superior double, $328 deluxe double. Rates include food, drink, nightly entertainment, nonmotorized watersports. AE, MC, V. Free parking. Children not accepted. **Amenities:** 2 restaurants; snack bar; 5 bars; nightly entertainment and shows; large beachfront pool with activities; smaller, quieter pool with wet bar; tennis court; spa with sauna, whirlpool tub, massage; nonmotorized watersports equipment; bikes; tour desk; car rental desk; small shopping strip with art and crafts shops; salon; laundry and dry cleaning service; safe-deposit boxes in reception area. *In room:* A/C, TV, hair dryer, safe-deposit boxes ($2 per day).

DOWNTOWN TO LOS MUERTOS BEACH

This part of town has recently undergone a renaissance; economical hotels and good-value guesthouses dominate the accommodations market. Several blocks off the beach, you can find numerous budget inns offering clean, simply furnished rooms; most offer discounts for long-term stays. Much of Vallarta's nightlife activity now centers in the areas south of the Río Cuale and along Olas Altas.

Hotel Molino de Agua ★ With an unrivaled location adjacent to both the Río Cuale and the ocean, this hotel is a mix of stone and stucco-walled bungalows and small beachfront buildings, spread out among winding walkways and lush tropical gardens. It's immediately past the Río Cuale—after crossing the southbound bridge, it's on your right. Although it's centrally located on a main street, open spaces, big trees, birds, and lyrical fountains lend it tranquillity. The individual bungalows are in the gardens between the entrance and the ocean. They are well maintained and simply furnished, with a wooden desk and chair, Mexican tile floors, beamed ceilings, and beautiful tile bathrooms. Wicker rocking chairs grace the private patios. Rooms and suites in the two small two- and three-story buildings on the beach have double beds and private terraces, and are decorated in rustic Mexican style.

Vallarta 130 (Apdo. Postal 54), Puerto Vallarta, Jal., 48380. ✆ **322/222-1957.** Fax 322/222-6056. www.molinodeagua.com. 60 units. High season garden bungalow $120 double, oceanfront room or suite $143–$195 double; low season bungalow $88 double, suite $106–$132 double. AE, MC, V. Free secured parking. **Amenities:** Restaurant; bar; beachside pool; pool with whirlpool; tour desk; car-rental desk. *In room:* A/C.

Hotel Playa Los Arcos ★★ This is one of Vallarta's perennially popular hotels and a favorite of mine, with a stellar location in the heart of Los Muertos Beach, central to the Olas Altas sidewalk-cafe action and close to downtown. The four-story structure is U-shaped, facing the ocean, with a small swimming pool in the courtyard. Rooms with private balconies overlook the pool. The 10 suites have ocean views; 5 of these have kitchenettes. The standard rooms are small but pleasantly decorated and immaculate, with carved wooden furniture painted pale pink. On the premises are a *palapa* beachside bar with occasional live entertainment, a gourmet coffee shop, and the popular Kaiser Maximilian's gourmet restaurant. It's seven blocks south of the river.

Olas Altas 380, Puerto Vallarta, Jal., 48380. ✆ **800/648-2403** in the U.S., or 322/222-1583. Fax 322/222-2418. www.playalosarcos.com. 175 units. High season $116–$140 double, $166 suite; low season $91 double, $137 suite. AE, MC, V. Limited street parking. **Amenities:** 2 restaurants; lobby bar; pool; tour desk; car-rental services; babysitting; laundry; safe-deposit boxes; money exchange at front desk. *In room:* A/C, TV.

Los Cuatro Vientos ★★ This quiet, secluded inn is in the center of downtown on a hillside overlooking Banderas Bay. Rooms surround a small central patio. A short flight of stairs takes you to the second-floor patio, which holds the pool, flowering trees, and the cozy Chez Elena restaurant. The cheerful, spotless rooms have fans, small tiled bathrooms, brick ceilings, red-tile floors, and glass-louvered windows. Each is colorfully decorated with simple Mexican furnishings, folk art, and antiques. The rooftop deck and El Nido bar have a panoramic view of the city; open from 3:30 to 10:30pm, it's great for late afternoon sunning, and the best place in the city for sunset drinks. The restaurant serves continental breakfast for guests only from 6 to 11am.

A favorite with solo women travelers, the hotel offers weeklong "Women's Getaway" packages several times a year.

Matamoros 520, Puerto Vallarta, Jal., 48300. ✆ **322/222-0161.** Fax 322/222-2831. www.cuatrovientos.com. 14 units. High season $55 double, $69 suite (up to 4 people); low-season discounts available. Rates higher at Christmas and New Year's. Rates include continental breakfast. MC, V. Very limited street parking. **Amenities:** Restaurant; rooftop bar; small courtyard pool.

SOUTH TO MISMALOYA

Camino Real ★★ The original luxury hotel in Puerto Vallarta, the Camino Real has retained its place as a premier property. Scores of loyal guests think only of staying here, and its free classical concerts on the first Thursday of each month occupy an integral place in the local community. It has the nicest beach of any Vallarta hotel, with soft white sand in a private cove. Set apart from other properties, with a lush mountain backdrop, it retains the exclusivity that made it popular from the beginning—yet it's only a 5- to 10-minute ride to town. The hotel consists of two buildings: the 250-room main hotel, which curves gently with the shape of the Playa Las Estacas, and the newer 11-story Camino Real Club tower, also facing the beach and ocean. An ample pool fronts the main building, facing the beach. Standard rooms in the main building are large; some have sliding doors opening onto the beach, and others have balconies. Royal Beach Club rooms (from the 6th floor up) feature balconies with whirlpool tubs. The top floor consists of six two-bedroom Fiesta Suites, each with a private swimming pool. All rooms have the signature vibrant colors of Camino Real hotels. Under new ownership, the already well-maintained hotel recently underwent renovations and upgrades but kept its 70s flavor.

Carretera Barra de Navidad Km 3.5, Playa Las Estacas, Puerto Vallarta, Jal., 48300. ✆ **800/722-6466** in the U.S. and Canada, or 322/221-5000. Fax 322/221-6000. www.caminoreal.com. 337 units. High season $180–$410 double, $600–$1,000 suite; low season $166–$242 double, $570–$880 suite. AE, DC, MC, V. Free secured parking. **Amenities:** 4 restaurants; lobby bar; pool bar; swimming pool; beach *palapas* with chair, towel, and dining service; 2 lighted grass tennis courts; fitness room with weights; children's program (Easter and Christmas vacations); convenience store; travel agency; car rental; 24-hr. room service; laundry. *In room:* A/C, TV, dataport, minibar, hair dryer, iron, safe-deposit box.

Casa Tres Vidas ★★ Value Terraced down a hillside to Conchas Chinas Beach, Casa Tres Vidas is three individual villas that make great, affordable lodgings for families or groups of friends. Set on a stunning private cove, Tres Vidas gives you the experience of your own private villa, complete with service staff. It offers outstanding value for the location—close to town, with sweeping panoramic views from every room—as well as for the excellent service. Each villa has at least two levels and over 465 sq. m (5,000 sq. ft.) of mostly open living areas, plus a private swimming pool, heated whirlpool, and air-conditioned bedrooms. The Vida Alta penthouse villa has three bedrooms, plus a rooftop deck with pool and bar. Vida Sol villa's three bedrooms sleep 10 (two rooms have two king-size beds each). Directly on the ocean, Vida Mar is a four-bedroom villa, accommodating eight people. The staff prepares gourmet meals in your villa twice a day—you choose the menu and pay only for the food.

Sagitario 134, Playa Conchas Chinas, Puerto Vallarta, Jal., 48300. ✆ **888/640-8100** or 801/531-8100 in the U.S., or 322/221-5317. Fax 322/221-5327. www.casatresvidas.com. 3 villas. High season $568–$597 villa; low season $410–$439 villa. Rates include services. Special summer 1- or 2-bedroom rates available; minimum 3 nights. AE, MC, V. Very limited street parking. **Amenities:** 2 prepared daily meals; private pool; concierge; tour desk; car rental. *In room:* Kitchen facilities, safe-deposit boxes.

La Jolla de Mismaloya All-Suites Resort ★★ On Mismaloya cove, the beach that originally drew visitors to Vallarta when it dazzled as the location of the film *Night of the Iguana,* La Jolla is a jewel of a resort. Set between the mountains and the bay, it shows off the area's natural beauty, yet it's just 15 minutes from downtown. Two towers face a central area that holds a spectacular pool complete with waterfalls, Jacuzzi, and children's waterslides. Each suite sleeps up to five people and has a comfortable seating area and a private balcony. Near La Noche de la Iguana Set Restaurant, the movie plays continually, so you can see what introduced this part of Mexico to the world spotlight. It is gaining recognition as the premier dive resort on Mexico's Pacific Coast. With its own dive boat and PADI instruction facility, La Jolla is a natural for divers—deep canyons are a short distance away, and excellent beach diving makes it easy to enjoy the marine life just offshore.

Carretera Barra de Navidad Km 11.5, Puerto Vallarta, Jal., 48300. ✆ **877/868-6124** in the U.S. and Canada, or 322/226-0660. Fax 322/2268-0500. www.lajollademismaloya.com. 303 units. High season $180–$410 double, $600–$1,000 suite; low season $166–$242 double, $570–$880 suite. Ask about honeymoon, diving, meeting, and all-inclusive packages. AE, MC, V. Free secured parking. **Amenities:** 4 restaurants; oceanfront bar; pool bar; swimming pool; tennis court; fitness room with weights; full-service spa; watersports center with dive boat and deep-sea fishing charters; Jollamigos children's program; travel agency; car rental; gift shop; boutique; 24-hr. room service; babysitting services; laundry. *In room:* A/C, TV, dataport, minibar, hair dryer, iron, safe-deposit box.

Quinta María Cortez ★★★ *Finds* A sophisticated, imaginative B&B on the beach, this is Puerto Vallarta's most original place to stay—and one of Mexico's most memorable inns. Most of the seven large suites, uniquely decorated with antiques, whimsical curios, and original art, have a kitchenette and balcony. Sunny terraces, a small pool, and a central gathering area with fireplace and *palapa*-topped dining area (where an excellent full breakfast is served) occupy different levels of the seven-story house. A rooftop terrace offers another sunbathing alternative—and is among the best sunset-watching spots in town. The Quinta is on a beautiful cove on Conchas Chinas beach. A terrace fronting the beach accommodates chairs for taking in the sunset.

The Quinta María wins my highest recommendation (in fact, I enjoyed living here for a few years when it still accepted long-term stays), but admittedly it's not for everyone. Air-conditioned areas are limited, due to the open nature of the suites and common areas. Those who love it return year after year, charmed by this remarkable place and by the consistently gracious service.

Sagitario 132, Playa Conchas Chinas, Puerto Vallarta, Jal., 48300. ✆ **888/640-8100** or 801/536-5850 in the U.S., or 322/221-5317. Fax 322/221-5327. www.quinta-maria.com. 7 units. High season $150–$275 double; low season $106–$205 double. Rates include breakfast. AE, MC, V. Very limited street parking. Children not accepted. **Amenities:** Small pool; concierge. *In room:* CD player, dataport, mini-refrigerator, coffeemaker, hair dryer, safe-deposit box.

YELAPA

Verana ★★★ *Finds* The magical Verana is my current favorite place to stay in Mexico. It has an unparalleled ability to inspire immediate relaxation and a deep connection with the natural beauty of the spectacular coast. Although Yelapa is 30 minutes by water taxi from town, even those unfamiliar with the village should consider it. Verana has six rustic yet sophisticated suites, set into a hillside with sweeping views of the mountains and ocean. Each is a work of art, hand-crafted with care and creativity by owners Heinz Leger, a former film production designer, and prop stylist Veronique Lieve. Each has a private terrace and two beds—but you won't find TVs, telephones, stereos, or other distractions. My favorite suite is the Studio; it's the most contemporary, with a wall of floor-to-ceiling windows that perfectly frame the spectacular view. The European-trained chef prepares scrumptious creations—global cuisine with a touch of Mexico. Compare this to the prices of the other rustic-chic resorts along Mexico's Pacific coast, and you'll find it's a true value. Verana also rents a villa in Puerto Vallarta, if you prefer a night in town upon arrival or departure. Adventurous travelers should not miss a stay at this unique place.

Yelapa, 48300. ✆ **800/677-5156** or 661/946-7477 in the U.S., or 322/222-2360; Cell 322/227-5420. www.verana.com. 6 villas. High season $220 per night per villa, 5-night minimum; 3-bedroom Casa Grande $400 per night, all based on double occupancy; extra person $85 per night. Mandatory daily breakfast and dinner charge $50 per person. Lunch and beverages extra. Shorter stays based on availability. AE, MC, V. Management helps arrange transportation from Puerto Vallarta to Boca, where a private boat runs to Yelapa; from there, Verana is a gentle hike or mule ride. **Amenities:** Restaurant/bar; 2 prepared daily meals; pool; spa with massage services; tours and excursions; library.

3 Where To Dine

Puerto Vallarta has the most exceptional dining scene of any resort town in Mexico. Over 250 restaurants serve cuisines from around the world, in addition to fresh seafood and regional dishes. Chefs from France, Switzerland, Germany, Italy, and Argentina have come for visits and stayed to open restaurants. In celebration of this diversity, Vallarta's culinary community hosts a 2-week-long Gourmet Dining Festival as part of its annual SeaFest each November.

Dining is not limited to high-end options—there are plenty of small, family-owned restaurants, local Mexican kitchens, and vegetarian cafes. Vallarta also has branches of the world food-and-fun chains: Hard Rock Cafe, Planet Hollywood, Outback Steakhouse, and even Hooters. I won't bother to review these restaurants, where the consistency and decor are so familiar.

Of the inexpensive local spots, one long-standing favorite for light meals and fresh fruit drinks is **Tutifruti,** Morelos 552 (✆ **322/222-1068**). It's open Monday through Saturday from 8am to 8pm. No credit cards accepted. A favorite for cheap eats is **Archi's,** Morelos 799 at Pípila, behind Carlos O'Brian's (✆ **322/222-4383**). It serves only chargrilled hamburgers, chicken burgers, fish filet burgers, hot dogs, and homemade fries in a surfer-inspired atmosphere. It's open Tuesday through Sunday from 11am to 1am; cash only. **El Planeta Vegetariano,** Iturbide 270, just down from the main church (✆ **322/222-3073**), serves an inexpensive, bountiful, and delicious vegetarian lunch buffet, as well as vegan and vegetarian breakfasts. It's open Monday through Saturday. Breakfast ($3.50) is served from 8:30 to 11:30am; the lunch buffet ($4.50) is served from 11:30am to 5:30pm; no credit cards. The restaurant serves dinner a la carte from 6 to 10pm.

MARINA VALLARTA

Contrary to conventional travel wisdom, most of the best restaurants in the Marina are in hotels. Especially notable are **Andrea** (fine Italian cuisine), at Velas Vallarta, and **Garibaldi** (exceptional seafood), on the beachfront of the Westin Regina Resort. (See "Where to Stay," earlier in this chapter, for more information.) Other choices are along the boardwalk bordering the marina yacht harbor. A notable stop is the **Café Gourmet,** next to the Vallarta

Adventures offices in Condominiums Marina Golf, Local 11 (© **322/221-0362**). It serves excellent coffee and espresso drinks, plus pastries and light snacks. Open Monday through Saturday from 8am to 10pm, Sunday from 5pm to 10pm.

Benitto's ★★ CAFE Wow! What a sandwich! Benitto's food would be reason enough to come to this tiny, terrific cafe inside the Plaza Neptuno—but added to that are the original array of sauces and the very personable service. This place is popular with locals for light breakfasts, filling lunches, and fondue and wine in the evenings. It's the best place in town to find pastrami, corned beef, or other traditional (gringo) sandwich fare, all served on your choice of gourmet bread. Draft beer and wine are available, as are the cafe's specialty infused waters. A second location opened last year downtown, on Josefa Ortiz de Domínguez and Juárez, with the same menu in a larger location. The bi-level downtown location offers late-night dining with full bar service—and great music!

Inside Plaza Neptuno. © **322/209-0287.** benittosdeli@prodigy.net.mx. Breakfast $3–$6; main courses $5–$7. No credit cards. Daily 8:30am–10:30pm.

Porto Bello ★ ITALIAN One of the first restaurants in the marina, Porto Bello remains a favorite for its authentically flavorful Italian dishes and exceptional service. For starters, fried calamari is delicately seasoned, and grilled vegetable antipasto could easily serve as a full meal. Signature dishes include fusilli prepared with artichokes, black olives, lemon juice, basil, olive oil, and Parmesan cheese, and sautéed fish filet with shrimp and clams in saffron tomato sauce. The elegant indoor dining room is air-conditioned, and there's also marina-front seating. The restaurant occasionally schedules live music in the evening.

Marina Sol, Local 7 (Marina Vallarta *malecón*). © **322/221-0003.** Main courses $7–$19. AE, MC, V. Daily noon–11pm.

DOWNTOWN

It's not that I'm particularly partial to Italian or Continental cuisine; it's just that the best restaurants here happen to fall into these categories. Although Vallarta has over 250 restaurants, it lacks in the categories of Mexican cuisine and seafood. It does boast an exceptional community of European chefs, however.

A great choice for lunch is **La Mejor Opción** ★, Josefa Ortiz de Domínguez 230 (© **322/222-2355**), where the home-style dishes have a gourmet flair, and chef-owner Gabriela Almada makes everyone feel special. The daily special of soup, salad, and entree runs around $10. Open Monday through Friday from 1 to 5pm for lunch, and Monday through Saturday from 5 to 10pm. No credit cards.

EXPENSIVE

Café des Artistes ★★ FRENCH/INTERNATIONAL This sophisticated restaurant is known as the place in town for that very special evening. Located in a restored house that resembles a castle, with an interior that combines murals, lush fabrics, and an array of original works of art, Café des Artistes is the creation of award-winning chef Thierry Blouet, a member of the French Academie Culinaire and Maitre Cuisinier de France. The Nobel Prize–winning Mexican novelist Carlos Fuentes wrote of this restaurant, "At Café des Artistes, there is no dish that is not a work of art, nor a work of art that does not feed the spirit."

There are three dining areas—the streetside balcony, the interior dining rooms, and my personal favorite, the terraced garden. Despite the decorative setting, the real star is the food. The menu is highly original, with dishes drawing heavily on chef Blouet's French training, yet using regional specialty ingredients. Noteworthy entrees include salmon filet *sarandeado* (smothered in sauce and grilled) with potato puree, and the renowned roasted duck glazed with agave honey, soy, ginger, and lime sauce, served with canelone gratin and pumpkin. And speaking of pumpkin, don't miss the signature starter, pumpkin and prawn soup served from a carved gourd. Chef Blouet started his culinary career as a pastry chef, so be sure to save room for one of his desserts. The only downside is that it is easily the most expensive restaurant in town, but it's worth the splurge.

Guadalupe Sánchez 740. ✆ **322/222-3228,** 322/222-3229, or 322/222-3230. www.cafedesartistes.com. Main courses $17–$31. AE, MC, V. Daily 6–11:30pm.

MODERATE

Daiquiri Dick's ★★ MODERN AMERICAN A Vallarta dining institution, Daiquiri Dick's has been around for over 20 years, evolving its winning combination of decor, service, and scrumptious cuisine. The menu is among Vallarta's most sophisticated, and the genuinely warm staff and open-air location fronting Los Muertos Beach add to the feeling of casual comfort. As lovely as the restaurant is, though, and as notorious as the fresh-fruit daiquiris are, the food is the main attraction. It incorporates touches of Tuscan, Thai, and Mexican. Start with grilled asparagus wrapped in prosciutto and topped with shaved asiago cheese, then try an entree such as sesame-crusted tuna, grilled rare and served with wild greens; pistachio chicken served with polenta; or my favorite, simple yet indulgent lobster tacos. Chocolate banana bread pudding makes a perfect finish. Daiquiri Dick's is a great place for groups—as well as for a romantic dinner. It's one of the few places that is equally enjoyable for breakfast, lunch, or dinner.

Olas Altas 314. ✆ **322/222-0566.** www.ddpv.com Main courses $6.50–$17. AE, MC, V. Daily 9am–10:30pm. Closed Sept.

de Santos ★★ MEDITERRANEAN After it opened a few years ago, de Santos quickly became the hot spot in town for late-night dining and bar action. Although the food initially didn't live up to the atmosphere and music, now it absolutely does. It's Mediterranean-inspired; best bets include lightly breaded calamari, paella Valenciana, and excellent thin-crust pizza. Also ask about nightly specials. The cool, refined interior feels more urban than resort, and it boasts the most sophisticated sound system in town—including a deejay who spins to match the mood of the crowd. It probably helps that one of the partners is also a member of the wildly popular Latin group Mana. There's open-air terrace dining in the back. Prices are extremely reasonable for the quality and overall experience of an evening here. Be sure to stay and check out the new, adjacent club—the hottest nightspot in town (see the "Puerto Vallarta After Dark" section beginning on p. 110).

Morelos 771, Centro. ✆ **322/223-3052.** www.desantos.com.mx. Reservations recommended during high season. Main courses $5–$20. AE, MC, V. Daily 5pm–1am; bar closes at 4am on weekends.

Las Palomas MEXICAN One of Puerto Vallarta's first restaurants, this is the power-breakfast place of choice—and a popular hangout for everyone else throughout the day. Authentic in atmosphere and menu, it's one of Puerto Vallarta's few genuine Mexican restaurants, with the atmosphere of a gracious home. Breakfast is the best value. The staff pours mugs of steaming coffee spiced with cinnamon as soon as you're seated. Try classic *huevos rancheros* or *chilaquiles* (tortilla strips, fried and topped with red or green spicy sauce, cheese, fried eggs, and cream). Lunch and dinner offer traditional Mexican specialties, plus a selection of stuffed crepes. The best places for checking out the *malecón* and watching the sunset while sipping an icy margarita are the spacious bar and upstairs terrace.

Paseo Díaz Ordaz 594. ✆ **322/222-3675.** Breakfast $8–$12; lunch $8.50–$22; main courses $8.50–$22. AE, MC, V. Daily 8am–midnight.

Pipis ★ MEXICAN Most of the people who come to Pipis tend to think of it as their own "find"—it's just enough off the beaten track to give a taste of a Vallarta neighborhood, and the ambience is an authentic glimpse at the Mexican belief that life is meant to enjoy. If you're looking for a casually good time, this is your place. Within moments of sitting down, your waiter will prepare homemade guacamole at your table and serve it with chips. The specialty here is sizzling fajitas—chicken, beef, or seafood, generous in portion, and absolutely delicious. Equally famous are the oversize margaritas, but be warned—these are serious drinks! That may account for the fact that the place is always a riot of laughter and conversation, mixed with the music of strolling mariachis. The gracious owners are always on hand, and the waitstaff seems dedicated to making certain you're happy and well fed. Pipis also has a full menu of other traditional Mexican dishes, but I've never moved beyond the fajitas—they're just too good.

Guadalupe Sánchez 804. ✆ **322/223-2767.** www.pipis.com.mx. Main courses $8–$21. AE, MC, V. Daily 1–11pm.

Rito's Baci ★★ ITALIAN If the food weren't reason enough to come here (and it definitely is!), then Rito himself would be. He directs gentle, devoted attention to every detail of this cozy *trattoria.* His grandfather emigrated from Italy, and the recipes and tradition of Italian food come naturally to him. So does his passion for food—it's obvious as he describes the specialties, which include lasagna (vegetarian, *verde,* or meat-filled); ravioli stuffed with spinach and ricotta; spaghetti with garlic, anchovy, and lemon zest; or a side of homemade Italian sausage. Everything is made by hand from fresh ingredients. Pizza-lovers favor the Piedmonte, with that famous sausage and mushrooms, and the Horacio, a cheeseless version with tomatoes, oregano, and basil. Sandwiches come hot or cold; arrive hungry—they're a two-handed operation. Because Rito offers home and hotel delivery, I enjoy his food more than any other restaurant's. It's 1½ blocks off the *malecón.*

Domínguez 181 (between Morelos and Juárez). ✆ **322/222-6448.** Pasta $8–$17; salads and sandwiches $3.50–$7; pizza $13–$17. MC, V. Daily 1–11:30pm.

Trio ★★★ *Finds* INTERNATIONAL Trio is the current darling of Vallarta restaurants, with diners beating a path to the modest but stylish cafe where chef-owner Bernhard Güth's undeniable passion for food imbues each dish. Trio is noted for its perfected melding of Mexican and Mediterranean flavors. Chef Güth combines local ingredients with impressive culinary experience; memorable entrees include San Blas shrimp in roasted red pepper and mango sauce; herb risotto with toasted sunflower seeds and barbecued quail; ricotta ravioli with sun-dried tomatoes; and pan-roasted sea bass with glazed grapes, mashed potatoes, and peppered sauerkraut, served in a white pepper sauce. These dishes may not be on the menu when you arrive, though—it's a constantly changing work of art. The atmosphere is always comfortable and welcoming, and the chef regularly chats with guests at the end of the evening. The rooftop bar area allows for a more comfortable wait for a table or for after-dinner coffee. A real treat!

Guerrero 264. ✆ **322/222-2196.** Reservations recommended. Main courses $14–$26. AE, MC, V. Year-round daily 6pm–midnight; high season Mon–Fri noon–3:30pm.

SOUTH OF THE RIO CUALE TO OLAS ALTAS

South of the river is the densest restaurant area, where you'll find the street Basilio Badillo, nicknamed "Restaurant Row." A second main dining drag has emerged along Calle Olas Altas, with a variety of cuisines and price categories. Cafes and espresso bars, generally open from 7am to midnight, line its wide sidewalks.

EXPENSIVE

Café Kaiser Maximilian ★★ INTERNATIONAL This bistro-style cafe has a casually elegant atmosphere with a genuinely European feel. It's the prime place to go if you want to combine exceptional food with great people-watching. Austrian-born owner Andreas Rupprechter is always on hand to ensure that the service is as impeccable as the food is delicious. Indoor, air-conditioned dining is at cozy tables; sidewalk tables are larger and great for groups of friends. The cuisine merges old-world European preparations with regional fresh ingredients. My favorite is filet of trout with watercress and beet sauce—so much so that I've never tried any other dish, although friends tell me mustard chicken with mashed potatoes is excellent, and the rack of lamb with polenta, endives, and lima beans is simply divine. The restaurant also offers northern European classics like *Rahmschnitzel* (sautéed pork loin and homemade noodles in creamy mushroom sauce). Desserts are especially tempting, as are gourmet coffees—Maximilian has an Austrian cafe and pastry shop next door.

Olas Altas 380-B (at Basilio Badillo, in front of the Hotel Playa Los Arcos), Zona Romántica. ✆ **322/223-0760.** Reservations recommended in high season. Main courses $16–$26. AE, MC, V. Mon–Sat 6–11pm.

Espresso ★★ ITALIAN This popular eatery is Vallarta's best late-night dining option. The two-level restaurant is on one of the town's busiest streets—across from El Torito's sports bar, and catercornered from the lively Señor Frog's—meaning that traffic noise is a factor, though not a deterrent. The food is superb, the service attentive, and the prices more than reasonable. Owned by a partnership of lively Italians, it serves food that is authentic in preparation and flavor, from thin-crust, brick-oven pizzas to savory homemade pastas. My favorite pizza is the "Quattro Stagioni," topped with artichokes, black olives, ham, and mushrooms. Excellent calzones and panini (sandwiches) are also options. I prefer the rooftop garden area for dining, but many patrons gravitate to the pool table in the air-conditioned downstairs, which features major sports and entertainment events on satellite TV. Espresso also has full bar service and draft beer and is especially popular with *Vallartenses* (locals).

Ignacio L. Vallarta 279. ✆ **322/222-3272.** Main courses $6.50–$13. AE, MC, V. Daily noon–4am.

Le Bistro ★★ MEXICAN/INTERNATIONAL A long-standing favorite, Le Bistro is especially enjoyable for breakfast. I consider a morning meal here one of Vallarta's best values. Le Bistro is known for its elegant decor, great recorded jazz music, and open-air setting on the island in the midst of the Río Cuale—all creating a singular experience that blends sophistication with a typically Vallarta atmosphere. Favorite choices at breakfast are eggs Benedict and eggs *motuleño* style (sunny side up, smothered in tomato-based sauce and served with cheese, peas, and fried plantains). The specialty is crepes, which come in a variety of flavors for breakfast, lunch, or dinner. Especially scrumptious are those filled with chicken breast and squash blossoms (a Mexican delicacy) in hollandaise sauce. The menu also has an excellent selection of innovative Mexican cuisine, including duck in Oaxacan black *mole,* and rock Cornish hen stuffed with herbed rice, dried tropical fruits, and nuts, finished in mango cilantro sauce. The vegetarian offerings are more creative than most. An impressive wine list and ample selection of specialty coffees complement the menu.

Isla Río Cuale 16-A (just east of northbound bridge). ✆ **322/222-0283.** www.lebistro.com.mx. Reservations recommended in high season. Breakfast $5–$8; main courses $19–$25. AE, MC, V. Mon–Sat 9am–midnight.

Los Pibes ★★ ARGENTINEAN/STEAKS You won't find a better steak anywhere in Vallarta—or many other places. Los Pibes offers signature thick cuts, exceptional quality, and a variety of preparations. Argentinean Cristina Juhas opened this restaurant in 1994 for her *pibes* (children), and the rave reviews have grown over the years. You select your huge portion of steak from a tray of fresh meat (all imported from the U.S.). While it's being prepared, try a wonderful *empanada* filled with meat or corn and cheese, or savor an order of *alubias,* marinated beans served with bread. The homemade sausage is also delicious, and you won't find a better *chimichurri* sauce. In addition to beef, Los Pibes has an ample selection of salads, side dishes, chicken, and pastas, as well as an excellent wine list. A second location, equally delicious, is on the Marina Vallarta *malecón* (✆ **322/221-0669**).

Basilio Badillo 261 (at Ignacio Vallarta). ✆ **322/223-1557.** Reservations recommended in high season. Main courses $19–$25. AE, MC, V. Mon–Sat 5–11:30pm.

MODERATE

Adobe Café ★★ INTERNATIONAL Adobe Café offers a classically chic atmosphere in which to enjoy innovative cuisine based on traditional Mexican specialties. Santa Fe–style decor with rustic wood accents provides a serene backdrop, and tables are comfortably large for enjoying a leisurely meal. Waiters are attentive without being intrusive. The menu features imaginative dishes, including grilled jumbo shrimp battered in coconut and served with homemade apple sauce, pork tenderloin in rum-tamarind sauce, and tenderloin of beef stuffed with *huitlacoche* in cheese sauce—to name just a few specialties. Owner Rodolfo Choperena is almost always on hand, which accounts for the consistently fine food and service.

Basilio Badillo 252 (at Ignacio Vallarta). ✆ **322/222-6720** or 322/223-1925. www.virtualvallarta.com/pv/adobecafe. Reservations recommended in high season. Main courses $12–$22. MC, V. Wed–Mon 6–11pm. Closed Aug–Sept.

Archie's Wok ★★★ *Finds* ASIAN/SEAFOOD Since 1986, Archie's has been legendary in Puerto Vallarta for serving original cuisine influenced by the intriguing flavors of Thailand, China, and the Philippines. Archie was Hollywood director John Huston's private chef during the years he spent in the area. Today his wife Cindy upholds his legacy at this tranquil retreat. The Thai Mai Tai and other tropical drinks, made from only fresh fruit and juices, are a good way to kick off a meal, as are the consistently crispy and delicious Filipino spring rolls. The popular Singapore fish filet features lightly battered filet strips in sweet-and-sour sauce; Thai garlic shrimp are prepared with fresh garlic, ginger, cilantro, and black pepper. Vegetarians have plenty of options, including broccoli, tofu, mushroom, and cashew stir-fry in black bean and sherry sauce. Finish with the signature Spice Islands coffee or a slice of lime cheese pie. Thursday through Saturday from 8 to 11pm, there's live classical harp and flute in Archie's Oriental garden.

Francisco Rodríguez 130 (½ block from the Los Muertos pier). ✆ **322/222-0411.** awok@pvnet.com.mx. Main courses $6–$21. AE, MC, V. Mon–Sat 2–11pm. Closed Sept–Oct.

La Palapa ★ SEAFOOD/MEXICAN This colorful, open-air, *palapa*-roofed restaurant on the beach is a decades-old local favorite, and with each recent visit, I have found the quality of both the food and service keeps improving. It's an exceptional dining experience, day or night. Enjoy a tropical breakfast by the sea, lunch on the beach, cocktails at sunset, or a romantic dinner (on a cloth-covered table in the sand). For lunch and dinner, seafood is the specialty; featured dishes include macadamia-and-coconut-crusted prawns, and poached red snapper with fresh cilantro sauce. Its location in the heart of Los Muertos Beach makes it an excellent place to start or end the day; I favor it for breakfast or, even better, a late-night sweet temptation and specialty coffee, while watching the moon over the bay. A particular draw is the all-you-can-eat Sunday brunch, which entitles you to a spot on popular Los Muertos beach for the day. There are acoustic guitars and vocals nightly from 8 to 11pm, generally performed by the owner, Alberto. La Palapa had a complete makeover in 2002 and retained its charm and gracious service.

Pulpito 103. ✆ **322/222-5225.** Reservations recommended for dinner in high season. Breakfast $2.50–$10; main courses $9.50–$25; salad or sandwiches $6.70–$10. AE, MC, V. Daily 9am–11:30pm.

INEXPENSIVE

Café San Angel CAFE This comfortable, classic sidewalk cafe is a local gathering place from sunrise to sunset. For breakfast, choose a burrito stuffed with eggs and *chorizo* sausage, a three-egg Western omelet, crepes filled with mushrooms, Mexican classics like *huevos rancheros* and *chilaquiles,* or a tropical fruit plate. Deli sandwiches, crepes, and pastries round out the small but ample menu. The cafe also serves exceptional fruit smoothies, like the Yelapa—a blend of mango, banana, and orange juice—and perfectly made espresso drinks. Note that the service is reliably slow and frequently frustrating, so choose this place if you have time on your side—and keep in mind that it offers the best people-watching in the area. Bar service and Internet access are available.

Olas Altas 449 (at Francisco Rodríguez). ✆ **322/223-2160.** Breakfast $3.50–$5; main courses $3.50–$6. Daily 7am–2am.

Fajita Republic ★★ MEXICAN/SEAFOOD/STEAKS Fajita Republic is consistently popular—and deservedly so. It has hit on a winning recipe: delicious food, ample portions, welcoming atmosphere, and low prices. The specialty is, of course, fajitas, grilled to perfection in every variety: steak, chicken, shrimp, combo, and vegetarian. All come with a generous tray of salsas and toppings. This "tropical grill" also serves sumptuous barbecued ribs, Mexican *molcajetes* with incredibly tender strips of marinated beef filet, and grilled shrimp. Starters include fresh guacamole served in a giant spoon and the ever-popular Mayan cheese sticks (breaded and deep-fried). Try an oversize mug or pitcher of Fajita Rita Mango Margaritas—or another spirited temptation. This is a casual, fun, festive place in a garden of mango and palm trees.

Pino Suárez 321 (at Basilio Badillo), 1 block north of Olas Altas. ✆ **322/222-3131.** Breakfast $3.60–$4.70; main courses $9–$17. MC, V. Daily 9am–midnight.

Red Cabbage Café (El Repollo Rojo) ★★ *Finds* MEXICAN This tiny, hard-to-find cafe is worth the effort—a visit here will reward you with exceptional traditional Mexican cuisine and a whimsical crash course in contemporary culture. The small room is covered wall-to-wall and table-to-table with photographs, paintings, movie posters, and news clippings about the cultural icons of Mexico. Frida Kahlo figures prominently in the decor, and a special menu duplicates dishes she and husband Diego Rivera prepared for guests.

Specialties from all over Mexico include divine *chiles en nogada* (poblanos stuffed with ground beef, pine nuts, and raisins, topped with sweet cream sauce and served cold), intricate chicken *mole* from Puebla, and hearty *carne en su jugo* (steak in its juice). In addition, the vegetarian menu is probably the most diverse and tasty in town (the owner offers cooking classes for groups of four or more). This is not the place for an intimate conversation, however—the poor acoustics cause everyone's conversations to blend together, although generally what you're hearing from adjacent tables are raves about the food. Also, this is a nonsmoking restaurant—the only one I'm aware of in town.

Calle Rivera del Río 204A (across from Río Cuale). ✆ **322/223-0411.** Main courses $8–$20. No credit cards. Daily 5–10:30pm.

JUNGLE RESTAURANTS

One of the unique attractions of Puerto Vallarta is its "jungle restaurants," south of town toward Mismaloya. They offer open-air dining in a tropical setting by the sea or beside a mountain river. The many varieties of "jungle" and "tropical" tours (see the "Organized Tours" section beginning on p. 191) include a stop for swimming and lunch. If you travel on your own, a taxi is the best transportation—the restaurants are quite a distance from the main highway. Taxis are usually waiting for return patrons.

The most recommendable of the jungle restaurants is the ecologically sensitive **El Nogalito** ★ (✆/fax **322/221-5225**). Located beside a clear jungle stream, the exceptionally clean, beautifully landscaped ranch serves lunch, beverages, and snacks on a shady, relaxing terrace. Several hiking routes depart from the grounds, and the restaurant provides a guide (whom you tip) to point out the native plants, birds, and wildlife. It's much closer to town than the other jungle restaurants: To find it, travel to Punta Negra, about 8km (5 miles) south of downtown Puerto Vallarta. A well-marked sign points up Calzada del Cedro, a dirt road, to the ranch. It's open daily from 11am to 5:30pm. No credit cards.

Just past Boca de Tomatlán, at Highway 200 Km 20, is **Chico's Paradise** (✆ **322/222-0747** or 322/223-0413; chicos@prodigy.net). It offers spectacular views of massive rocks—some marked with petroglyphs—and the surrounding jungle and mountains. There are natural pools and waterfalls for swimming, plus a small *mercado* selling pricey trinkets. The menu features excellent seafood as well as Mexican dishes. The quality is quite good, and the portions are generous, although prices are higher than in town—remember, you're paying for the setting. Open daily from 10am to 7pm. No credit cards.

The mediocre, somewhat unkempt restaurants up the hill from the entrance to Mismaloya, at Highway 200 Km 6.5, are **Chino's Paraíso** (no phone) and **El Edén** (no phone). El Nogalito and Chico's Paradise are better options.

3

Exploring Puerto Vallarta & Beyond

Beyond its cobblestone streets, graceful cathedral, and welcoming atmosphere, Puerto Vallarta offers a wealth of natural beauty and man-made pleasures.

Ecotourism activities are gaining ground here—from mountain biking the Sierra foothills to whale-watching, ocean kayaking, and diving with giant mantas in Banderas Bay. Forty-two kilometers (26 miles) of beaches, many in pristine coves accessible only by boat, extend around the bay. High in the Sierra Madre Mountains, the mystical Huichol Indians still live in relative isolation in an effort to protect their centuries-old culture from outside influences.

Villages such as **Rincón de Guayabitos, Barra de Navidad,** and **Melaque** are laid-back and almost undiscovered. Starkly different from the spirited resort towns, they offer travelers a glimpse into local culture. Excursions to these smaller villages make easy day trips or extended stays.

1 Beaches, Activities & Excursions

Travel agencies can provide information on what to see and do in Puerto Vallarta and can arrange tours, fishing trips, and other activities. Most hotels have a tour desk on-site. Of the many travel agencies in town, I highly recommend **Tukari Servicios Turísticos,** Av. España 316 (✆ **322/224-7177;** fax 322/224-2350), which specializes in ecological and cultural tours. Another source is **Xplora Adventours** (✆ **322/223-0661**), in the Huichol Collection shop on the *malecón.* It has listings of all locally available tours, with photos, explanations, and costs; however, be aware that a timeshare resort owns the company, so part of the information you receive will be an invitation to a presentation, which you may decline. **American Express Travel Services,** Morelos 660 (✆ **322/223-2955**), also has a varied selection of high-quality, popular tours. One of the tour companies with the largest—and best quality—selection of boat cruises and land tours is **Vallarta Adventures** (© **866/256-2739** toll-free from the U.S., or 322/297-1212, ext. 3; www.vallarta-adventures.com). I can highly recommend any of their offerings. Book with them directly and get a 10% discount when you mention Frommer's.

THE BEACHES

For years, beaches were Puerto Vallarta's main attraction. Although visitors today are exploring more of the surrounding geography, the sands are still a powerful draw. Over 42km (26 miles) of beaches extend around the broad Bay of Banderas, ranging from action-packed party spots to secluded coves accessible only by boat.

IN TOWN The easiest to reach is **Playa Los Muertos** (also known as Playa Olas Altas or Playa del Sol), just off Calle Olas Altas, south of the Río Cuale. The water can be rough, but the wide beach is home to an array of *palapa* restaurants that offer food, beverages, and beach-chair service. The most popular are the adjacent El Dorado and La Palapa, at the end of Pulpito Street. On the southern end of this beach is a section known as "Blue Chairs"—the most popular gay beach. Vendors stroll Los Muertos, and beach volleyball, parasailing, and jet-skiing are all popular pastimes. The **Hotel Zone** is also known for its broad, smooth beaches, accessible primarily through the hotel lobbies.

SOUTH OF TOWN **Playa Mismaloya** is in a beautiful sheltered cove about 10km (6 miles) south of town along Highway 200. The water is clear and beautiful, ideal for snorkeling off the beach. Entrance to the public beach is just to the left of the **Jolla de Mismaloya All-Suites Resort** (© **322/226-0600**). The movie *Night of the Iguana* was filmed at Mismaloya, and the resort has a restaurant on the restored film set—**La Noche de la Iguana Set Restaurant,** open daily from noon to 11pm. The movie runs continuously in a room below the restaurant, and still photos from the filming hang in the restaurant. The restaurant is accessible by land on the point framing the south side of the cove. Just below the restaurant is **John Huston's Bar & Grill,** serving drinks and light snacks daily from 11am to 6pm.

The beach at **Boca de Tomatlán,** just down the road, has numerous *palapa* restaurants where you can relax for the day—you buy drinks, snacks, or lunch, and you can use their chairs and *palapa* shade.

The two beaches are accessible by public buses, which depart from the corner of Basilio Badillo and Insurgentes every 15 minutes from 5:30am to 10pm and cost just 40¢.

Las Animas, Quimixto, and **Yelapa** beaches offer a true sense of seclusion; they are accessible only by boat (see "Getting Around," in chapter 2, for information about water-taxi service). They are larger than Mismaloya, offer intriguing hikes to jungle waterfalls, and are similarly set up, with restaurants fronting a wide beach. Overnight stays are available at Yelapa (see "Side Trips from Puerto Vallarta," later in this chapter).

NORTH OF TOWN The beaches at **Marina Vallarta** are the least desirable in the area, with darker sand and seasonal inflows of stones.

The entire northern coastline from Bucerías to Punta Mita is a succession of sandy coves alternating with rocky inlets. For years the beaches to the north, with their long, clean breaks, have been the favored locale for surfers. The broad, sandy stretches at **Playa Anclote, Playa Piedras Blancas,** and **Playa Destiladeras,** which all have *palapa* restaurants, have made them favorites with local residents looking for a quick getaway. The stellar white sand beach at Punta Mita, home of the Four Seasons, is closed to road access, except for guests of the resort development.

One option for visiting a north shore beach is to spend a day at the **Villa Vera Beach Club** (**© 322/221-1401**), 20 miles north of Puerto Vallarta, just past Destiladeras beach on the highway to Punta Mita. To get there, take a taxi, a public bus bound for Punta Mita, or a shuttle bus from Club Regina at the Westin Regina Resort. Two pools—one reserved for adults—and marble baths with changing rooms and showers complement an exquisite beach. There's also a *palapa*-topped restaurant and bar, gym, kids' play area with water slides and splashes, and small shopping area. The entrance fee of $16 for adults, $12 for children, includes a welcome drink, towel service, and the use of all the facilities for the day. Extra charges apply for food, drinks, horseback riding, or massage.

ORGANIZED TOURS

BOAT TOURS Puerto Vallarta offers a number of boat trips, including sunset cruises and snorkeling, swimming, and diving excursions. They generally travel one of two routes: to the **Marietas Islands,** a 30- to 45-minute boat ride off the northern shore of Banderas Bay, or to **Yelapa, Las Animas,** or **Quimixto** along the southern shore. The trips to the southern beaches make a stop at **Los**

Arcos, an island rock formation south of Puerto Vallarta, for snorkeling. Don't base your opinion of underwater Puerto Vallarta on this, though—dozens of tour boats dump quantities of snorkelers overboard at the same time each day, exactly when the fish know *not* to be there. It is, however, an excellent site for night diving. When comparing boat cruises, note that some include lunch, while most provide music and an open bar on board. Most leave around 9:30am, stop for 45 minutes of snorkeling, and arrive at the beach destination around noon for a 2½-hour stay before returning around 3pm. At Quimixto and Yelapa, visitors can take a half-hour hike to a jungle waterfall or rent a horse for the ride. Prices range from $45 for a sunset cruise or a trip to one of the beaches with open bar, to $85 for an all-day outing with open bar and meals.

One boat, the ***Marigalante*** (**© 322/223-0309**), is an exact replica of Columbus's ship the *Santa María,* built in honor of the 500th anniversary of his voyage to the Americas. It features a daytime "pirate's cruise" ($60 per person), complete with picnic barbecue and treasure hunt, and a sunset dinner cruise ($70 per person) with fireworks and disco dance.

One of the best trips is a day trip to Caletas ★★, the cove where John Huston made his home for years. Vallarta Adventures (& 866/256-2739 toll-free in the U.S., or 322/297-1212, ext. 3; www.vallarta-adventures.com) holds the exclusive lease on the private cove and has done an excellent job of restoring Huston's former home, adding exceptional day-spa facilities and landscaping the beach, which is wonderful for snorkeling. The facilities and relative privacy have made this excursion ($70 per person) one of the most popular. The evening cruise includes dinner and a spectacular contemporary dance show, "Rhythms of the Night" (see p. 111).

Travel agencies sell tickets and distribute information on all cruises. If you prefer to spend more time at Yelapa or Las Animas without snorkeling and cruise entertainment, see the information about travel by water taxis, under "Getting Around" in chapter 2.

Whale-watching tours become more popular each year. Viewing humpback whales is almost a certainty from mid- to late November to March. The majestic whales have migrated to this bay for centuries (in the 1600s, it was called "Humpback Bay") to bear their calves. The noted local authority is **Open Air Expeditions,** Guerrero 339 (©/fax **322/222-3310;** openair@vivamexico.com). It offers ecologically oriented, oceanologist-guided 4-hour tours on the soft boat *Prince of Whales,* the only boat in Vallarta specifically designed for whale-watching. Cost is $80, and travel is in a group of

Moments Art Along the *Malecón*

One of the great pleasures of strolling Puerto Vallarta's *malecón* is taking in the fanciful sculptures that line the seaside promenade. Among the notable works on display is *Nostalgia,* across from Carlos O'Brian's restaurant. Created by Ramiz Barquett, it depicts a couple sharing a romantic moment while gazing out to the bay. Farther south is the sculpture group at the *Rotonda del Mar,* locally known as *Fantasy by the Sea.* It's an array of sculpture "chairs" by renowned Mexican artist Alejandro Colunga. This wildly creative series—a large octopus head tops one chair, and another bench has two giant ears for backrests—always seems to draw a crowd. (Although one of the original sculptures washed out to sea in a 2002 hurricane, at press time a stunning replacement that pays homage to the power of the sea was in the works.) Closer to the main square is the *Boy on the Seahorse* sculpture, an image that has come to represent Puerto Vallarta. Don't miss the fountain across from the main square; its three bronze dolphins seem ready to leap right into the bay. Other sculptures along the *malecón* include the controversial "ladder to heaven" by Sergio Bustamante, and Mathis Lidice's interpretation of the passage of time, across from Hotel Rosita at the northernmost edge of the *malecón.*

up to 12. Twice-daily departures (8:30am and 1:30pm) include a healthful snack and T-shirt. **Vallarta Adventures** (✆ **866/256-2739** toll-free in the U.S., or 322/297-1212, ext. 3; www.vallarta-adventures.com) offers whale-watching photo excursions in small boats for $80. The trip includes a predeparture briefing on whale behaviors. The company also features whale-watching on tours to the Marietas Islands. For $60 you get lunch, time at a private beach, and a more festive than educational ambience aboard large catamarans.

LAND TOURS **Tukari Servicios Turísticos** (see p. 189) can arrange trips to the fertile birding grounds near **San Blas,** 3 to 4 hours north of Puerto Vallarta in the state of Nayarit, and shopping trips to **Tlaquepaque and Tonalá** (6 hr. inland, near Guadalajara). A day trip to **Rancho Altamira,** a 50-acre working ranch, includes a barbecue lunch and horseback riding, then a stroll through **El Tuito,** a small nearby colonial-era village. The company can also arrange an unforgettable morning at **Terra Noble Art & Healing Center** (✆ **322/223-3530** or 322/222-5400), a mountaintop day spa and center for the arts where participants can get a massage, *temazcal* (ancient, indigenous sweat lodge), or treatment, work in clay and paint, and have lunch in a heavenly setting overlooking the bay. Call ahead for reservations, and make sure to advise if you want to have lunch there.

Hotel travel desks and travel agencies, including Tukari and American Express, can also book the popular **Tropical Tour** or **Jungle Tour** ($25), a basic orientation to the area. These excursions are expanded city tours that include a drive through the workers' village of Pitillal, the affluent neighborhood of Conchas Chinas, the cathedral, the market, the Taylor-Burton houses, and lunch at a jungle restaurant. Any stop for shopping usually means the driver picks up a commission for what you buy.

The **Sierra Madre Expedition** is another excellent tour offered by **Vallarta Adventures** (✆ **866/256-2739** toll-free from the U.S., or 322/297-1212, ext. 3; www.vallarta-adventures.com). The daily excursion travels in Mercedes all-terrain vehicles north of Puerto Vallarta through jungle trails, stops at a small town, ventures into a forest for a brief nature walk, and winds up on a pristine secluded beach for lunch and swimming. The $70 outing is worthwhile because it takes tourists on exclusive trails into scenery that would otherwise be off-limits.

AIR TOURS Speaking of off-limits, you can explore some of the most remote and undiscovered reaches of the Sierra Madre mountains in Vallarta Adventures' **San Sebastián Air Adventure** (✆ **866/256-2739** toll-free from the U.S., or 322/297-1212, ext. 3; www.vallarta-adventures.com). A 15-minute flight aboard a 14-seat turbo-prop Cessna Caravan takes you into the heart of the Sierra Madre. The plane is equipped with raised wings, which allow you to admire—and photograph—the mountain scenery. The plane arrives on a gravel landing strip in the old mining town of San Sebastián, a beautiful village that dates to 1603. One of the oldest mining towns in Mexico, it reached its prosperous peak in the 1800s, with over 30,000 inhabitants. Today, San Sebastián remains an outstanding example of how people lived and worked in a remote Mexican mountain town—it's a living museum. The half-day adventure costs $130, which covers the flight, a walking tour of the town (including a stop at the old Hacienda Jalisco, a favored getaway of John Huston, Liz and Dick, and their friends), and brunch in town. Other excursions include overnight stays and return trips by bike or horseback. There's also a **Jeep tour** to San Sebastián. The cost of $75 per person, for up to four people per Jeep, includes a guide. This tour departs at 9am and returns at 5pm. Call Pacific Travel (✆ **322/225-2270**) to reserve.

Anyone for a taste of tequila? We're talking about the town, and a sampling of the best of the spirit of Mexico. Vallarta Adventures (see above) offers a trip that takes you to the classic town, where you visit one of the original haciendas and tequila (agave) fields. A comfortable 35-minute flight aboard a private 16-passenger plane takes you to the town of Tequila. This is the only region in the world where the legendary spirit is distilled. The visit centers around Herradura Tequila's impressive 18th-century Hacienda San Jose, where you learn about the myth and the tradition of producing tequila from the stately plants that line the hillsides of the town. Departures are every Thursday at 10am from the Aerotron private airport (adjacent to the Puerto Vallarta International Airport); the group returns to Puerto Vallarta by 8pm. Cost is $290, which includes all air and ground transportation, tours, lunch, and beverages.

TOURS IN TOWN Every Wednesday and Thursday in high season (late Nov to Easter), the **International Friendship Club** (✆ **322/222-5466**) offers a **private home tour** of four villas in town. It costs $30 per person, with proceeds donated to local charities. Arrive early, because this tour sells out quickly. It starts at the Hotel Molino de Agua, Av. Ignacio L. Vallarta 130, adjacent to the southbound bridge over the Río Cuale. Get there at 10am, and you can buy breakfast while you wait for the group to gather. The tour departs at 11am and lasts approximately 2½ hours.

You can also tour the **Taylor/Burton villas** (Casa Kimberley; ✆ **322/222-1336**), at Calle Zaragoza 445. Tours of the two houses owned by Elizabeth Taylor and Richard Burton cost $8. Call ahead daily between 9am and 6pm, and if the manager is available, he will take you through the house.

STAYING ACTIVE

DIVING Underwater enthusiasts from beginner to expert can arrange scuba diving through **Vallarta Adventures** (✆ **866/256-2739** toll-free from the U.S., or 322/297-1212, ext. 3; www.vallarta-adventures.com), a five-star PADI dive center. Dives take place at Los Arcos, a company-owned site at Caletas Cove, Quimixto Coves, the Marietas Islands, or the offshore La Corbeteña, Morro, and Chimo reefs. The company also offers a full range of certification courses (through Instructor). **Chico's Dive Shop,** Díaz Ordaz 772–5, near Carlos O'Brian's (✆ **322/222-1895;** www.chicos-diveshop.com), offers similar dive trips and is also a PADI five-star dive center. Chico's is open daily from 8am to 10pm and has branches at the Marriott, Las Palmas, Holiday Inn, Fiesta Americana, Krystal, San Marino, Villa del Palmar, Paradise Village, and Playa Los Arcos hotels.

ECOTOURS & ACTIVITIES **Open Air Expeditions** (✆/fax **322/222-3310;** openair@vivamexico.com) offers nature-oriented trips, including birding and ocean kayaking in Punta Mita. **Ecotours de México,** Ignacio L. Vallarta 243 (✆/fax **322/222-6606**), has eco-oriented tours, including seasonal (Aug–Nov) trips to a turtle preservation camp where you can witness hatching baby Olive Ridley turtles.

Vallarta's newest adventure activity is **Canopy Tours.** You glide from treetop to treetop, getting an up-close-and-personal look at a tropical rainforest canopy and the trails far below. Expert guides assist you to the special platforms, and you move from one to another using pulleys on horizontal traverse cables, while the guides explain the tropical flora surrounding you. They also offer assistance—and moral support!—as you rappel back down to the forest floor. Tours depart from the **Vallarta Adventures** (✆ **866/256-2739** toll-free from the U.S., or 322/297-1212, ext. 3; www.vallarta-adventures.com) offices in both Marina Vallarta and Nuevo Vallarta at 8am, returning at 2pm. The price ($65 for adults, $33 for children 8–12) includes the tour, unlimited non-alcoholic beverages, and light snacks.

FISHING Arrange fishing trips through travel agencies or through the **Cooperativa de Pescadores (Fishing Cooperative),** on the *malecón* north of the Río Cuale, next door to the Rosita Hotel (✆ **322/222-1202** or 322/224-7886). Fishing charters cost $250 to $400 a day for four to eight people; price varies with the size of the boat. Although the posted price at the fishing cooperative is the same as you'll find through travel agencies, you may be able to negotiate a lower price at the cooperative, which does not accept credit cards. It's open Monday through Saturday from 7am to 10pm, but make arrangements a day ahead. You can also arrange fishing trips at the Marina Vallarta docks, or by calling **Fishing with Carolina** (✆ **322/224-7250;** cell 044-322/292-2953;

fishingwithcarolina@hotmail.com), which uses a 30-foot Uniflite sportsfisher, fully equipped with an English-speaking crew. Fishing trips cost $350 for up to six people and include equipment and bait, but drinks, snacks, and lunch are optional, at $10 per person. If you mention Frommer's when you make your reservation, they'll offer a free lunch with your booking.

GOLF Puerto Vallarta is an increasingly popular golf destination; five courses have opened in the past 4 years, bringing the total in the region to nine. The Joe Finger–designed private course at the **Marina Vallarta Golf Club** (✆ **322/221-0073**) is an 18-hole, par-74 course that winds through the Marina Vallarta peninsula and affords ocean views. It's for members only, but most luxury hotels in Puerto Vallarta have memberships for their guests. Greens fees are $136 in high season, $115 in low season. Fees include golf cart, range balls, and tax. Hiring a caddy costs $8 to $10. Club rentals, lessons, and special packages are available.

North of town in the state of Nayarit, about 16km (10 miles) beyond Puerto Vallarta, is the 18-hole, par-72 **Los Flamingos Club de Golf** (✆ **329/296-5006**). It features beautiful jungle vegetation and has just undergone a renovation and upgrade of the course. It's open from 7am to 5pm daily, with a snack bar (but no restaurant) and full pro shop. The greens fee is $95 and includes the use of a golf cart; hiring a caddy costs $12 plus tip, and club rental is $22 to $44. A free shuttle runs from downtown Puerto Vallarta; call for pickup times and locations.

The breathtaking Jack Nicklaus Signature course at the **Four Seasons Punta Mita** (✆ **329/291-6000;** fax 329/291-6060) has eight oceanfront holes and an ocean view from every hole. Its hallmark is the optional Hole 3B, the "Tail of the Whale," with a long drive to a green on a natural island—the only natural-island green in the Americas. It requires an amphibious cart to take you over when the tide is high, and there's an alternate hole for when the ocean or tides are not accommodating. It's open only to guests of the Four Seasons resort or to members of other golf clubs with a letter of introduction from their pro. Selected other area hotels also have guest privileges—ask your concierge. Greens fees for nonguests are $260, including cart, with (Calloway) club rentals for $60. Lessons are available from PGA pro Rick Avina.

A second Jack Nicklaus course is at the **Vista Vallarta Golf Club** (✆ **322/290-0030**), along with one designed by Tom Weiskopf. These courses were the site of the 2002 PGA World Cup Golf

Championships. It's in the foothills of the Sierra Madre, behind the bullring in Puerto Vallarta. A round costs $167 per person, including cart.

The Robert von Hagge–designed **El Tigre** course at Paradise Village (© **322/297-0773;** www.paradisemexico.com), in Nuevo Vallarta, opened in March 2002. The 7,239-yard course is on a relatively flat piece of land, but the design incorporates challenging bunkers, undulating fairways, and water features on several holes. Troon Golf manages El Tigre, which offers lessons and has an expansive clubhouse. Greens fees are $185 a round, or $85 if you play after 2pm.

American Golf Tours of Mexico (© **322/225-2056;** www.mexicogolftours.com) offers professionally guided tours to area courses as well as some tours further south along the Costa Alegre. Prices vary according to the number of golfers and whether you choose optional overnight stays. Personalized packages can be arranged, and club and shoe rentals are available.

HORSEBACK-RIDING TOURS Travel agents and local ranches can arrange guided horseback rides. **Rancho Palma Real,** Carretera Vallarta, Tepic 4766 (© **322/221-2120**), has an office 5 minutes north of the airport; the ranch is in Las Palmas, approximately 40 minutes northeast of Vallarta. It is by far the nicest horseback riding tour in the area. The horses are in excellent condition, and you enjoy a tour of local farms on your way to the ranch. The price ($62; Amex only) includes breakfast and lunch.

Rancho El Charro, Av. Francisco Villa 895 (© **322/224-0114;** cell 322/292-0122; www.ranchoelcharro.com), and **Rancho Ojo de Agua,** Cerrada de Cardenal 227, Fracciónamiento Las Aralias (©/fax **322/224-0607**), also offer high-quality tours. Both ranches are about a 10-minute taxi ride north of downtown toward the Sierra Madre foothills. The morning and sunset rides last 3 hours and take you up into the mountains overlooking the ocean and town. The cost is $39. The ranches have their own comfortable base camp for serious riders who want to stay out overnight.

Rancho El Charro offers an exclusive "Fly-away to a Hide-away in San Sebastián" day trip from 9:30am to 5pm. A 15-minute flight takes you to the 17th-century mining town (see "Side Trips from Puerto Vallarta," later in this chapter). A bilingual guide meets you at the airstrip, well-tended horses in tow; after a short ride to the Hacienda Jalisco, you'll get a light breakfast and a tour of the hacienda. The ride continues into town along a riverside trail used by the locals since mining days. A thorough tour of the town touches on the historic buildings, church, carpenter shop, and coffee plantation, before heading back to the hacienda for a gourmet lunch. Overnight stays can be arranged. The cost is $278 per person, minimum four people, and advance reservations are required.

Rancho El Charro also organizes a "Horseback on Mexico's Hacienda Trail" tour. The 3- to 7-day journeys by horseback into the mountains are offered November through April. There's a four-person minimum and a 15-person maximum. The cost ($270 per person per day; no credit cards) includes food, horses, camping en route, and stays in centuries-old haciendas. For details, contact Pam Aguirre of Rancho El Charro (see above).

MOUNTAIN BIKING & HIKING **Bike Mex** ★, Calle Guerrero 361 (✆ **322/223-1834** or 322/223-1680; www.bikemex.com), offers expert guided biking and hiking tours up the Río Cuale canyon and to outlying areas. The popular Río Cuale bike trip costs $42 for 4 hours and includes bike, helmet, gloves, insurance, water, lunch, and an English-speaking guide. Trips take off at 9am or 2pm, but starting times are flexible; make arrangements a day ahead.

Who says Yelapa is accessible only by boat? Well, most people, but I've traveled with Bike Mex on its all-day, advanced-level bike trip to this magical cove (see "Side Trips from Puerto Vallarta," later in this chapter). Riders depart at 7:30am in a van, traveling to the starting point in the town of El Tuito. The 53km (33-mile) ride includes 30km (19 miles) of climbs to a peak elevation of 1,091m (3,600 ft.). The journey consists of switchbacks, fire roads, single tracks, awesome climbs, and steep downhills before ending up at a beachfront *palapa* restaurant in Yelapa. You have the option of staying the night in Yelapa or returning that afternoon by small boat. This tour costs $160, takes 4 to 6 hours, and includes all bike gear, drinks, lunch, boat and land transportation, guide, and *ample* encouragement. Other bicycle trips, such as those along the beachfront of Punta Mita, are also available. Bike Mex also arranges guided **hiking tours** along the same routes; prices start at $30, depending on the route.

SAILING **Sail Vallarta,** Club de Tenis Puesta del Sol, Local 7-B, Marina Vallarta (✆ **322/221-0096;** fax 322/221-0097; gallonavarro@aol.com), offers a variety of sailing vessels for hire. A group day sail, including crew, use of snorkeling equipment, drinks, food, and music, plus a stop at a beach for swimming and lunch, costs $82. Most trips include a crew, but you can make arrangements to sail yourself. Prices vary for full boat charters, depending on the vessel and amount of time. **Vallarta Adventures** (✆ **866/256-2739** toll-free from the U.S., or 322/297-1212, ext. 3; www.vallarta-adventures.com) offers two beautiful sailboats for charter or small-group sails (up to 12 people). The service is superb, as is the quality of the food and beverages. These are known as the boats that are most frequently under sail—many other sailing charters prefer to motor around the bay.

SWIMMING WITH DOLPHINS Ever been kissed by a dolphin? Take advantage of a unique opportunity to swim with Pacific bottlenose dolphins in one of two facilities—a clear lagoon or a special swim facility that's part of the Vallarta Adventures offices. **Dolphin Adventure** ★★ (✆ **866/256-2739** toll-free from the U.S., or 322/297-1212, ext. 3; www.vallarta-adventures.com) operates an interactive dolphin-research facility—considered the finest in Latin America—that allows limited numbers of people to swim with dolphins Monday through Saturday at scheduled times. Cost for the swim is $130. Reservations are required, and they generally sell out at least a week in advance. You may prefer the **Dolphin Encounter** ($60), which allows you to touch and learn about the dolphins in smaller pools, so you're ensured up-close-and-personal time with them. I give this my highest recommendation. Not only does the experience leave you with an indescribable sensation, but it's also a joy to see these dolphins—they are well cared for, happy, and spirited. The program is about education and interaction, not entertainment or amusement, and is especially popular with children 10 and older.

TENNIS Many hotels in Puerto Vallarta offer excellent tennis facilities; they often have clay courts. The full-service **Continental Plaza Tennis Club** (✆ **322/224-0123**) is at the Continental Plaza hotel in the Hotel Zone. It offers indoor and outdoor courts (including a clay court), full pro shop, lessons, clinics, and partner matches.

Tips **A Spectator Sport**

Bullfights are held December through April beginning at 5pm on Wednesday at the La Paloma bullring, across the highway from the town pier. Travel agencies can arrange tickets, which cost around $25.

PARASAILING Parasailing and other watersports are available at many beaches along the Bay of Banderas. The most popular spot is at Los Muertos Beach. WaveRunners, banana boats, and parasailing are available by the hour, half day, or full day.

A STROLL THROUGH TOWN

Puerto Vallarta's cobblestone streets are a pleasure to explore; they're full of tiny shops, rows of windows edged with curling wrought iron, and vistas of red-tile roofs and the sea. Start with a walk up and down the *malecón.*

Among the sights you shouldn't miss is the **municipal building** on the main square (next to the tourism office), which has a large Manuel Lepe mural inside by its stairwell. Nearby, up Independencia, sits the **Parish of Nuestra Señora de Guadalupe church,** Hidalgo 370 (© **322/222-1326**), topped with a curious crown held in place by angels—a replica of the one worn by Empress Carlota during her brief time in Mexico as Emperor Maximilian's wife. On its steps, women sell religious mementos; across the narrow street, stalls sell native herbs for curing common ailments. Services in English are held Sunday at 10am. Regular hours are Monday through Saturday from 7:30am to 8:30pm, Sunday from 6:30am to 8:30pm.

Three blocks south of the church, head east on Libertad, lined with small shops and pretty upper windows, to the **municipal market** by the river. (It's the Río Cuale Mercado, but I recently overheard a tourist ask for the "real quality" market!) After exploring the market, cross the bridge to the island in the river; sometimes a painter is at work on its banks. Walk down the center of the island toward the sea, and you'll come to the tiny **Museo Río Cuale** (no phone), which has a small but impressive permanent exhibit of pre-Columbian figurines. It's open Monday through Saturday from 10am to 4pm. Admission is free.

Retrace your steps to the market and Libertad, and follow Calle Miramar to the brightly colored steps up to Zaragoza. Midway is a magnificent view over rooftops to the sea, plus a cute cafe, **Graffiti** (no phone), where you can break for a cappuccino and a snack. Up Zaragoza to the right 1 block is the famous **pink arched bridge** that once connected Richard Burton's and Elizabeth Taylor's houses. In this area, known as **"Gringo Gulch,"** many Americans have houses.

2 Shopping

Shopping in Puerto Vallarta is generally concentrated in small, eclectic, independent shops rather than impersonal malls. You can

Downtown Puerto Vallarta

find excellent **folk art,** original **clothing** designs, fine jewelry, and creative home accessories at great prices. Vallarta is known for having the most diverse and impressive selection of **contemporary**

Mexican fine art outside Mexico City. It also has an abundance of tacky T-shirts and the ubiquitous **silver jewelry.**

THE SHOPPING SCENE

There are a few key shopping areas: central downtown, the Marina Vallarta *malecón,* the popular *mercados,* and on the beach—where the merchandise comes to you. Some of the more attractive shops are 1 to 2 blocks in **back of the *malecón.*** Start at the intersection of Corona and Morelos streets—interesting shops spread out in all directions from here. **Marina Vallarta** has two shopping plazas, Plaza Marina and Neptuno Plaza, on the main highway from the airport into town, which offer a limited selection of shops. Although still home to a few interesting shops, the marina boardwalk *(marina malecón)* is dominated by real estate companies, timeshare vendors, restaurants, and boating services.

Puerto Vallarta's **municipal market** is just north of the Río Cuale, where Libertad and A. Rodríguez meet. The *mercado* sells clothes, jewelry, serapes, shawls, leather accessories and suitcases, papier-mâché parrots, stuffed frogs and armadillos, and, of course, T-shirts. Be sure to comparison-shop, and definitely bargain before buying. The market is open daily from 9am to 7pm. Upstairs, a **food market** serves inexpensive Mexican meals—for more adventurous diners, it's probably the best value and most authentic dining experience in Vallarta. An **outdoor market** is along Río Cuale Island, between the two bridges. Stalls sell crafts, gifts, folk art, and clothing.

Along any public beach, walking **vendors** will probably approach you. Their merchandise ranges from silver jewelry to rugs and T-shirts to masks. "Almost free!" they'll call out. If you're too relaxed to think of shopping in town, this can be an entertaining alternative for picking up souvenirs, and remember: Bargaining is expected. The most reputable beach vendors concentrate at Los Muertos Beach in front of the El Dorado and La Palapa restaurants (Calle Pulpito).

In most of the better shops and galleries, shipping, packing, and delivery to Puerto Vallarta hotels are available. Some will also ship to your home address. Note that while bargaining is expected in the *mercados* and with beach vendors, stores generally charge fixed—and fair—prices for their wares.

THE LOWDOWN ON HUICHOL INDIAN ART

Puerto Vallarta offers the best selection of Huichol art in Mexico. Descendants of the Aztec, the Huichol are one of the last remaining

Tips Beware the Silver Scam

Much of the silver sold on the beach is actually alpaca, a lower-quality silver metal (even though many pieces are stamped with the designation ".925," supposedly indicating true silver). Prices for silver on the beach are much lower, as is the quality. If you're looking for a more lasting piece of jewelry, you're better off in a silver shop.

indigenous cultures in the world that has remained true to its ancient traditions, customs, language, and habitat. The Huichol live in adobe structures in the high Sierras (at an elevation of 1,394m/4,600 ft.) north and east of Puerto Vallarta. Due to the decreasing fertility (and therefore productivity) of the land surrounding their villages, they have come to depend more on the sale of their artwork for sustenance.

Huichol art has always been cloaked in a veil of mysticism—probably one of the reasons serious collectors seek out this form of *artesanía.* Colorful, symbolic yarn "paintings," inspired by visions experienced during spiritual ceremonies, characterize Huichol art. In the ceremonies, artists ingest peyote, a hallucinogenic cactus, which induces brightly colored visions; these are considered messages from their ancestors. The visions' symbolic and mythological imagery influences the art, which encompasses not only yarn paintings but also fascinating masks and bowls decorated with tiny colored beads.

The Huichol might be geographically isolated, but they are savvy businesspeople and have adapted their art to meet consumer demand. Original Huichol art, therefore, is not necessarily traditional. Iguanas, jaguars, sea turtles, frogs, eclipses, and eggs appear in response to consumer demand. For more traditional works, look for pieces that depict deer, scorpions, wolves, or snakes.

The Huichol have also had to modify their techniques to create more pieces in less time and meet increased demand. Patterned fill-work, which is faster to produce, sometimes replaces the detailed designs that used to fill the pieces. The same principle applies to yarn paintings. While some are beautiful depictions of landscapes and even abstract pieces, they are not traditional themes.

You may see Huichol Indians on the streets of Vallarta—they are easy to spot, dressed in white clothing embroidered with colorful designs. A number of fine Huichol galleries are in downtown Puerto

Fun Fact A Huichol Art Primer: Shopping Tips

Huichol art falls into two main categories: yarn paintings and beaded pieces. All other items you might find in Huichol art galleries are either ceremonial objects or items used in everyday life.

Yarn paintings are made on a wood base covered with wax and meticulously overlaid with colored yarn. Designs represent the magical vision of the underworld, and each symbol gives meaning to the piece. Paintings made with wool yarn are more authentic than those made with acrylic; however, acrylic yarn paintings are usually brighter and have more detail because the threads are thinner. It is normal to find empty spaces where the wax base shows. Usually the artist starts with a central motif and works around it, but it's common to have several independent motifs that, when combined, take on a different meaning. A painting with many small designs tells a more complicated story than one with only one design and fill-work on the background. Look for the story of the piece on the back of the painting. Most Huichol artists write in pencil in Huichol and Spanish.

Beaded pieces are made on carved wooden shapes depicting different animals, wooden eggs, or small bowls made from gourds. The pieces are covered with wax and tiny *chaquira* beads are applied one by one to form designs. Usually the beaded designs represent animals; plants; the elements of fire, water, or air; and certain symbols that give a special meaning to the whole. Deer, snakes, wolves, and scorpions are traditional elements; other figures, such as iguanas, frogs, and any animals not indigenous to Huichol territory, are incorporated by popular demand. Beadwork with many small designs that do not exactly fit into one other is more time-consuming and has a more complex symbolic meaning. This kind of work has empty spaces where the wax shows.

Vallarta (see individual listings under "Crafts & Gifts" and "Decorative & Folk Art," below).

One place to learn more about the Huichol is **Huichol Collection,** Morelos 490, across from the sea-horse statue on the *malecón*

(© **322/223-2141**). Not only does this shop offer an extensive selection of Huichol art in all price ranges, but it also has a replica of a Huichol adobe hut, informational displays explaining more about their fascinating way of life and beliefs, and usually a Huichol artist at work. However, note that this is a timeshare sales location, so don't be surprised if you're hit with a pitch for a "free" breakfast and property tour in the process of your Huichol education.

CLOTHING

Vallarta's single true department store is **LANS,** with branches at Juárez 867 (© **322/226-9100;** www.lans.com.mx), and in Plaza Caracol, next door to the supermarket Gigante, in the Hotel Zone (© **322/226-9100**). Both offer a wide selection of brand-name clothing, accessories, footwear, cosmetics, and home furnishings. Along with the nationally popular **LOB, Carlos 'n' Charlie's,** and **Bye-Bye** brands, Vallarta offers a distinctive shop featuring original designs.

Laura López Labra Designs The most comfortable clothing you'll ever enjoy, LLL is renowned for her trademark all-white (or natural) designs in 100% cotton or lace. Laura's fine gauze fabrics float in her designs of seductive skirts, romantic dresses, blouses, beachwear, and baby dolls. Men's offerings include cotton drawstring pants and lightweight shirts. Other designs include a line of precious children's clothing and some pieces with elaborate embroidery based on Huichol Indian designs. Personalized wedding dresses are also available. Open Monday through Saturday from 10am to 2pm and 5 to 9pm. Basilio Badillo 324. © **322/222-3074.**

Mar de Sueños This small shop carries stunning swimsuits and exquisite lingerie. Without a doubt, the finest women's beachwear, intimate apparel, and evening wear in Vallarta for those special occasions—or just to make you feel extra special. The shop also stocks a selection of fine linen clothing—and it's one of the few places in Mexico that carries the renowned Italian line La Perla. Other name brands include Gottex, Calvin Klein, and DKNY. Open Monday through Saturday from 10am to 2pm and 5 to 9pm. Leona Vicario 220-C. © **322/222-2662.**

CONTEMPORARY ART

Known for sustaining one of the stronger art communities in Latin America, Puerto Vallarta has an impressive selection of fine galleries featuring quality original works. Several dozen galleries get together to offer art walks almost every week between November and April.

Galería AL (Arte Latinoamericano) This gallery showcases contemporary works created by young, primarily Latin American artists, as well as Vallarta favorite Marta Gilbert. Feature exhibitions take place every 2 weeks during high season. The historic building (one of Vallarta's original structures) has exposed brick walls; small rooms of exhibition spaces on the second and third floors surround an open courtyard. It's also rumored to have a friendly resident ghost, who partner Susan Burger says has been quite welcoming. Open Monday through Saturday from 10:30am to 9pm. Josefa Ortiz Domínguez 155. ✆/fax **322/222-4406.**

Galería Dante This gallery-in-a-villa showcases contemporary art as well as sculptures and classical reproductions of Italian, Greek, and Art Deco bronzes—against a backdrop of gardens and fountains. Located on the "Calle de los cafés," the gallery is open during the winter Monday through Saturday from 10am to 5pm, and by appointment. Basilio Badillo 269. ✆ **322/222-2477.** Fax 322/222-6284. www.galleriadante.com.

Galería Pacífico Since opening in 1987, Galería Pacífico has been considered one of the finest galleries in Mexico. On display is a wide selection of sculptures and paintings in various media by midrange masters and up-and-comers alike. The gallery is 1½ blocks inland from the fantasy sculptures on the *malecón.* Among the artists whose careers Galería Pacífico has influenced are rising talent Brewster Brockman, internationally renowned sculptor Ramiz Barquet, and Patrick Denoun. Open Monday through Saturday from 10am to 3pm and 5 to 9pm, and Sunday by appointment. Between May and October, check for reduced hours or vacation closings. Aldama 174, 2nd floor. ✆ **322/222-5502.** www.artmexico.com.

Galería Rosas Blancas This notable member of Puerto Vallarta's gallery community features contemporary painters from throughout Mexico. The downstairs courtyard exhibition space showcases a featured artist, while the upstairs offers a sampling of the artists who regularly exhibit here. A shop next door sells art supplies and books on Mexican art in English and Spanish. Owner Marcella García Alegría also runs the adjacent folk-art store, Querubines (see "Decorative & Folk Art," below). Open Monday through Saturday from 9am to 9pm. Juárez 523. ✆ **322/222-1168.**

Galería Uno One of Vallarta's first galleries, the Galería Uno features an excellent selection of contemporary paintings by Latin American artists, plus a variety of posters and prints. During the high season, featured exhibitions change every 2 weeks. In a classic adobe building with open courtyard, it's also a casual, *salón*-style gathering place for friends of owner Jan Lavender. Open Monday through Saturday from 10am to 9pm. A branch, **Arte de las Américas** (✆ **322/221-1985**), is at Marina Vallarta between La Taberna and the Yacht Club. It exhibits some of the same artists but has a decidedly more abstract orientation. It's open Monday through Saturday from 10am to 2pm and 5 to 9pm. Morelos 561 (at Corona). ✆ **322/222-0908.**

Studio Cathy Van Rohr This lovely studio showcases the work of Cathy Von Rohr, one of the most respected artists in the area. For years, Cathy lived in the secluded cove of Majahuitas, on the bay's southern shore, and much of her work reflects the tranquillity and deep connection with the natural world that resulted. Paintings, prints, and sculptures are featured. It's open by appointment and does not accept credit cards. Manuel M. Dieguez 321. ✆ **866/256-2739** toll-free in the U.S., or 322/222-5875. www.cathyvonrohr.com.

CRAFTS & GIFTS

Alfarería Tlaquepaque Opened in 1953, this is Vallarta's original source for Mexican ceramics and decorative crafts, all at excellent prices. Talavera pottery and dishware, colored glassware, bird cages, baskets, and wood furniture are just a few of the many items in this warehouse-style store. Open Monday through Sunday from 9am to 9pm. Av. México 1100. ✆ **322/223-2121.** www.at.com.mx.

Safari Accents Flickering candles glowing in colored-glass holders welcome you to this highly original shop overflowing with creative gifts, one-of-a-kind furnishings, and reproductions of paintings by Frida Kahlo and Botero. Open daily from 9am to 11pm. Olas Altas 224, Local 5. ✆ **322/223-2660.**

DECORATIVE & FOLK ART

Azul Siempre Azul Religious figurative pieces, antique *retablos* (painted scenes on tin backgrounds depicting the granting of a miracle), artistic jewelry, and beeswax candles in grand sizes come together in this tiny store brimming with captivating treasures. Open Monday through Saturday from 10am to 9pm. Ignacio L. Vallarta 228, across from Club Roxy, just over the southbound bridge. ✆ **322/223-0060.**

La Tienda Fine antiques and decorative objects for the home, including unique furniture, religious-themed items (such as *retablos*), glassware, and pewter. La Tienda also carries an outstanding selection of rustic candlesticks and beeswax candles, both in a

walkway by the water's edge and check out the action at the various clubs, which extend from **Bodeguita del Medio** on the north end to **Hooters** just off the central plaza.

Marina Vallarta's clubs offer a more upscale, indoor, air-conditioned atmosphere. South of the Río Cuale, the **Olas Altas** zone's small cafes and martini bars buzz with action. In this zone, there's also an active gay and lesbian club scene.

PERFORMING ARTS & CULTURAL EVENTS

Truth be told, cultural nightlife beyond the **Mexican Fiesta** is limited. Culture centers on the visual arts; the opening of an exhibition has great social and artistic significance. Puerto Vallarta's gallery community comes together to present almost weekly **art walks,** where new exhibits are presented, featured artists attend, and complimentary cocktails are served. These social events alternate between the galleries along the Marina Vallarta *malecón* and those in the central downtown area. Check listings in the daily English-language newspaper, *Vallarta Today,* to see what's on the schedule during your stay.

FIESTA NIGHTS

Major hotels in Puerto Vallarta feature frequent fiestas for tourists—extravaganzas with open bars, Mexican buffet dinners, and live entertainment. Some are fairly authentic and make a good introduction for first-time travelers to Mexico; others can be a bit cheesy. Shows are usually held outdoors but move indoors when necessary. Reservations are recommended.

NH Krystal Vallarta Hotel One of the best fiesta nights is here on Tuesday and Saturday at 7pm. These things are difficult to quantify, but Krystal's program is probably less tacky than those at most of its counterparts. Av. de las Palmas, north of downtown off the airport road. ✆ **322/224-1041.** kvallart@krystal.com.mx. Cover $48.

Rhythms of the Night (Cruise to Caletas) ★★★ *Moments* This is an unforgettable evening under the stars at John Huston's former home at the pristine cove called Las Caletas. The smooth, fast Vallarta Adventures catamaran travels here, entertaining guests along the way. Tiki torches and native drummers greet you at the dock. There's no electricity—you dine by the light of candles, the stars, and the moon. The buffet dinner is delicious—steak, seafood, and generous vegetarian options: Everything is first-class. The entertainment showcases indigenous dances in contemporary style. The cruise departs at 6pm and returns by 11pm. Departs from Terminal Marítima.

✆ **866/256-2739** toll-free from the U.S., or 322/297-1212, ext 3. www.vallarta-adventures.com. Cost $75 (includes cruise, dinner, open bar, entertainment).

THE CLUB & MUSIC SCENE

RESTAURANT/BARS

Bianco The newest and most sophisticated lounge in Vallarta is the sleek Bianco. It has a long glass-top bar and cozy seating areas where conversation is possible. This is the spot—finally—for anyone over 30 who wants to enjoy an evening out, listening to contemporary music. The air-conditioned lounge also features occasional live music. You can't miss the dramatic entrance, and the lounge even has valet parking—a first in Vallarta. Open daily from 5pm to 4am. Insurgentes 109, Col. Emiliano Zapata. ✆ **322/222-2748.**

Carlos O'Brian's Vallarta's original nightspot was once the only place for an evening of revelry. Although the competition is stiffer nowadays, COB's still packs them in—especially the 20-something set. Late at night, the scene resembles a college party. Open daily from noon to 2am; happy hour is from noon to 6pm. Paseo Díaz Ordaz (malecón) 786, at Pípila. ✆ **322/222-1444** or 322/222-4065. Weekend cover $11 (includes 2 drinks); no cover weekdays.

Kit Kat Club It's swank and sleek and reminiscent of a New York club, but don't be fooled—the Kit Kat Club also has a terrific sense of humor. In the golden glow of candlelight, lounge around on cushy leopard-patterned chairs or cream-colored overstuffed banquettes, listening to swinging tunes while you sip a martini. Not only does the place attract a very hip, generally gay crowd, but it also serves good food, with especially tasty appetizers—which can double as light meals—and scrumptious desserts. Michael, the owner, describes his air-conditioned lounge and cafe as cool, crazy, wild, jazzy, and sexy. Often, in high season, you'll be treated to a cabaret-style floorshow performed by a cross-dressing songstress. Open daily from 6pm to 2am. Pulpito 120, Playa Los Muertos. ✆ **322/223-0093.** No cover.

La Bodeguita del Medio This authentic Cuban restaurant and bar is known for its casual energy, terrific live music, and mojitos—stiff rum-based drinks with fresh mint and lime juice. It is a branch of the original Bodeguita in Havana (reputedly Hemingway's favorite restaurant there), which opened in 1942. If you can't get to that one, the Vallarta version has successfully imported the essence—and has a small souvenir shop that sells Cuban cigars, rum, and other items. The downstairs has large wooden windows that open to the *malecón* street action, while the upstairs offers terrific views of the bay. Walls throughout are decorated with old photographs and patrons' signatures—if you can, find a spot and add yours! I feel the food is less memorable here then the music and atmosphere, so I suggest drinks and dancing, nothing more. Open daily from 11:30am to 2am. Paseo Díaz Ordaz (malecón), at Allende. ✆ **322/223-1585.** No cover.

La Cantina de los Remedios Cantinas are a centuries-old tradition, and this one has retained the fundamentals while updating the concept to a hip club. Cantinas serve little complimentary plates of food as your table orders drinks. La Cantina does this from 1 to 5pm; dishes might include *carne con chile* (meat in chile sauce), soup of the day, or quesadillas. In the evenings, recorded music alternates between sultry boleros and the hottest in Mexican rock, at a volume that permits conversation, creating a romantic, clubby atmosphere. If you require more stimulation, play a board game in one of the smaller rooms or on the larger open-air patio. Beers cost $1.50, bar drinks $2.50. Open Sunday through Wednesday from noon to 2am, Thursday through Saturday from noon to 4am. No credit cards. Morelos 709, downtown. ✆ **322/222-7701.** No cover.

ROCK, JAZZ & BLUES

Club Roxy Currently the most popular live-music club in Vallarta, Club Roxy features a hot house band led by club owner Pico, playing a mix of reggae, blues, rock, and anything by Santana. Live music jams between 10pm and 2am Monday through Saturday. It's open daily from 6pm to 2am. Ignacio L. Vallarta 217 (between Madero and Cárdenas, south of the river). ✆ **322/223-2402.** No cover.

El Faro Lighthouse Bar A circular cocktail lounge at the top of the Marina lighthouse, El Faro is one of Vallarta's most romantic nightspots. Live or recorded jazz plays, and conversation is manageable. Drop by at twilight for the magnificent panoramic views, but don't expect anything other than a drink and, if you get lucky, some popcorn. Open daily from 5pm to 2am. Royal Pacific Yacht Club, Marina Vallarta. ✆ **322/221-0541** or 322/221-0542. elfaropv@pvnet.com.mx. No cover.

Mariachi Loco This live and lively mariachi club features singers belting out boleros and ranchero classics. The mariachi show begins at 9pm—the mariachis stroll and play as guests join in impromptu singing—and by 10pm it gets going. After midnight the mariachis play for pay, which is around $11 for each song played at your table. There's Mexican food until 1am. Open daily from 1pm to 4am. Lázaro Cárdenas 254 (at Ignacio Vallarta). ✆ **322/223-2205.** No cover.

CLUBS & DISCOS

A few of Vallarta's clubs or discos charge admission, but generally you pay just for drinks—$4 for a margarita, $2.50 for a beer, more for whiskey and mixed drinks. Keep an eye out for discount passes frequently available in hotels, restaurants, and other tourist spots. Most clubs are open from 10pm to 4am.

Christine Proving that disco is alive and well, this dazzling club draws a crowd with an opening laser-light show, pumped-in dry ice and oxygen, flashing lights, and a dozen large-screen video panels. The sound system is truly amazing, and the mix of music can get almost anyone dancing. Dress code: No shorts for men, tennis shoes, or thongs. Open daily from 10pm to 4am; the light show begins at 11pm. In the Krystal Vallarta Hotel, north of downtown off Av. Francisco Medina Ascencio. ✆ **322/224-0202.** Cover free to $6.

Collage A multilevel monster of nighttime entertainment, Collage includes a pool salon, video arcade, bowling alley, and the always-packed Disco Bar, with frequent live entertainment. It's just past the entrance to Marina Vallarta, air-conditioned, and very popular with a young, mainly local crowd. Open daily from 10am to 6am. Calle Proa s/n, Marina Vallarta. ✆ **322/221-0505** or 322/221-0861. Cover $5.50–$25. Call ahead as cover varies depending on the theme—Mardi Gras, Foam Party, Black Light party, and so on.

de Santos Vallarta's chicest dining spot is known more for the urban, hip crowd the bar draws. In 2003 it added a stunning state-of-the-art club, which quickly became the place for the super-chic to party. The lower level holds an air-conditioned bar and dance floor, where a deejay spins the hottest of house and techno. Upstairs, there's an open-air rooftop bar with chill-out music and acid jazz. Enjoy the tunes and the fresh air while lounging around on one of the several oversize beds. One partner, a member of the super-hot Latin rock group Mana, uses Vallarta as a home base for writing new songs. The crowd, which varies in age from 20s on up, shares a common denominator of cool style. The restaurant bar is open daily from 5pm to 1am; the club is open Wednesday through Saturday from 10pm to 6am, and often waives the cover charge for women. Morelos 771. ✆ **322/223-3052** or 322/223-3053. Cover usually $10 (includes 1 drink).

J & B Salsa Club This is the locally popular place to go for dancing to Latin music—from salsa to samba, the dancing is hot! On Fridays, Saturdays, and holidays the air-conditioned club features live bands. Open Monday through Saturday from 10pm to 6am. Av. Francisco Medina Ascencio Km 2.5 (Hotel Zone). ✆ **322/224-4616.** Cover $9.

The Palm Video & Show Bar The big screen above the dance floor of this colorful, lively club plays the most danceable videos in town. They're certain to get you moving. The pool table is regularly in play, and the air-conditioned club frequently books live shows featuring female impersonators. This is a gay-friendly but not exclusively gay club, with a spirited, festive atmosphere. Open daily from 7pm to 2am. Olas Altas 508. ✆ **322/223-4813.** www.thepalmbar.com. Cover $3 on show nights only.

Señor Frog's The sheer size of this outpost of the famed Carlos 'n' Charlie's chain is daunting, but it fills up and rocks until the early morning hours. Cute waiters are a signature of the chain, and one never knows when they'll assemble on stage and call on a bevy of beauties to join them in a tequila-drinking contest. Occasionally live bands appear. Although mainly popular with the 20s set, all ages will find the air-conditioned club fun. There's food service, but it's better known for its dance-club atmosphere. Open daily from 11am to 4am. Ignacio L. Vallarta and Venustiano Carranza. ✆ **322/222-5171** or 322/222-5177. Cover free to $11 (includes 2 drinks).

Zoo Your chance to be an animal and get wild in the night. The Zoo even has cages to dance in if you're feeling unleashed. This popular club has a terrific sound system and a great variety of dance music, including techno, reggae, and rap. Every hour's happy hour, with two-for-one drinks. It opens daily at noon and closes in the wee hours. Paseo Díaz Ordaz (malecón) 630. ✆ **322/222-4945.** Cover $11 (includes 2 drinks).

A SPORTS BAR & A STRIP JOINT

Micky's No Name Cafe With a multitude of TVs and enough sports memorabilia to start a mini-museum, Micky's is a great venue for catching your favorite game. It shows all NBA, NHL, NFL, and MLB broadcast events, plus pay-per-view. Mickey's also serves great barbecued ribs and USDA imported steaks. It's open daily from 9am to midnight. Morelos 460 (malecón), at Mina. ✆ **322/223-2508.** No cover.

Q'eros This air-conditioned adult nightclub features exotic dancers, private shows, and stripteases. It's open nightly from 9pm to 6am. Av. Francisco Medina Ascencio, in front of Plaza Genovesa. ✆ **322/222-4367.** Cover $5.

GAY & LESBIAN CLUBS

Vallarta has a vibrant gay community with a wide variety of clubs and nightlife options, including special bay cruises and evening excursions to nearby ranches.

Club Paco Paco This combination disco, cantina, and rooftop bar stages a spectacular "Trasvesty" transvestite show every Thursday, Friday, Saturday, and Sunday night at 1:30am. It's open daily from 1pm to 6am and is air-conditioned. Ignacio L. Vallarta 278. ✆ **322/222-1899.** www.pacopaco.com. Cover $6 (includes 1 drink) after 10pm or start of 1st show, whichever is earlier.

Los Balcones One of the original gay clubs in town, this air-conditioned bi-level space boasts several dance floors and an excellent sound system. It earned a few chuckles when *Brides* magazine listed it as one of the most romantic spots in Vallarta. It posts nightly specials, including exotic male dancers. Open from 9pm to 4am, daily November through March, closed Sunday in the off season. Juárez 182. ✆ **322/222-4671.** No cover.

Ranch Disco Bar This place is known for the nightly "Ranch Hand's Show," at 11:30pm and 2am. The club also has a new dance floor. Open daily from 9pm to 6am. Venustiano Carranza 239 (around the corner from Paco Paco). ✆ **322/223-0537.** Cover $4.50 (includes 1 drink).

4 Side Trips from Puerto Vallarta

YELAPA: ROBINSON CRUSOE MEETS JACK KEROUAC

It's a cove straight out of a tropical fantasy, and only a 45-minute trip by boat from Puerto Vallarta. **Yelapa** ★ has no cars, has one sole paved (pedestrian-only) road, and got electricity only in the past 2 years. It's accessible only by boat. Its tranquillity, natural beauty, and seclusion have made it a popular home for hippies, hipsters, artists, writers, and a few ex-pats (looking to escape the stress of the world, or perhaps the law). A seemingly strange mix, but you're unlikely to ever meet a stranger—Yelapa remains casual and friendly.

To get there, travel by excursion boat or inexpensive water taxi (see "Getting Around," in chapter 2). There's also a challenging mountain bike trip with Bike Mex (see "Mountain Biking & Hiking" on p. 99). You can spend an enjoyable day, but I recommend a longer stay—it provides a completely different perspective.

Once you're in Yelapa, you can lie in the sun, swim, snorkel, eat fresh grilled seafood at a beachfront restaurant, or sample the local moonshine, *raicilla.* The local beach vendors specialize in the most amazing pies you've ever tasted (coconut, lemon, or chocolate). Equally amazing is how the pie ladies walk the beach while balancing the pie plates on their heads; they sell crocheted swimsuits, too. You can also tour this tiny town or hike up a river to see one of two waterfalls. The closest to town is about a 30-minute walk from the beach. ***Note:*** If you use a local guide, agree on a price before you start out. Horseback riding, guided birding, fishing trips, and paragliding are also available.

For overnight accommodations, local residents frequently rent rooms, and there's also the rustic **Hotel Lagunita** (✆ **329/298-0554;** www.hotel-lagunita.com). Its 27 cabañas have private bathrooms, and the hotel has electricity, a saltwater pool, massage, and an amiable restaurant and bar. Though the prices are high for what you get—and you may need to bring your own towels, which are known to be in short supply—it is the most accommodating place for most visitors. It's quite popular for yoga students and other groups. Double rates run $78 during the season and $55 in the off-season (MasterCard, Visa).

A stylish alternative is the fashionable **Verana** ★★★ (✆ **800/677-5156** or 322/222-2360; www.verana.com). See p. 77 for details.

If you stay over on a Wednesday or Saturday during the winter, don't miss the regular dance at the **Yelapa Yacht Club** ★ (no phone). Typically tongue-in-cheek for Yelapa, the "yacht club" consists of a cement dance floor and a disco ball, but the deejay spins a great range of tunes, from Glenn Miller to Eminem, attracting all ages and types. Dinner ($5–$12) is a bonus—the food may be the best anywhere in the bay. The menu changes depending on what's fresh. Ask for directions; it's in the main village, on the beach.

NUEVO VALLARTA & NORTH OF VALLARTA: ALL-INCLUSIVE

Many people assume Nuevo Vallarta is a suburb of Puerto Vallarta, but it's a stand-alone destination over the state border in Nayarit. It was designed as a mega-resort development, complete with marina, golf course, and luxury hotels. Although it got off to a slow start, it is finally coming together, with a collection of mostly all-inclusive hotels on one of the widest, most attractive beaches in the bay. The biggest resort, Paradise Village, has a growing marina and just opened an 18-hole golf course inland from the beachfront strip of hotels. The Mayan Palace also just opened an 18-hole course. The

Paradise Plaza shopping center, next to Paradise Village, adds much to the area's shopping, dining, and services. It's open daily from 10am to 10pm. To get to the beach, you travel down a lengthy entrance road from the highway, passing by fields (great for birding) and nearby lagoons (great for kayaking).

Also worthwhile is a day spent at the **Etc. Beach Club,** Paseo de los Cocoteros 38, Nuevo Vallarta (✆ **322/297-0174**). This beach club has a volleyball net, showers, restroom facilities, and food and drink service on the beach, both day and night. To get there, take the second entrance to Nuevo Vallarta coming from Puerto Vallarta and turn right on Paseo de los Cocoteros; it is past the Vista Bahía hotel. It's open daily during the winter from 11am to 10:30pm, summer from 11am to 7pm. Drinks cost $2.50 to $7, entrees $4.50 to $17; cash only.

A trip into downtown Puerto Vallarta takes about 30 minutes by taxi, costs about $15, and is available 24 hours a day. The ride is slightly longer by public bus, which costs $1.20 and operates from 7am to 11pm.

Hotel Club Marival This all-inclusive hotel sits almost by itself at the northernmost end of Nuevo Vallarta. Done in Mediterranean style, it's a refreshing alternative to the mega-resorts that dominate the area. This smaller property has a large variety of rooms, ranging from standard units with no balconies to large master suites with whirlpools. The master suites have minibars and hair dryers. The broad white-sand beach is one of the real assets here—it stretches over 500 yards. There is also an extensive activities program, including fun for children.

Paseo de los Cocoteros and Bulevar Nuevo Vallarta s/n, Nuevo Vallarta, Nay. 63735. ✆ **322/297-0100.** Fax 322/297-0160. www.clubmarival.com. 646 units. High season $246 double; low season $230 double. Upgrade to junior suite $50 per day, to master suite with whirlpool $300 per day. Rates are all-inclusive. Ask for seasonal specials. AE, MC, V. From the Puerto Vallarta airport, enter Nuevo Vallarta from the 2nd entrance; Club Marival is the 1st resort to your right on Paseo de los Cocoteros. **Amenities:** 6 restaurants; 8 bars; 3 pools and a whirlpool for adults; 2 pools and a water park for children; 4 lighted tennis courts; spa; business center; salon. *In room:* A/C, TV, safe-deposit boxes.

Paradise Village ★★ Truly a village, this self-contained resort on an exquisite stretch of beach offers a full array of services, from an on-site disco to a full-service European spa and health club. The collection of pyramid-shaped buildings, designed in Maya-influenced style, houses well-designed all-suite accommodations in studio, one-bedroom, and two-bedroom configurations. All have sitting areas and kitchenettes, making the resort ideal for families or groups of friends. The Maya theme extends to both oceanfront pools, with mythical creatures forming water slides and waterfalls. The exceptional spa is reason enough to book a vacation here, with treatments, hydrotherapy, massage (including massage on the beach), and fitness and yoga classes. Special spa packages are always available.

Paseo de los Cocoteros 001, Nuevo Vallarta, Nay. 63731. ✆ **800/995-5714** or 322/226-6770. Fax 322/226-6713. www.paradisemexico.com. 490 units. High season $235–$433 double, 2-bedroom suite $334, 3-bedroom suite $581; low season $151–$292 double, 2-bedroom suite $280, 3-bedroom suite $435. AE, DC, MC, V. **Amenities:** 2 restaurants; 2 beachfront snack bars; theme nights; nightclub; 2 oceanfront swimming pools; lap pool; championship golf club with 18-hole course; 4 tennis courts; European spa and complete fitness center; watersports center; Kid's Club; travel services desk; guests-only rental-car fleet; basketball court; beach volleyball; petting zoo; full marina. *In room:* A/C, TV, dataport, minibar, coffeemaker, hair dryer, iron, safe-deposit box.

BUCERIAS: A COASTAL VILLAGE

Only 18km (11 miles) north of the Puerto Vallarta airport, **Bucerías** (boo-seh-*ree*-ahs, meaning "place of the divers") ★ is a small coastal fishing village of 10,000 people in Nayarit state on Banderas Bay. It's caught on as an alternative to Puerto Vallarta for those who find the pace of life there too invasive. Bucerías offers a seemingly contradictory mix of accommodations—trailer-park spaces and exclusive villa rentals tend to dominate, although there's a small selection of hotels as well.

To reach the town center by car, take the exit road from the highway and drive down the shaded, divided street that leads to the beach. Turn left when you see a line of minivans and taxis (which serve Bucerías and Vallarta). Go straight ahead 1 block to the main plaza. The beach, with a lineup of restaurants, is half a block farther. You'll see cobblestone streets leading from the highway to the beach, and hints of villas and town homes behind high walls. Second-home owners and about 1,500 transplanted Americans have already sought out this peaceful getaway; tourists have discovered its relaxed pace as well.

If you take the bus to Bucerías, exit when you see the minivans and taxis to and from Bucerías line up on the street that leads to the beach. To use public transportation from Puerto Vallarta, take a minivan or bus marked BUCERIAS (they run from 6am–9pm). The last minivan stop is Bucerías's town square. There's also 24-hour taxi service.

EXPLORING BUCERÍAS Come here for a day trip from Puerto Vallarta just to enjoy the long, wide, uncrowded beach, along with the fresh seafood served at the beachfront restaurants or at one of the unusually great cafes listed below. If you are inclined to stay a few days, you can relax inexpensively and explore more of Bucerías. Sunday is street-market day, but it doesn't get going until around noon, in keeping with the town's casual pace.

The **Coral Reef Surf Shop,** Heroe de Nacozari 114-F (✆ **329/298-0261**), sells a great selection of surfboards and gear, and offers surfboard and boogie board rentals, surf lessons, and ATV and other adventure tours to surrounding areas.

WHERE TO STAY Unfortunately, I cannot recommend any of the hotels in Bucerías; they're run-down, and most people who choose to stay here opt for a private home rental. Check out the villa rental bulletin board at **www.sunworx.com**. **Las Palmas** in Bucerías (✆ **329/298-0060;** fax 329/298-1100) will book accommodations, including villas, houses, and condos. Call ahead, or ask for directions to the office when you get to Bucerías. It's open Monday through Friday from 9am to 2pm and 4 to 6pm, Saturday from 9am to 2pm.

WHERE TO DINE Besides those mentioned below, there are many seafood restaurants fronting the beach. The local specialty is *pescado sarandeado,* a whole fish smothered in tasty sauce and slow-grilled.

Cafe Magaña BARBECUED RIBS Famous for its ribs and chicken, Cafe Magaña gives you a choice of 10 original homemade sauces, including the "legendary" Salsa Magaña. Flavors have mythological names and contain creative ingredients like ginger, garlic, oranges, apples, cinnamon, and chiles. The sauces have been such a hit that British owner Jeff Rafferty also sells bottled versions and says to look for them commercially soon. This casual, colorful cafe and take-out restaurant also features TV sports and an occasional live band.

Lázaro Cárdenas 40. ✆ **329/298-1091.** www.sunworx.com/salsa. Main courses $7–$12. No credit cards. Fri–Wed 5–11pm.

Karen's Place ★ INTERNATIONAL/MEXICAN This casual oceanside restaurant offers classic cuisine, plus Mexican favorites in a style that appeals to North American appetites. Known for Sunday Champagne brunch (9am–3pm), it also is a great place to spend the day on the beach while enjoying a light lunch, and makes a romantic dining spot. The best-selling dinner is a Parmesan herb-crusted fish filet with a salad of baby greens. The casual, comfortable restaurant also features live music on Tuesday and Thursday. It recently added a terrace dining area with spectacular views, and a sushi menu.

On the beach at the Costa Dorada, Calle Lázaro Cárdenas. ✆ **329/298-1499.** Breakfast $4.50–$5.50; Sun brunch (9am–3pm) $12; main courses $5.50–$13. No credit cards. Tues–Sun 9am–10pm.

Le Fort ★★★ *Finds* FRENCH What an unforgettable dining experience! It's more than dinner—the evening consists of watching as Chef Gilles Le Fort prepares your gourmet meal and teaches you how to re-create it. The U-shaped bar in the intimate kitchen accommodates diners, who sip fine wines and nibble on paté while the master works. Chef Le Fort is the winner of numerous culinary awards, and his warm conviviality is the real secret ingredient of this unusual experience. Once dinner is served, the chef and his wife, Margarita, will join the table, entertaining with stories of their experiences in Mexico. The first group of six to book for the evening chooses the menu; the maximum class size is 16, so groups often blend together. Le Fort has probably the most extensive wine cellar in the bay—some 4,000 bottles. Hand-rolled Cuban cigars, homemade sausages, patés, and more delicacies are available in the adjoining shop.

Calle Lázaro Cárdenas 71, 1 block from the Hotel Royal DeCameron. ✆ **329/298-1532.** www.lefort.com.mx. 3-course dinner, wines, and recipes $40 per person. No credit cards. Daily 8–10:30pm; cooking classes available 10am-1:30pm. Reservations required.

Mark's ★★ *Finds* ITALIAN/STEAK/SEAFOOD It's worth a special trip to Bucerías just to eat at this covered-patio restaurant. The most popular American hangout in town, Mark's offers a great assortment of thin-crust pizzas and flatbread, baked in its brick oven and seasoned with fresh herbs grown in the garden. Everything has exquisite flavorings—some favorites include shrimp in angel-hair pasta, pesto-crusted fish filet, ahi tuna served rare, and filet mignon with bleu-cheese ravioli. Multitalented chef Jan Marie (Mark's charming wife and partner) runs an adjacent boutique, with the nicest selection of women's resort wear in town, plus ceramics from Pueblo, and her own line of dressings and chutneys. The bar televises all major sporting events.

Lázaro Cárdenas 56, ½ block from the beach. ✆ **329/298-0303.** Pasta $8.70–$19; main courses $13–$22. MC, V. High season daily noon–11pm; low season Wed–Mon 5:30–11pm. From the highway, turn left just after the bridge, where there's a small sign for Mark's. Double back left at next street (immediately after you turn left) and turn right at next corner. Mark's is on the right.

PUNTA MITA: EXCLUSIVE SECLUSION

At the northern tip of the bay is an arrowhead-shaped piece of land called **Punta Mita** ★★★. Considered a sacred place by the Indians, this is the point where Banderas Bay, the Pacific Ocean, and the Sea of Cortez come together. It's magnificent, with white-sand beaches and coral reefs just offshore. Stately rocks jut out along the shoreline, and the water is a dreamy translucent blue. Punta Mita is evolving into one of Mexico's most exclusive developments. The master plan calls for a total of five luxury hotels, several high-end residential communities, and three championship golf courses. It is the first luxury residential development in Mexico intended for the foreign market. Today, all you'll find is the elegant Four Seasons Resort and its Jack Nicklaus Signature golf course, but by next year, a new 68-unit all-suite Rosewood resort will open.

Four Seasons Resort Punta Mita ★★★ *Finds* The Four Seasons Resort has brought a new standard of luxury to Mexico's Pacific Coast. The boutique hotel, on 1,000 acres of land bordered on three sides by the ocean, artfully combines seclusion and pampering service with a welcoming sense of comfort. Accommodations are in three-story *casitas* surrounding the main building, which holds the lobby, cultural center, restaurants, and pool.

Every guest room offers breathtaking views of the ocean from a large terrace or balcony. Most suites also offer a private plunge pool, a separate sitting room, a bar, and a powder room. Room interiors are typical Four Seasons—plush and spacious, with a king or two double beds, plus a seating area and oversize bathroom with a deep soaking tub, separate glass-enclosed shower, and dual vanity sink.

More than the stylish luxury, this hotel boasts unerring service that is both warm and unobtrusive. It's a place to completely get away—at least 45 minutes from Puerto Vallarta's activities—but then, most guests feel so relaxed and at ease, it's hard to think of places beyond the resort. The full-service spa, tennis center, and private championship golf course seem to be options enough.

Bahía de Banderas, Nay. 63734. ✆ **800/332-3442** or 329/291-6000. Fax 329/291-6060. www.fourseasons.com. 140 units. High season $691–$796 double, $1,814–$2,048 suite; low season $457–$656 double, $1,170–$1,287 suite. AE, DC, MC, V. Free valet parking. **Amenities:** 2 restaurants; lobby bar; heated infinity pool surrounded by private cabañas; tennis center with 4 courts of various surfaces; full-service fitness center; European-style spa; watersports equipment including sea kayaks, windsurfers, surfboards, and sunfish sailboats; Kids for All Seasons children's activity program; daily activity agenda; tour desk; 24-hr. concierge service; 24-hr. room service; cultural center with lectures and activities; complimentary video library. *In room:* A/C, TV/VCR, dataport, minibar, coffeemaker, hair dryer, iron, safe-deposit box.

SAYULITA: MUCH MORE THAN A GREAT SURF SPOT

Sayulita is only 40km (25 miles) northwest of Puerto Vallarta, on Highway 200 to Tepic, yet it feels worlds away. It captures the simplicity and tranquillity of beach life that has long since left Vallarta. For years, Sayulita has been principally a surfers' destination—the main beach in town is known for its consistent break and long, rideable waves. Recently, visitors and locals who find Vallarta becoming too cosmopolitan have started to flock to Sayulita.

An easygoing attitude seems to permeate the air in this beach town. Yet despite its simplicity, a few niceties are popping up among the basic accommodations, inexpensive Mexican food stands, and hand-made, hippie-style baubles.

Sayulita is a popular stage for surfing tournaments and raves; on any given weekend you might encounter a flock of techno-beat-loving ravers or perfect-swell-seeking surfers—or a Huichol Indian family that has come down to sell their wares. This eclectic mix of the cool, the unusual, and the authentic Mexican makes Sayulita such a special place.

To get to Sayulita, you can rent a car, or take a taxi from the airport or downtown Vallarta. The rate is about $50 to get to the town plaza. You can also take a taxi back to Vallarta. Agustín (✆ **327/275-0234**) has the best local service, making trips to the Puerto Vallarta airport for $44 and to downtown for $50. The stand is on the main square, or you can call for pickup at your hotel. Another option is to contact the professional, bilingual tour guide service run by Mónico (✆ **311/258-4024** or 311/258-4151). The trip from the airport to Sayulita costs $55. Guides also lead tours to Vallarta, Punta Mita, and other surrounding areas, including a Huichol Indian community.

WHERE TO STAY Sayulita offers several private homes for rent. Your best option is to contact **Upi Viteri** (upiviteri@prodigy.net.mx), who has access to some of the nicest rental properties.

Aurinko Bungalows ★ Located half a block from the beach, these are classic beach accommodations—quiet, rustic, and casual. With tall palms all around, you may feel as if you're on a South Sea island. The rooms are impeccably clean, with cotton linens and fluffy white towels. Each room has a ceiling fan, open-air seating area, and fully equipped kitchenette.

Calle Marlín 7 Centro, Sayulita, Nay. 63732. ✆ **327/275-0010.** www.sayulita-vacations.com. 6 units. $57–$67 1-bedroom suite, $88–$103 2-bedroom suite. 20% low-season discount. MC, V. *In room:* Kitchenette, coffeemaker.

Villa Amor ★★★ *Finds* A personal favorite, Villa Amor is a collection of inviting, airy, perfectly appointed guest rooms—think of it as your private villa by the sea. Owner Rod Ingram and his design team have carefully crafted each space and individual suite into something truly special. The exterior walls curve invitingly and open up to breathtaking views all around. The one- and two-bedroom suites have fully equipped kitchenettes, plus open-air seating or dining areas (or both), and some have plunge pools. TVs are available on request. Construction of 24 new villas is under way; it makes the place a bit unsightly from the road, but once you're there, you'll find the peace and beauty you came for.

Camino Playa a Los Muertos s/n, Sayulita, Nay. 63732. ✆ **329/291-3010.** Fax 329/291-3018. www.villaamor.com. 21 units. $50–$75 double; $85–$125 1-bedroom villa; $180–$250 2-bedroom villa. No credit cards. **Amenities:** Restaurant; kayaks; bicycles; boogie boards; surfboards; concierge; tour desk; room service; massage. *In room:* Fan.

WHERE TO DINE If you are in Sayulita, chances are you heard about it because of **Don Pedro's,** the most popular restaurant in town (in the heart of the main beach), which serves gourmet Mexican food as well as seafood.

El Tigre MEXICAN El Tigre is the local favorite for real Mexican food at real Mexican prices. The place is basic—except for the two huge-screen TVs that broadcast every sporting event of any relevance, from the Super Bowl to Mexican soccer. Dishes include smoked fish, chiles rellenos, and fresh fish and seafood cooked in a variety of ways.

East side of the main square, next to the church. No phone. Main courses $4–$14. No credit cards. High season daily 5–11pm; low season hours vary. From Av. Revolución, go left on pedestrian street by Choco-Banana.

L'Ultima Spiaggia ITALIAN Paolo, an Italian chef, runs this tiny restaurant by the seashore. The menu is simple and classic, with salads, pizzas, and pastas. Paolo picks the freshest ingredients at the market every morning for his daily specials. They usually include fresh fish and seafood pasta dishes. Start with dorado carpaccio. The pizzas, baked in a wood-burning oven, have thin, crispy crusts. Don't miss the gnocchi, homemade fresh every day. The restaurant has a table out by the sea, which is perfect for romantic dinners. Breakfast features European-style offerings, including light omelets and fresh fruit. The espressos and cappuccinos are by far the best in Sayulita.

Camino Playa a los Muertos s/n, downstairs from Villa Amor. ✆ **322/100-6879.** Breakfast $3–$8; pizza $7–$11; main courses $8–$17. No credit cards. Tues–Sun 8:30–11am and 6–11pm.

Rollie's BREAKFAST Breakfast heaven! This family restaurant emanates a happy aura that puts its patrons in a good mood. The menu reflects the tone of the place, with options such as Rollie's Delight (blended fresh orange and banana), Adriana's Rainbow (an omelet with cheese, tomatoes, green peppers, and onions), and my personal favorite, Indian Pipe Pancakes. All dishes come with Rollie's famous potatoes (lightly seasoned pan-fried new potatoes). The place tends to be very crowded on weekends, so be prepared to sit and wait—the wait is worthwhile.

Av. Revolución, 2 blocks west of the main square. ✆ **329/291-3053.** Breakfast $3–$8. No credit cards. Daily Nov–Apr 8am–noon. Closed May–Oct.

SAN SEBASTIAN: AN AUTHENTIC MOUNTAIN HIDEAWAY

If you haven't heard about **San Sebastián** ★★★ yet, it probably won't be long—its remote location and historic appeal have made it the media's new darling destination in Mexico. Originally discovered in the late 1500s and settled in 1603, the town peaked as a center of mining operations, swelling to a population of over 30,000 by the mid-1800s. Today, with roughly 600 year-round residents, San Sebastián retains all the charm of a village locked in time, with an old church, a coffee plantation, and an underground tunnel system—and without a T-shirt shop.

GETTING THERE By car, it's a 2½-hour drive up the Sierra Madre from Puerto Vallarta on an improved road, but it can be difficult during the summer rainy season, when the road washes out frequently. **Vallarta Adventures** (✆ **866/256-2739** toll-free from the U.S., or 322/297-1212, ext. 3; www.vallarta-adventures.com) runs a daily plane service for half-day tours and can occasionally accommodate overnight visitors. The small private airport can arrange flights. **Aerotrón** (✆ **322/221-1921**) charges about $130 round-trip, **Taxis Aéreos de Nayarit** (✆ **322/221-1990**) about $88 round-trip, depending on the type of plane and number of passengers. For more information on air tours and horseback-riding excursions, see the "Organized Tours" section, earlier in this chapter.

WHERE TO STAY There are two places to stay in San Sebastián. The first is the very basic **El Pabellón de San Sebastián,** which faces the town square. Its nine simply furnished rooms surround a central patio. Don't expect extras here; rates run $40 per double. The town's central phone lines handle reservations—you call (© **322/297-0200**) and leave a message or send a fax, and hopefully the hotel will receive it. More secure is e-mail: ssb@pvnet.com.mx. Except on holidays, there is generally room at this inn. No credit cards.

A more enjoyable option is the stately **Hacienda Jalisco,** built in 1850 and once the center of mining operations in this mining town. The beautifully landscaped, rambling old hacienda is near the airstrip a 15-minute walk from town. Proprietor Bud Acord has welcomed John Huston, Liz Taylor, Richard Burton, Peter O'Toole, and a cast of local characters over the years.

The 10 extra-clean rooms have wood floors, rustic furnishings and antiques, and working fireplaces; some are decorated with pre-Columbian reproductions. The ample bathrooms are beautifully tiled and have skylights. Hammocks grace the upstairs terrace, while a sort-of museum on the lower level attests to the celebrity guests and importance the hacienda has enjoyed over the years. Because of its remote location, all meals are included. Rates are $120 per couple per night, including meals; alcoholic beverages are extra. Reserve through e-mail (ssb@pvnet.com.mx), or through the town telephone number listed above. Group rates and discounts for longer stays are available. No credit cards. Guided horseback, walking, or mine tours can be arranged through the Hacienda.

4

Costa Alegre: From Puerto Vallarta to Barra de Navidad

Costa Alegre is one of Mexico's most spectacular coastal areas, a 232km (145-mile) stretch that connects tropical forests with a series of dramatic cliff-lined coves. Tiny outpost towns line the coast, while dirt roads trail down to a succession of magical coves with pristine beaches, most of them steeped in privileged exclusivity. Considered one of Mexico's greatest undiscovered treasures, this area is becoming a favored hideaway for publicity-fatigued celebrities and those in search of natural seclusion.

The area is referred to as **Costa Alegre (Happy Coast)**—the marketer's term—and **Costa Careyes (Turtle Coast),** after the many sea turtles that nest here. It is home to an eclectic array of the most captivating and exclusive places to stay in Mexico, with a selective roster of activities that includes championship golf and polo. Along the line, however, you will encounter the funky beach towns that were the original lure for travelers who discovered the area.

Stops along Highway 200, as it meanders between Puerto Vallarta to the north and Manzanillo to the south, can be an enjoyable day trip, but travelers usually make the drive en route to a destination along the coast.

EXPLORING COSTA ALEGRE Costa Alegre is more an ultimate destination than a place to rent a car and take a drive. Most of the beaches are tucked into coves accessible by dirt roads that can extend for miles inland. If you do drive along this coast, Highway 200 is safe, but it's not lit and it curves through the mountains, so travel only during the day. A few buses travel this route, but they stop only at the towns that line the highway; many of them are several kilometers inland from the resorts along the coast.

1 Along Costa Alegre (from North to South)

CRUZ DE LORETO'S LUXURY ECO-RETREAT

Hotelito Desconocido ★★★ *Moments* The fact that the Hotelito Desconocido ("little unknown hotel") is ecologically minded is a bonus, but it's not the principal appeal. A cross between *Out of Africa* and *Blue Lagoon,* it is among my favorite places in Mexico. Think camping out with luxury linens, romantic candles everywhere, and a symphony performed by cicadas, birds, and frogs.

The rustic, open-air rooms, called *palafitos,* are in cottages perched on stilts over a lagoon. A grouping of suites are on the ample sand bar that separates the tranquil estuary from the Pacific Ocean. However, these are the least desirable units, and are often damp from the ocean air. Also here is a saltwater pool—the ocean is too aggressive for even seasoned swimmers.

The rooms have cotton sheets, oversize bath towels, and gauzy mosquito nets. Ceiling fans cool the air, and water is solar-heated. It's easy to disconnect here. In fact, it's mandatory: There's no electricity, no phones, no neighboring restaurants, nightclubs, or shopping—only delicious tranquillity. What the service lacks in polish it makes up for in enthusiasm. Rates do not include meals or drinks; a meal plan is mandatory, because there are no other options nearby, which makes the whole package somewhat pricey—but it's a unique experience.

Playón de Mismaloya s/n, Cruz de Loreto, Tomatlán, Jal. 48360. ✆ **800/851-1143** in the U.S. and Canada. Reservations ✆ **01-800/851-1143** in Mexico, 322/222-2526, or 322/222-2546; fax 322/223-0293. At the hotel ✆ 322/281-4010. www.hotelito.com. 30 units. High season *palafito* double $590, *palafito* suite $680; low season *palafito* double $470, *palafito* suite $590. Mandatory daily meal plan $75 per person. Children stay free in parent's room and pay $75 per day for meals; accepted with prior authorization only. AE, MC, V. Take Highway 200 south for 1 hr., turn off at exit for Cruz de Loreto, and continue on clearly marked route on unpaved road for about 25 min. **Amenities:** 2 restaurant/bars; primitive-luxury spa with massage and spa treatments, sauna, and whirlpool; birding tours; windsurfing; kayaking; mountain biking; hiking; horseback riding; billiards; beach volleyball. All activities are subject to an extra charge.

LAS ALAMANDAS: AN EXCLUSIVE LUXURY RESORT

Las Alamandas ★★★ Almost equidistant between Manzanillo (1½ hr.) and Puerto Vallarta (1¾ hr.) lies Mexico's original ultra-exclusive resort. A dirt road winds for about a mile through a tiny village to the guardhouse of Las Alamandas, on 70 acres set against low hills that are part of a 1,500-acre estate. The resort, owned by Isabel Goldsmith, daughter of British financier Sir James Goldsmith, consists of villas and *palapas* spread among four beaches, gardens, lakes, lagoons,

Costa Alegre & Central Pacific Coast

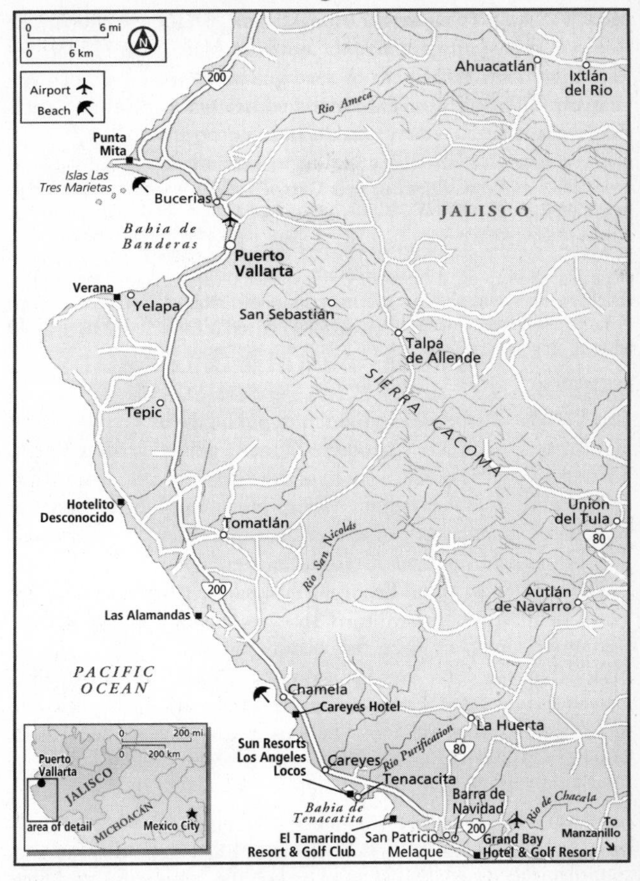

and a bird sanctuary. It's designed for privacy—to the point that guests rarely catch a glimpse of one another. The resort has air-conditioning, telephones, and a new beachfront massage *palapa,* yet manages to keep the experience as natural as possible. The resort accommodates only 22 guests.

The six spacious villas have tiled verandas with ocean views. They have several bedrooms (each with its own bathroom) and can be rented separately; guests who rent whole villas have preference for reservations. Some villas are on the beach, others across a cobblestone plaza. TVs with VCRs are available on request, but there's no outside reception. Van transportation to and from Manzanillo ($293 one-way) and Puerto Vallarta ($293 one-way) can be arranged when you reserve your room. Air transport from Puerto Vallarta is also available; call for details.

Hwy. 200, Manzanillo–Puerto Vallarta, Jal. 48800. (Mailing address: Domicilio Conocido Costa Alegre QUEMARO Jalisco, Apdo. Postal 201, San Patricio Melaque, Jal. CP 48980.) ✆ **888/882-9616** in the U.S. and Canada, or 322/285-5500. Fax 322/285-5027. www.alamandas.com. 14 units. High season $567–$1,998 unit, $2,039–$4,235 villa; low season $495–$1,312 unit, $1,496–$2,978 villa. Meal plans available. AE, MC, V. **Amenities:** Restaurant; 60-ft. pool; lighted tennis court; weight room; mountain bikes; concierge; tour desk; room service; horses; hiking trails; boogie boards; birding boat tours; book and video library; landing strip (make advance arrangements). *In room:* A/C, dataport, minibar.

CAREYES

The Careyes Hotel ★★ The Careyes is a gem of a resort nestled on a small, pristine cove between dramatic cliffs that are home to the exclusive villas of Careyes. This area has practically defined the architectural style that defines Mexico beach chic—bold washes of vibrant colors, open spaces, and gardens that showcase the tropical flowers and palms indigenous to the area.

The hotel, a Starwood Luxury Collection property, recently completed significant upgrades in services and facilities. The pampering accommodations all face the ocean and are stylishly simple. Although guests come here for isolation, you can enjoy many services, including a full European spa and polo. It's both rustic and sophisticated, with the room facades awash in scrubbed pastels forming a U around the center lawn and freeform pool. Rooms have a dramatic feel, from the colony shutters and white-tile floors to the handsome loomed bedspreads and colorful pillows. Some units have balconies; all have ocean views. Twenty rooms have private pools, and villas are available for rent. The hotel is popular for weddings and small corporate retreats.

The hotel offers a number of special-interest activities for guests. Named after the hawksbill turtle (*carey* in Spanish), the hotel sponsors a Save the Turtle program in which guests can participate between July and December.

The hotel is roughly 160km (100 miles) south of Puerto Vallarta. It's about a 2-hour drive north of Manzanillo on Highway 200, and about a 1-hour drive from the Manzanillo airport. Taxis from the Manzanillo airport charge around $100 one-way. There are car-rental counters at the Manzanillo and Puerto Vallarta airports. A car would be useful only for exploring the coast—Barra de Navidad and other resorts, for example—and the hotel can make touring arrangements.

Km 53.5 Hwy. 200, Careyes, Jal. CP 48970. (Mailing address: Apdo. Postal 24, Cihuatlán, Jal. CP 48970.) ✆ **800/525-4800** in the U.S. and Canada, or 315/351-0000 and 315/351-0606. Fax 315/351-0100. www.grupoplan.com. 48 units. High season $265 double, $415–$485 suite; low season $225 double, $350–$450 suite. AE, MC, V. **Amenities:** Restaurant and bar; deli; large oceanfront pool; privileges at exclusive El Tamarindo resort (40km/25 miles south), with 18-hole mountaintop golf course; 2 tennis courts; fully equipped, state-of-the-art spa with massage, hot and cold plunge pools, steam, sauna, weight equipment; kayaks; windsurf boards; Aquafins; "Just for Kids" children's activity program (during Christmas and Easter vacation); room service; laundry; paddle court; book and video library. *In room:* A/C, TV, minibar, small fridge, hair dryer, robes.

TENACATITA BAY

Located 60 minutes (53km/33 miles) north of the Manzanillo airport, this jewel of a bay is accessible by an 8km (5-mile) dirt road that passes through a small village set among banana plants and coconut palms. Sandy, serene beaches dot coves around the bay (frolicking dolphins are a common sight), and exotic birds fill a coastal lagoon. Swimming and snorkeling are good, and the bay is a popular stop for luxury yachts. Just south of the entrance to Tenacatita is a sign for the all-inclusive **Sun Resorts Los Angeles Locos,** as well as the exclusive **El Tamarindo** resort and golf club. There is no commercial or shopping area, and dining options outside hotels are limited to a restaurant or two that may emerge during the winter months (high season). Relax—that's what you're here for.

El Tamarindo ★★★ *Finds* A personal favorite, El Tamarindo is a gem that combines stunning jungle surroundings with exquisite facilities, gracious service, and absolute tranquillity. The area's most luxurious resort, part of Starwood Hotels' Luxury Collection, it comes complete with its own golf course.

The bungalows exude an air of exclusivity—each thatched-roof villa has a splash pool and whirlpool, plus lounging and dining areas that complement the stunning bedrooms. A personal "butler" is on call to meet your every need. The bedrooms—with dark hardwood floors and furnishings—can be closed off for air-conditioned comfort, but the remaining areas are open to the sea breezes and heady tropical air.

The categories of bungalows denote their location—Beachfront (on a calm cove, but not as private as the others), Palm Tree, Garden, and Forest. The non-beachfront bungalows all have similar decor and amenities but feature more closed-in areas. Anyone squeamish about creepy-crawlies may be uncomfortable in the beginning, but listening to the life around you is a spectacular sensation. On 2,000 acres of tropical rainforest bordering the Pacific Ocean, you'll feel as if you've found your own personal bit of heaven.

El Tamarindo has a championship 18-hole golf course; the approach to the first hole is through a forest of palms so tall they block the sun. The course has seven oceanside holes and dramatic views.

The resort restaurant is the only dining option, but you won't be disappointed. Noted chef Patricia Quintana created the divine menu, which changes daily, based on her book, *Cuisine of the Water Gods.*

Km 7.5 Carretera Melaque–Puerto Vallarta, Cihuatlan, Jal. CP 48970. ✆ **315/351-5032.** Fax 315/351-5070. www.luxurycollection.com. 29 bungalows. High season Beachfront bungalow $669, 2-bedroom Palm Tree bungalow $550, Forest bungalow $437; low season Beachfront bungalow $617, 2-bedroom Palm Tree bungalow $525, Forest bungalow $385. AE, MC, V. From Puerto Vallarta (3 hr.) or the Manzanillo airport (40 min.), take Highway 200, then turn west at the clearly marked exit for El Tamarindo. Follow signs for about 25 min. **Amenities:** Restaurant and bar; large beachfront pool with whirlpool; 2 clay tennis courts; estuary bird-watching tours; windsurfing; kayaking; Aquafin sailboats; horseback riding; mountain biking; hiking; in-suite dining; spa services; yoga classes; *temazcal* (pre-Hispanic sweat lodge). *In room:* A/C, dataport, hair dryer, safe, bathrobes.

Sun Resorts Los Angeles Locos ✪ On a 3-mile stretch of sandy beach, Los Angeles Locos offers an abundance of activities and entertainment. An extensive activities program and an ample selection of dining and entertainment options offer guests excellent value. It's a good choice for families and groups of friends. All rooms have ocean views, with either balconies or terraces. The three-story hotel is basic in decor and amenities, but comfortable. The attraction here is the wide array of on-site activities, plus a "Jungle River" cruise excursion (included in the room rate). **La Lagarta Disco** is a little on the dark and smoky side but can really rock, depending on the crowd—it's basically the only option on the bay.

Km 20 Carretera Federal 200, Tenacatita 48989, Municipio de la Huerta, Jal. ✆ **315/351-5020** or 315/351-5100. Fax 315/351-5050. www.sunresorts.com. 204 units. High season $140 double; low season $95 double; children 5–12 $30 year-round. Rates are all-inclusive. Ask about family specials. AE, MC, V. **Amenities:** 2 restaurants and snack bar (with buffets and a la carte dining); 3 bars; disco; nightly shows and entertainment; adult pool; kids' pool adjacent to the beach; 3 tennis courts; exercise room; windsurfing; kayaks; Hobie cats; Kid's Club; massage; babysitting; laundry; pool tables; horseback riding; basketball court. *In room:* A/C, TV.

2 Barra de Navidad & Melaque

This pair of rustic beach villages (only 5km/3 miles apart) has been attracting travelers for decades. Only 30 minutes north of Manzanillo's airport, and 104km (65 miles) north of downtown, Barra has a few brick or cobblestone streets, good budget hotels and restaurants, and funky beach charm. All of this lies incongruously next to the super-luxurious Grand Bay Hotel, which sits on a bluff across the inlet from Barra. Melaque offers budget hotels on and off the beach, fewer restaurants, and little in the way of charm, although the beach is as wide as and more beautiful than Barra's. Both villages appeal to those looking for a quaint, quiet, inexpensive retreat rather than a modern, sophisticated destination.

In the 17th century, Barra de Navidad was a harbor for the Spanish fleet; from here, galleons first set off in 1564 to find China. Located on a crescent-shaped bay with curious rock outcroppings, Barra de Navidad and neighboring Melaque are connected by a continuous beach on the same wide bay. It's safe to say that the only time Barra and Melaque hotels are full is during Easter and Christmas weeks. **Barra de Navidad** has more charm, more tree-shaded streets, better restaurants, more stores, and more conviviality between locals and tourists. Barra is very laid-back; faithful returnees adore its lack of flash. Other than the Grand Bay Hotel, on the cliff across the waterway in what is called Isla Navidad (although it's not on an island), nothing is new or modern. But there's a bright edge to Barra, with more good restaurants and limited—but existent—nightlife.

Melaque, on the other hand, is larger, rather sun-baked, treeless, and lacking in attractions. It does, however, have plenty of cheap hotels available for longer stays, and a few restaurants. Although the beach between the two is continuous, Melaque's beach, with deep sand, is more beautiful than Barra's.

Isla Navidad Resort has a manicured 27-hole golf course and the super-luxurious Grand Bay Hotel, but the area's pace hasn't quickened as fast as expected. The golf is challenging and delightfully uncrowded, with another exceptional course at nearby El Tamarindo. It's a serious golfer's dream.

ESSENTIALS

GETTING THERE Buses from Manzanillo frequently run up the coast along Highway 200 on their way to Puerto Vallarta and

Guadalajara. The fare is about $3.50. Most stop in the central villages of Barra de Navidad and Melaque. From the Manzanillo airport, it's only around 30 minutes to Barra, and taxis are available. The fare from Manzanillo to Barra is around $40; from Barra to Manzanillo, $30. From Manzanillo, the highway twists through some of the Pacific Coast's most beautiful mountains. Puerto Vallarta is a 3-hour (by car) to 5-hour (by bus) ride north on Highway 200 from Barra.

VISITOR INFORMATION The **tourism office** for both villages is at Jalisco 67 (between Veracruz and Mazatlán), Barra (✆/fax **315/355-5100**). The office is open Monday through Friday from 9am to 5pm. The **Travel Agency Isla Navidad Tours,** Veracruz 204-A, Barra de Navidad (✆ **315/355-5666** or 315/355-5667), can handle arrangements for plane tickets and sells bus tickets from Manzanillo to Puerto Vallarta and Guadalajara. It's open Monday through Saturday from 10am to 8pm.

ORIENTATION In Barra, hotels and restaurants line the main beachfront street, **Legazpi.** From the bus station, beachfront hotels are 2 blocks straight ahead, across the central plaza. Two blocks behind the bus station and to the right is the lagoon side. More hotels and restaurants are on its main street, **Morelos/Veracruz.** Few streets are marked, but 10 minutes of wandering will acquaint you with the village's entire layout. There's a taxi stand at the intersection of Legazpi and Sinaloa streets. Legazpi, Jalisco, Sinaloa, and Veracruz streets border Barra's **central plaza.**

ACTIVITIES ON & OFF THE BEACH

Swimming and enjoying the attractive beach and views of the bay take up most tourists' time. You can hire a small boat for a coastal ride or fishing in two ways. Go toward the *malecón* on Calle Veracruz until you reach the tiny boatmen's cooperative, with fixed prices posted on the wall, or walk two buildings farther to the water taxi ramp. The water taxi is the best option for going to Colimilla (5 min., $2) or across the inlet (3 min., $1) to the Grand Bay Hotel. Water taxis make the rounds regularly, so if you're at Colimilla, wait, and one will be along shortly. At the cooperative, a 30-minute **lagoon tour** costs $20, and a **sea tour** costs $25. **Sportfishing** is $80 for up to four people for half a day in a small *panga* (open fiberglass boat, like the ones used for water taxis).

To arrange unusual **area tours, real estate rentals,** and **sports-equipment rental,** contact **The Crazy Cactus,** Jalisco 8, half a

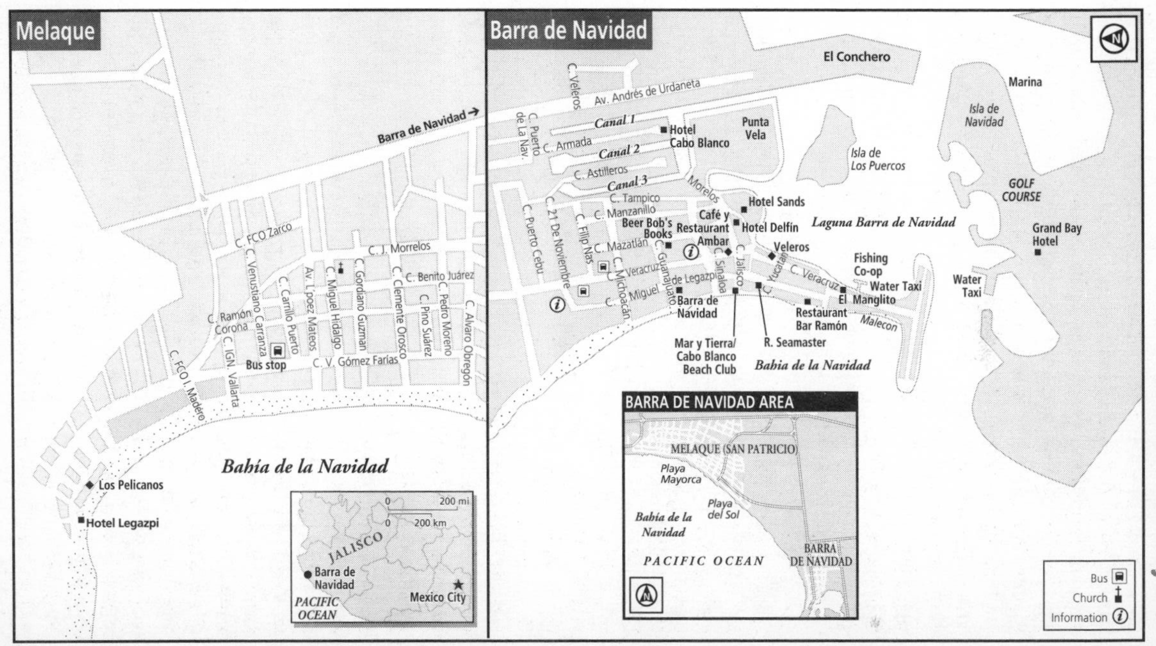
Melaque
Barra de Navidad
El Conchero
Marina
Isla de Navidad
GOLF COURSE
Grand Bay Hotel
Isla de Los Puercos
Laguna Barra de Navidad
Water Taxi
Fishing Co-op
Water Taxi
El Manglito
Malecon
Restaurant Bar Ramón
R. Seamaster
Bahía de la Navidad
Mar y Tierra/ Cabo Blanco Beach Club
Punta Vela
Hotel Cabo Blanco
Hotel Sands
Hotel Delfín
Veleros
Café y Restaurant Ambar
Beer Bob's Books
Barra de Navidad
C. Veleros
Av. Andrés de Urdaneta
Canal 1
Canal 2
Canal 3
C. Puerto de La Nav.
C. Armada
C. Astilleros
C. Tampico
C. Manzanillo
C. Mazatlán
C. Veracruz
C. Yucatán
C. Jalisco
C. Sinaloa
Morelos
de Legazpi
C. Guanajuato
C. Miguel
C. Michoacán
C. Filip Nas
C. 21 De Noviembre
C. Puerto Cebu
Barra de Navidad →
C. FCO Zarco
C. J. Morrelos
C. Benito Juárez
C. Venustiano Carranza
C. Carrillo Puerto
Av. L'poez Mateos
C. Miguel Hidalgo
C. Gordiano Guzman
C. Clemente Orosco
C. Pino Suárez
C. Pedro Moreno
C. Alvaro Obregón
C. Ramón Corona
C. IGN. Vallarta
Bus stop
C. V. Gómez Farías
C. FCO I. Madéro
Bahía de la Navidad
Los Pelicanos
Hotel Legazpi
0 200 mi
0 200 km
JALISCO
Barra de Navidad
PACIFIC OCEAN
Mexico City
BARRA DE NAVIDAD AREA
MELAQUE (SAN PATRICIO)
Playa Mayorca
Playa del Sol
Bahía de la Navidad
PACIFIC OCEAN
BARRA DE NAVIDAD
Bus
Church
Information

block inland from the town church on Legazpi (✆/fax **315/ 355-6099;** crazycactusmx@yahoo.com). Trayce Ross, who also rents cars and handles real estate sales, operates it. Her daughter, who does custom building, runs the adjoining gift shop. The store may be closed May through October.

The Grand Bay Hotel's beautiful and challenging 27-hole, 7,053-yard, par-72 **golf course** is open to the public. Hotel guests pay greens fees of $166 for 18 holes, $192 for 27 holes; nonguests pay $216 and $240, respectively. Prices include a motorized cart. Caddies are available, as are rental clubs. The Crazy Cactus (see above) can arrange golf at El Tamarindo's gorgeous mountaintop course, about 32km (20 miles) north of Barra.

Beer Bob's Books, Av. Mazatlán 61, between Sinaloa and Guanajuato, is a book-lover's institution in Barra and a sort of community service that the rather grouchy Bob does for fun. His policy of "leave a book if you take one" allows vacationers to select from hundreds of neatly shelved paperbacks, as long as they leave a book in exchange. It's open Monday through Friday from 1 to 4pm and occasionally in the evenings. "Beer Bob" got his name because in earlier days, when beer was cheap, he kept a cooler stocked, and book browsers could sip and read. (When beer prices went up, Bob put the cooler away.)

WHERE TO STAY

Low season in Barra is any time except Christmas and Easter weeks. Except for those 2 weeks, it doesn't hurt to ask for a discount at the inexpensive hotels.

VERY EXPENSIVE

Grand Bay Hotel ★ *Overrated* Across the yacht channel from Barra de Navidad, this luxurious hotel opened in 1997 on 1,200 acres next to its 27-hole golf course. It overlooks the village, bay, Pacific Ocean, and Navidad lagoon. The hotel's beach is narrow and on the lagoon. A better beach is opposite the hotel on the bay in Barra de Navidad. The spacious rooms are sumptuously outfitted with marble floors, large bathrooms, and hand-carved wood furnishings. Prices vary according to view and size of room, but even the modest rooms are large; all have cable TV. Each comes with a king-size or two double beds, a glass-top desk, ceiling fans plus air-conditioning, and a balcony. All suites have a steam sauna and telephones in the bathroom as well as a sound system. The hotel is a short water-taxi ride across the inlet from Barra de Navidad; it is also on a paved road from Highway 200. Although the hotel bills itself as being on the Island of Navidad at Port Navidad, the port is the marina, and the hotel is on a peninsula, not an island.

Isla Navidad, Col. 45110. ✆ **310/536-9278** in the U.S., 315/355-5050, or 315/331-0500. Fax 315/355-6070. www.grandbay.com. 199 units. High season $381–$460 double, $550–$680 suite; low season $275–$321 double, $468–$614 suite. Ask about tennis, golf, fishing, and honeymoon packages. Rates include round-trip transportation to and from Manzanillo airport. AE, DC, DISC, MC, V. **Amenities:** 2 restaurants; 2 bars; golf club with food and bar service; swimming pool with water slides and swim-up bar; 27-hole, par-72 golf course designed by Robert Von Hagge; golf club with pro shop and driving range; 3 lighted grass tennis courts with stadium seating; small but sufficient workout room; Kid's Club with activity program; business center; salon; 24-hr. concierge; room service; babysitting; laundry and dry cleaning; 150-slip marina with private yacht club. Fishing, boat tours, and other excursions can be arranged. *In room:* A/C, TV, dataport, minibar, hair dryer, iron, security box, robes.

MODERATE

Hotel Cabo Blanco ★★ Located on the point where you cross over to Isla Navidad, the Cabo Blanco is an outstanding option for family vacations or longer-term stays. Rooms are pleasantly rustic, with tile floors, large tile tubs, separate dressing areas, and stucco walls. The hotel overlooks the bay, but it's a 5-minute walk to the beach. The beamed-ceiling lobby is in its own building; rooms are in hacienda-style buildings surrounded by gardens. The atmosphere is generally tranquil, except during weekends and Mexican holidays, when this hotel tends to fill up. Because the Cabo Blanco doesn't front the beach, it has an affiliated beach club and restaurant, Mar y Tierra (see "Where to Dine," below).

Armada y Bahía de la Navidad s/n, 48987 Barra de Navidad, Jal. ✆ **315/355-5103** or 315/355-5136. Fax 315/355-6494. 101 units. $90 double; $256 suite with kitchenette. Prices are all-inclusive. Room-only option $39 double, $125 suite. AE, MC, V. **Amenities:** 2 restaurants; 4 pools (2 adults only); 2 tennis courts; concierge; tour desk; car-rental desk; laundry service. *In room:* A/C, TV.

INEXPENSIVE

Hotel Barra de Navidad ★ At the northern end of Legazpi, this popular, comfortable beachfront hotel is by far the nicest in the town. It has friendly management, and some rooms with balconies overlooking the beach and bay. Other, less expensive rooms afford only a street view. Only the oceanview rooms have air-conditioning. A nice swimming pool is on the street level to the right of the lobby.

Legazpi 250, 48987 Barra de Navidad, Jal. ✆ **315/355-5122.** Fax 315/355-5303. 59 units. $50–$72 double. MC, V. **Amenities:** Pool.

Hotel Delfín One of Barra's better-maintained hotels, the four-story (no elevator) Delfín is on the landward side of the lagoon. It offers pleasant, basic, well-maintained, well-lit rooms. Each has red-tile floors and one double, two double, or two single beds. The tiny courtyard, with a small pool and lounge chairs, sits in the shade of an enormous rubber tree. From the fourth floor, there's a view of the lagoon. A breakfast buffet is served from 8:30 to 10:30am (see "Where to Dine," below).

Morelos 23, 48987 Barra de Navidad, Jal. ✆ **315/355-5068**. Fax 315/355-6020. 24 units. $36–$45 double; ask about low-season discounts. MC, V. Free parking. **Amenities:** Restaurant; pool.

Hotel Sands The colonial-style Sands, across from the Hotel Delfín (see above) on the lagoon side at Jalisco, offers small but homey rooms with red-tile floors and windows with both screens and glass. The remodeled bathrooms have new tiles and fixtures. Lower rooms look onto a public walkway and wide courtyard filled with greenery and singing birds; upstairs rooms are brighter. Twelve rooms (suites or bungalows) have air-conditioning and kitchenette facilities. The hotel is known for its warm hospitality and high-season happy hour (2–6pm) at the pool terrace bar beside the lagoon. On weekends from 9pm to 4am, an adjacent patio "disco" plays recorded music for dancing. Breakfast is served from 7:30am to noon. Fishing trips can be arranged, and tours to nearby beaches are available.

Morelos 24, 48987 Barra de Navidad, Jal. ✆/fax **315/355-5018** or ✆ 315/616-2859. 42 units. High season $61 double; low season $42 double. Rates include breakfast. Room-only rates $10 less. Discounts for stays of 1 week or more. MC, V (6% surcharge). **Amenities:** Restaurant and bar; pool with whirlpool overlooking lagoon beach; children's play area; tour desk.

WHERE TO DINE

El Manglito ★ SEAFOOD/INTERNATIONAL On the placid lagoon, with a view of the palatial Grand Bay Hotel, El Manglito serves home-style Mexican food to a growing number of repeat diners. The whole fried fish accompanied by drawn garlic butter, boiled vegetables, rice, and french fries, is a crowd-pleaser. Other enticements include boiled shrimp, chicken in orange sauce, and shrimp salad.

Veracruz, near the boatmen's cooperative. No phone. Main courses $5–$10. No credit cards. Daily 9am–11pm.

Hotel Delfín INTERNATIONAL The second-story terrace of this small hotel is a pleasant place to begin the day. The self-serve buffet offers an assortment of fresh fruit, juice, granola, yogurt, milk, pastries, and unlimited coffee. The price includes made-to-order eggs and delicious banana pancakes—for which the restaurant is known.

Morelos 23. ✆ **315/355-5068.** Breakfast buffet $4. No credit cards. Daily 8:30am–noon.

Mar y Tierra INTERNATIONAL Hotel Cabo Blanco's beach club is also a popular restaurant and bar, and a great place to spend a day at the beach. On the beach, there are shade *palapas* and beach chairs, and a game of volleyball seems constantly in progress. The colorful restaurant is decorated with murals of mermaids. Perfectly seasoned shrimp fajitas come in plentiful portions.

Legazpi s/n (at Jalisco). ✆ **315/355-5028.** Main courses $10–$17. AE, MC, V. Wed–Sun 2–10pm (opens at 10am Wed–Mon for hotel guests).

Restaurant Bar Ambar CREPES/SPANISH/FRENCH This cozy, thatched-roof, upstairs restaurant is open to the breezes. The crepes are named after towns in France; the delicious *crêpe Paris,* for example, is filled with chicken, potatoes, spinach, and green sauce. Sweet dessert crepes are also available. International main dishes include imported (from the U.S.) rib-eye steak in Dijon mustard sauce, mixed brochettes, quiche, and Caesar salad. Ambar serves Spanish-style tapas from noon until 6pm, and adds French specialties during dinner.

Av. Veracruz 101-A (at Jalisco). No phone. Crepes $5–$13; main courses $5–$15. No credit cards. Daily noon–midnight (happy hour 1pm–midnight). Closed July–Oct.

Restaurant Bar Ramón ★ *Value* SEAFOOD/MEXICAN It seems that everybody eats at Ramón's, where the chips and fresh salsa arrive unbidden, and service is prompt and friendly. The food is especially good—however, most options are fried. Try fresh fried shrimp with French fries, or any daily special that features vegetable soup or chicken-fried steak. Great value!

Legazpi 260. ✆ **315/355-6435.** Main courses $6–$10. MC, V. Daily 7am–11pm.

Seamaster SEAFOOD/INTERNATIONAL This cheery, colorful restaurant on the beach facing the ocean is a great place for sunsets and margaritas, or a meal anytime. Specialties include steamed shrimp (peeled or unpeeled), fried calamari, barbecue chicken, ribs, steak, chicken wings, hamburgers, and other sandwiches. During high season, it turns into a popular disco at night.

Legazpi (at Yucatán). No phone. Main courses $5–$15. No credit cards. Daily noon–midnight.

BARRA DE NAVIDAD AFTER DARK

When dusk arrives, visitors and locals alike find a cool spot to sit outside, sip cocktails, and chat. Many outdoor restaurants and stores in Barra accommodate this relaxing way to end the day, adding extra tables and chairs for drop-ins.

During high season, the **Hotel Sands** poolside and lagoon-side bar has happy hour from 2 to 6pm. The colorful **Sunset Bar and Restaurant,** facing the bay at the corner of Legazpi and Jalisco, is a favorite for sunset watching, and then a game of oceanside pool or dancing to live or taped music. It's most popular with travelers ages 20 to 30. In the same vein, **Chips Restaurant,** on the second floor facing the ocean at the corner of Yucatán and Legazpi near the southern end of the *malecón,* has an excellent sunset vista. Live music follows the last rays of light, and patrons stay for hours. **Piper's Lover Bar & Restaurant,** on Legazpi, is done in the style of the Carlos Anderson's chain—but it's not one of them. Still, it is lively, with pool tables and occasional live music.

At the **Disco El Galeón,** in the Hotel Sands on Calle Morelos, cushioned benches and cement tables encircle the round dance floor. It's all open-air, and about as stylish as you'll find in Barra. It serves drinks only. Admission is $6, and it's open Friday and Saturday from 9pm to 4am.

A VISIT TO MELAQUE (SAN PATRICIO)

For a change of scenery, you may want to wander over to Melaque (also known as San Patricio), 5km (3 miles) from Barra on the same bay. You can walk on the beach from Barra or take one of the frequent local buses from the bus station near the main square in Barra. The bus is marked MELAQUE. To return to Barra, take the bus marked CIHUATLAN.

Melaque's pace is even more laid-back than Barra's, and though it's a larger village, it seems smaller. It has fewer restaurants and less to do. Although there are more hotels, or "bungalows," as they are usually called, few manage the charm of those in Barra. If Barra hotels are full on a holiday weekend, Melaque would be a second choice. The paved road ends where the town begins. A few yachts bob in the harbor, and the palm-lined beach is gorgeous.

If you come by bus from Barra, you can exit anywhere in town or stay on until the last stop, which is the bus station in the middle of town a block from the beach. Restaurants and hotels line the beach. Coming into town from the main road, you'll be on the town's main street, **Avenida López Matéos.** You'll pass the main square on the way to the waterfront, where there's a trailer park. The street going left (southeast) along the bay is **Avenida Gómez Farías;** the one going right (northwest) is **Avenida Miguel Ochoa López.**

WHERE TO STAY & DINE At the north end of Melaque beach is **Los Pelicanos** (✆ **315/355-5415**). It serves the usual seafood specialties; the tender fried squid is delectable. In addition, you can find burritos, nachos, and hamburgers. Many Barra guests come here to stake a place on the beach and use the restaurant as headquarters for sipping and nipping. Open daily from 9am to 10pm, it's a peaceful place to watch the pelicans bobbing. The restaurant is at the far end of the bay before the **Hotel Legazpi** (✆ **315/355-5397**), a pleasant place to stay. It has 20 rooms, charges $32 for a double, and doesn't accept credit cards.

In addition to the Los Pelicanos, there are many rustic ***palapa* restaurants** on the beach and farther along the bay at the end of the beach.

5

Manzanillo

Manzanillo has long been known as a resort town with wide, curving beaches, legendary sportfishing, and a highly praised diversity of dive sites. Golf is also an attraction here, with two of Mexico's most popular courses in the area.

One reason for its popularity could be Manzanillo's enticing tropical geography—vast groves of tall palms, abundant mango trees, and successive coves graced with smooth sand beaches. To the north, mountains blanketed with palms rise alongside the shoreline. And over it all lies the veneer of perfect weather, with balmy temperatures and year-round sea breezes. Even the approach by plane into Manzanillo showcases the promise—you fly in over the beach and golf course. Once on the ground, you exit the airport through a palm grove.

Manzanillo is a dichotomous place—it is both Mexico's busiest commercial seaport and a tranquil, traditional town of multicolor houses cascading down the hillsides to meet the central commercial area of simple seafood restaurants, shell shops, and a few salsa clubs. The activity in Manzanillo divides neatly into two zones: the downtown commercial port and the luxury Santiago Peninsula resort zone to the north. The busy harbor and rail connections to Mexico's interior dominate the downtown zone. A visit to the town's waterfront *zócalo* provides a glimpse into local life. The exclusive Santiago Peninsula, home to the resorts and golf course, separates Manzanillo's two golden sand bays.

1 Manzanillo Essentials

256km (160 miles) SE of Puerto Vallarta; 267km (167 miles) SW of Guadalajara; 64km (40 miles) SE of Barra de Navidad

GETTING THERE & DEPARTING **By Plane** **Aeromexico,** its sister airline, **Aerolitoral** (both can be reached at ✆ **800/237-6639** in the U.S., 314/334-1226 at the airport), and **Mexicana** (✆ **800/531-7921** in the U.S., 314/333-2323 at the airport) offer flights to and from Mexico City, Durango, Chihuahua, and

Manzanillo Area

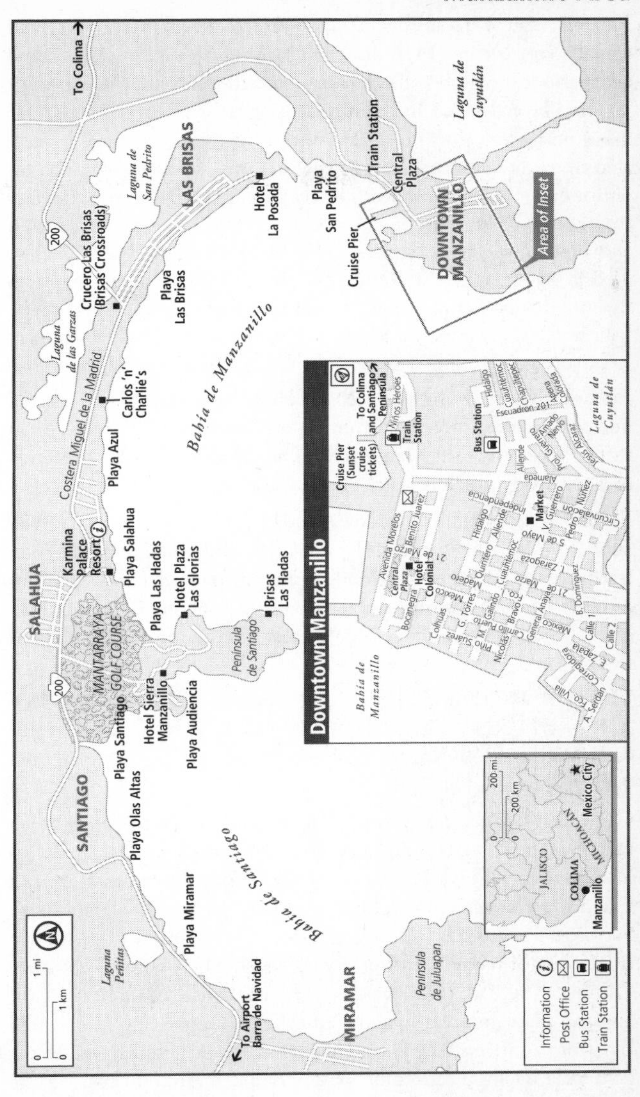

Mazatlán and to cities in the United States and Canada. **Alaska Airlines** (© **800/426-0333** in Mexico, or 314/334-2211) offers service from Los Angeles; **America West** (© **800/235-9292**) flies from

Phoenix; and **Aerocalifornia** (✆ **800/237-6225** in the U.S. and Canada, or 314/334-1414) has flights from Los Angeles. Ask a travel agent about the numerous **charters** from the States in the winter.

The **Playa de Oro International Airport** is 40km (25 miles; 45 min.) northwest of town. *Colectivo* (minivan) airport service is available from the airport; hotels arrange returns. Make reservations for return trips 1 day in advance. The *colectivo* fare is based on zones and runs $8 to $10 for most hotels. Private taxi service between the airport and downtown area is around $25. **Budget** (✆ **800/527-0700** or 314/333-1445) and **AutoRentas** (✆ **314/333-2580**) have counters in the airport open during flight arrivals; they will also deliver a car to your hotel. Daily rates run $56 to $78. You need a car only if you plan to explore surrounding cities and the Costa Alegre beaches.

By Car **Coastal Highway 200** leads from Acapulco (south) and Puerto Vallarta (north). From Guadalajara, take Highway 54 through Colima into Manzanillo. Outside Colima you can switch to a toll road, which is faster but less scenic.

By Bus Buses run to Barra de Navidad (1½ hr. north), Puerto Vallarta (5 hr. north), Colima (1½ hr. east), and Guadalajara (4½ hr. north), with deluxe service and numerous daily departures. Manzanillo's **Central Camionera** (bus station) is about 12 long blocks east of town. If you follow Hidalgo east, the station will be on your right.

VISITOR INFORMATION The **tourism office** (✆ **314/333-2277** or 314/333-2264; fax 314/333-1426) is on the Costera Miguel de la Madrid 4960, Km 8.5. It's open Monday through Friday from 9am to 3pm and 5 to 7pm.

CITY LAYOUT The town lies at one end of a 7-mile-long beach facing Manzanillo Bay and its commercial harbor. The beach has four sections—**Playa Las Brisas, Playa Azul, Playa Salahua,** and **Playa Las Hadas.** At the other end of the beaches is the high, rocky **Santiago Peninsula.** Santiago is 11km (7 miles) from downtown; it's the site of many beautiful homes and the best hotel in the area, Camino Real Las Hadas, as well as the hotel's Mantarraya Golf Course. The peninsula juts out into the bay, separating Manzanillo Bay from Santiago Bay. Playa Las Hadas is on the south side of the peninsula, facing Manzanillo Bay, and **Playa Audiencia** is on the north side, facing Santiago Bay. The inland town of **Santiago** is opposite the turnoff to Las Hadas.

Activity in downtown Manzanillo centers on the **central plaza,** or *zócalo,* officially known as the Jardín Alvaro Obregón. A railroad, shipyards, and a basketball court with constant pick-up games separate it from the waterfront. The plaza has flowering trees, a fountain, twin kiosks, and a view of the bay. It is a staple of local life, where people congregate on park benches to swap gossip and throw handfuls of rice to the ever-present *palomas* ("doves"—really just pigeons). Large ships dock at the pier nearby. **Avenida México,** the street leading out from the plaza's central gazebo, is the town's principal commercial thoroughfare.

Once you leave downtown, the highway (the **Costera Miguel de la Madrid,** or the Costera Madrid) runs through the neighborhoods of Las Brisas, Salahua, and Santiago to the **hotel zones** on the Santiago Peninsula and at Miramar. Shell shops, mini-malls, and several restaurants are along the way.

There are two main lagoons. **Laguna de Cuyutlán,** almost behind the city, stretches south for miles, paralleling the coast. **Laguna de San Pedrito,** north of the city, parallels the Costera Miguel de la Madrid; it's behind Playa Las Brisas beach. Both are good birding sites. There are also two bays. **Manzanillo Bay**

FAST FACTS: Manzanillo

American Express The local representative is **Bahías Gemelas Travel Agency,** Km 10, Costera Miguel de la Madrid (✆ **314/333-1000** or 314/333-1053; fax 314/333-0649). It's open Monday through Friday from 10am to 2pm and 4 to 6pm, Saturday from 10am to 2pm.

Area Code The telephone area code is **314.**

Bank **Banamex,** just off the plaza on Avenida México, downtown (✆ **314/332-0115**), is open Monday through Friday from 9am to 4pm, but changes foreign currency only until 12:30pm.

Internet Access The air-conditioned **Net Café,** Calle Benito Juárez 115, Int. 7-B (✆ **314/332-2660;** mayocomp@bay.net.mx), is half a block from the central plaza. It charges $3 per hour. It's open Monday through Friday from 10am to 2pm and 4:30 to 8:30pm, Saturday from 10am to 2pm.

Post Office The *correo,* Dr. Miguel Galindo 30, opposite Farmacia de Guadalajara, downtown (✆ **314/332-0022**), is open Monday through Saturday from 9am to 1pm.

encompasses the harbor, town, and beaches. The Santiago Peninsula separates it from the second bay, **Santiago.** Between downtown and the Santiago Peninsula is **Las Brisas,** a flat peninsula with a long stretch of sandy golden beach, a lineup of inexpensive but run-down hotels, and a few good restaurants.

GETTING AROUND By Taxi Taxis in Manzanillo are plentiful. Fares are fixed by zones; rates for trips within town and to more distant points should be posted at your hotel. Daily rates can be negotiated for longer drives outside the Manzanillo area.

By Bus The local buses *(camionetas)* make a circuit from downtown in front of the train station, along the Bay of Manzanillo, to the Santiago Peninsula and the Bay of Santiago to the north; the fare is 30¢. The ones marked LAS BRISAS go to the Las Brisas crossroads, to the Las Brisas Peninsula, and back to town; MIRAMAR, SANTIAGO, and SALAHUA buses go to outlying settlements along the bays and to most restaurants mentioned below. Buses marked LAS HADAS go to the Santiago Peninsula and pass the Las Hadas resort and the Sierra Manzanillo and Plaza Las Glorias hotels. This is an inexpensive way to see the coast as far as Santiago and to tour the Santiago Peninsula.

2 Activities On & Off the Beach

Activities in Manzanillo revolve around its golden sand beaches, which frequently accumulate a film of black mineral residue from nearby rivers. Most of the resort hotels are completely self-contained. Manzanillo's public beaches provide an opportunity to see more local color and scenery. They are the daytime playground for those staying at places off the beach or without pools.

BEACHES Playa Audiencia, on the Santiago Peninsula, offers the best swimming as well as snorkeling, but **Playa San Pedrito,** shallow for a long way out, is the most popular beach for its proximity to downtown. **Playa Las Brisas** offers an optimal combination of location and good swimming. **Playa Miramar,** on the Bahía de Santiago past the Santiago Peninsula, is popular with bodysurfers, windsurfers, and boogie boarders. It's accessible by local bus from town. The major part of **Playa Azul** drops off sharply but is noted for its wide stretch of golden sand.

BIRDING Several lagoons along the coast offer good birding. As you go from Manzanillo past Las Brisas to Santiago, you'll pass **Laguna de Las Garzas (Lagoon of the Herons),** also known as

Downtown Manzanillo

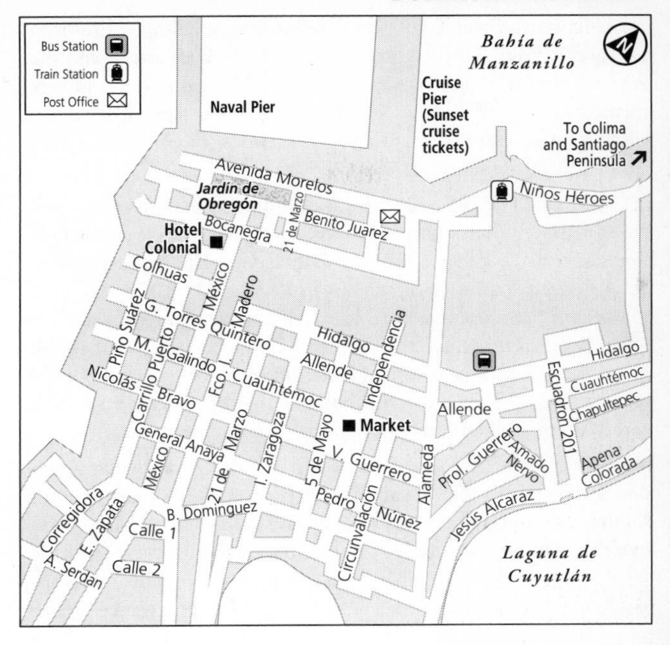

Laguna de San Pedrito, where you can see many white pelicans and huge herons fishing in the water. They nest here in December and January. Directly behind downtown is the **Laguna de Cuyutlán** (follow the signs to Cuyutlán), where you'll usually find birds in abundance; species vary between summer and winter.

DIVING Underworld Scuba (©/fax **314/333-0642;** cell 314/358-0327; www.gomanzanillo.com), owned by longtime resident and local diving expert Susan Dearing, conducts highly professional diving expeditions and classes. Susan's warm enthusiasm and intimate knowledge of the area make this one of my top recommendations for dive outfitters in Mexico. Many locations are so close to shore that there's no need for a boat. Close-in dives include the jetty with coral growing on the rocks at 14m (45 ft.), and a nearby sunken frigate downed in 1959 at 8m (28 ft.). Divers can see abundant sea life, including coral reefs, seahorses, giant puffer fish, and moray eels. A dive requiring a boat costs $50 per person for one tank (with a three-person minimum), or $70 for two tanks ($10 discount if you have your own equipment). You can also rent weights and a tank for beach dives for $10. A three-stop snorkel trip costs $35. All guides are certified divemasters, and the shop offers certification classes (PADI, YMCA, and CMAS) in very intensive courses of various durations. The owner offers a 10% discount on your certification when you mention Frommer's. MasterCard and Visa are accepted.

ESCORTED TOURS Because Manzanillo is so spread out, you might consider a city tour. Reputable local tour companies include **Hectours** (© **314/333-1707**) and **Bahías Gemelas Travel Agency,** the American Express representative (© **314/333-1000;** fax 314/333-0649). Schedules are flexible; a half-day city tour costs around $25. Other tours include the daylong Colima Colonial Tour ($67), which stops at a sugar-cane plantation, Colima's Archaeological Museum, and principal colonial buildings, and passes the active volcano. Offerings change regularly, so ask about new tours.

FISHING Manzanillo is famous for its fishing, particularly sailfish. Marlin and sailfish are abundant year-round. Winter is best for dolphin fish and dorado (mahimahi); in summer, wahoo and rooster fish are in greater supply. The international sailfish competition is held around the November 20 Revolution Day holiday, and the national sailfish competition is in February. You can arrange fishing through travel agencies or directly at the fishermen's cooperative (© **314/332-1031**), located downtown where the fishing boats moor. Call from 7am to 7pm. A fishing boat is approximately $35 to $65 per hour, with most trips lasting about 5 hours.

GOLF The 18-hole **La Mantarraya Golf Course** (© **314/331-0101**) is open to nonguests as well as guests of Brisas Las Hadas. At one time, La Mantarraya was among the top 100 courses in the world, but newer entries have passed it. Still, the compact, challenging 18-hole course designed by Roy and Pete Dye is a beauty, with banana trees, blooming bougainvillea, and coconut palms at every turn. A lush and verdant place (12 of the 18 holes are played over water), it remains in the top 10 of Mexico's 125 courses.

When the course was under construction, workers dug up pre-Hispanic ceramic figurines, idols, and beads where the 14th hole now lies. It is believed to have been an important ancient burial site. The course culminates with its signature 18th hole, with a drive to the island green off El Tesoro (the treasure) beach, directly in front of the Karminda Palace Resort. Local lore says this beach still may hold buried treasure from Spanish galleons, whose crews were the first to recognize the perfection of this natural harbor, and who used it during the 16th century as their starting point for voyages to the Pacific Rim. Greens fees are $101 for 18 holes, $60 for 9 holes; cart rental costs $50.

The fabulous 27-hole golf course associated with the **Grand Bay Hotel** in Barra de Navidad, an easy distance from Manzanillo, is also open to the public. The Robert Von Hagge design is long and lovely, with each hole amid rolling, tropical landscapes. It is wide open, with big fairways and big greens, and features plenty of water (2 lagoon holes, 13 lakeside holes, and 8 holes along the Pacific). The greens fees are $166 for 18 holes, $192 for 27 holes for hotel guests, $216 and $240, respectively, for nonguests, including a motorized cart. Barra is about a 1- to 1½-hour drive north of Manzanillo on Highway 200. (See "Activities On & Off the Beach" under "Barra de Navidad & Melaque," in chapter 4.)

A MUSEUM The **Museum of Archaeology and History** (✆ **314/332-2256**) is a small but impressive structure that houses exhibits depicting the region's history, plus rotating displays of contemporary Mexican art. It's on Avenida Niños Heroes at Avenida Teniente Azueta, on the road leading between the downtown and Las Brisas areas. Every Friday evening, the museum hosts free cultural events, which might be a trio playing romantic ballads or a chamber music ensemble. Performances begin at 8pm. Hours are Tuesday through Saturday from 10am to 2pm and 5 to 8pm, Sunday from 10am to 1pm.

SHOPPING Manzanillo has a selection of shops carrying Mexican crafts and clothing, mainly from nearby Guadalajara. Almost all are downtown on the streets near the central plaza. Shopping downtown is an experience—for example, you won't want to miss the shop bordering the plaza that sells a combination of shells, religious items (including shell-framed Virgin of Guadalupe nightlights), and orthopedic supplies. The Plaza Manzanillo is an American-style mall on the road to Santiago, and there's a traditional *tianguis* (outdoor) market in front of the entrance to Club Maeva, with touristy items from around Mexico. Most resort hotels also have boutiques or shopping arcades.

SUNSET CRUISES To participate in this popular activity, buy tickets from a travel agent or downtown at La Perlita Dock (across from the train station), fronting the harbor. Tickets are on sale at La Perlita daily from 8:30am to 2pm and cost around $25. The trips vary in their combinations of drinks, music, and entertainment and last 1½ to 2 hours.

3 Where to Stay

Manzanillo's strip of coastline consists of three areas: **downtown,** with its shops, markets, and commercial activity; **Las Brisas,** the hotel-lined beach area immediately north of the city; and **Santiago,** the town and peninsula, now virtually a suburb, to the north at the end of Playa Azul. Transportation by bus or taxi makes all three areas fairly convenient to each other. Reservations are recommended during the Easter, Christmas, and New Year's holidays.

DOWNTOWN

Hotel Colonial ★ An old favorite, this three-story colonial-style hotel in the central downtown district added five new units in 2000. Popular for its consistent quality, ambience, and service, it has beautiful blue-and-yellow tile, and colonial-style carved doors and windows in the lobby and restaurant. Rooms are decorated with minimal furniture, red-tile floors, and basic comforts. The hotel is 1 block inland from the main plaza at the corner of Juárez and Galindo.

Av. México 100 and González Bocanegra, 28200 Manzanillo, Col. ✆ **314/332-1080,** 314/332-0668, 314/332-1230, or 314/332-1134. 42 units. $28 double. AE, MC, V. **Amenities:** Restaurant and bar; tour desk. *In room:* A/C, TV.

LAS BRISAS

Earthquake damage Las Brisas suffered in 1995 left many buildings damaged and abandoned. This makes parts of the Las Brisas area look run-down. However, it still lays claim to one of the best beaches in the area and is known for its constant gentle sea breezes—a pleasure in the summer.

Hotel La Posada This small inn has a bright-pink stucco facade with a large arch that leads to a broad tiled patio right on the beach. The rooms have exposed brick walls and simple furnishings with Mexican decorative accents. Mattresses are beginning to sag, and the place could use some upkeep, but it remains popular with longtime travelers to Manzanillo. The atmosphere is casual and informal—help yourself to beer and soft drinks, and at the end of your stay, owner Bart Varelmann (a native of Ohio) counts the bottle caps you deposited in a bowl labeled with your room number. The restaurant, which is open to nonguests, is open daily during high season from 8 to 11am and 1:30 to 8pm. A meal costs around $7. During low season, the restaurant is open from 8am to 3pm. Stop by for a drink at sunset; the bar's open until 9pm all year. The hotel is at the end of Las Brisas Peninsula, closest to downtown, and is on the local Las Brisas bus route.

Film Fact

The movie *10* featured Manzanillo's signature property, Las Hadas—along with Bo Derek.

Av. Lázaro Cárdenas 201, Las Brisas (Apdo. Postal 135), 28200 Manzanillo, Col. ✆/fax **314/333-1899.** www.mexonline.com/laposada.htm. 24 units. High season $70 double; low season $39 double. Rates include breakfast. AE, MC, V. **Amenities:** Restaurant and bar; laundry service; money exchange; safe-deposit boxes.

SANTIAGO

Five kilometers (3 miles) north of Las Brisas is the wide Santiago Peninsula. The settlement of Salahua is on the highway where you enter the peninsula to reach the hotels Las Hadas, Plaza Las Glorias, and Sierra Manzanillo, as well as the Mantarraya Golf Course. Buses from town marked LAS HADAS pass by these hotels every 20 minutes. Past the Salahua turnoff, at the end of the settlement of Santiago, an obscure road on the left is marked ZONA DE PLAYAS and leads to the hotels on the other side of the peninsula and Playa de Santiago.

Brisas Las Hadas ★★★ For me, Las Hadas is the most compelling reason to visit Manzanillo. This elegant beachfront resort, a member of the Leading Hotels of the World, is built in Moorish style into the side of the rocky peninsula. The service is gracious, warm, and unobtrusive. Rooms spread over meticulously landscaped grounds and overlook the bay; cobbled lanes lined with colorful flowers and palms connect them. The resort is large but maintains an air of seclusion. (Motorized carts are on call for transportation within the property.)

Views, room size, and amenities differentiate the six types of accommodations, which can vary greatly. If you're not satisfied with your room, ask to be moved—a few of the rooms are significantly less attractive than others. Understated and spacious, the better units have white-marble floors, sitting areas, and large, comfortably furnished balconies. Nine suites have private pools. The lobby is a popular place for curling up in one of the overstuffed seating areas or, at night, for enjoying a drink and live music. Pete and Roy Dye designed La Mantarraya, the hotel's 18-hole, par-71 golf course.

Av. de los Riscos s/n, Santiago Peninsula, 28200 Manzanillo, Col. ✆ **800/722-6466** in the U.S. and Canada, or 314/334-0000. 233 units. High season $250–$300 double, $462–$557 Fantasy Suite; low season $190–$232 double, $395–$495 Fantasy Suite. AE, DC, MC, V. Free guarded parking. **Amenities:** 4 restaurants, including the elegant Legazpi (see "Where to Dine," below); 4 lounges and bars; theme nights ($50 per person); 2 pools; 10 tennis courts (8 hard-surface, 2 clay); small workout room; scuba diving, snorkeling, sailing, and trimaran cruises; concierge; tour desk; travel agency; car rental; shopping arcade; in-room massage; babysitting; laundry and dry cleaning; marina for 70 vessels; shade tents on the beach. *In room:* A/C, TV, dataport, minibar, hair dryer, safe-deposit box, robes.

Hotel Plaza Las Glorias ★★ The sunset-colored walls of this pueblo-like hotel ramble over a hillside on the Santiago Peninsula. The restaurant on top and most rooms afford a broad vista of other red-tiled rooftops and either the palm-filled golf course or the bay. It's one of Manzanillo's undiscovered resorts, known more to wealthy Mexicans than to Americans. Originally conceived as private condominiums, the accommodations were designed for living; each spacious unit is stylishly furnished, and very comfortable. Each has a huge living room; a small kitchen/bar; one, two, or three large bedrooms with tile or brick floors; large Mexican-tiled bathrooms; huge closets; and large furnished private patios with views. Some units contain whirlpool tubs, and a few rooms can be partitioned off and rented by the bedroom only. Rooms can be a long walk from the main entrance, through a succession of stairways and paths. If stair climbing bothers you, try to get a room by the restaurant and pool—you'll have a great view, and a hillside rail elevator goes straight from top to bottom.

Av. de Tesoro s/n, Santiago Peninsula. 28200 Manzanillo, Col. ✆ **314/334-1098.** Fax 314/333-1395. lasglorias@delfin.colimanet.com. 103 units. $95 double. Packages available. AE, MC, V. **Amenities:** Restaurant (with occasional live music); pool; game area; beach club on Las Brisas beach, with pool and small restaurant; transportation to and from beach club (once daily in each direction); room service; babysitting (with advance notice); laundry service. *In room:* A/C, TV, security box.

Hotel Sierra Manzanillo ★ *Kids* This all-inclusive hotel has 21 floors overlooking La Audiencia beach, and a full program of activities, dining, and entertainment. Its excellent kids' program makes it a top choice for families. Architecturally, it mimics the white Moorish style of Las Hadas that has become so popular in Manzanillo. Inside, it's palatial in scale and awash in pale-gray marble. Room decor picks up the pale-gray theme with armoires that conceal the TV and minibar. Most standard rooms have two double beds or a king-size bed, plus a small table, chairs, and desk. Several rooms at the end of most floors are small, with one double bed, small porthole-size windows, no balcony, and no view. Most rooms, however, have balconies and ocean or hillside views. The 10 honeymoon suites have sculpted shell-shaped headboards, king-size beds, and chaises. Junior suites have a sitting area with couch, and large bathrooms.

Scuba-diving lessons take place in the pool, and excellent scuba-diving sites are within swimming distance of the shore.

Av. La Audiencia 1, Los Riscos, 28200 Manzanillo, Col. ✆ **800/448-5028** in the U.S., or 314/333-2000. Fax 314/333-2611. 332 units. High season $342 double, $392–$412 suite; low season $175 double, $248–$308 suite. Rates are all-inclusive. AE, MC, V. **Amenities:** 3 restaurants; 4 bars; grand pool on the beach; children's pool; 4 lighted tennis courts; health club with exercise equipment, aerobics, hot tub, and men's and women's sauna and steam rooms; travel agency; salon with massage; room service; laundry service; 24-hr. currency exchange. *In room:* A/C, TV, dataport, minibar, hair dryer.

Karmina Palace ★★★ Kids The quality of rooms and services at this all-inclusive resort makes the newest of Manzanillo's hotels probably one of the area's best values. It's also the best choice for families in Manzanillo. The buildings resemble Maya pyramids, and even though the architecture at first might seem a little overdone, somehow it works. Rooms are all very large suites, with rich wood accents, comfortable recessed seating areas with pull-out couches, and two 27-inch TVs in each room. The extra-large bathrooms have marble floors, twin black marble sinks, separate tubs, and glassed-in showers. Most rooms have terraces or balconies with views of the ocean, overlooking the tropical gardens and swimming pools. Master suites have spacious sun terraces with private splash pools, plus a full wet bar, full refrigerator, and a large living room area with a 42-inch TV. Two full-size bedrooms close off from the living/dining area.

The Kid's Club offers a host of activities, while adults have numerous choices for fun—all included in the price. There's also an exceptionally well-equipped gym and European-style spa.

Bulevar Miguel de la Madrid s/n, Península de Santiago, Manzanillo, Col. ✆ **314/334-1313.** Fax 314/334-1108. www.karminapalace.com. 324 units. $240 double. Rates are all-inclusive. 2 children under 12 stay free in parent's room. Ask about seasonal specials. AE, MC, V. **Amenities:** 2 restaurants; snack bar; 5 bars; 8 connected swimming pools; tennis courts; health club with treadmills and Cybex equipment; full spa facilities, including men's and women's sauna and steam rooms; kids' activity program; 24-hr. concierge; car rental; 24-hr. room service; beach volleyball; windsurfing; money exchange; safe-deposit box in reception area. *In room:* A/C, TV, dataport, minibar, hair dryer, iron, safe-deposit box ($2).

4 Where to Dine

DOWNTOWN

Roca del Mar MEXICAN/INTERNATIONAL Join the locals at this informal cafe facing the plaza. The large menu includes club sandwiches, hamburgers, *carne asada a la tampiqueña* (thin grilled steak served with rice, poblano pepper, an enchilada, and refried beans), fajitas, fish, shrimp, and vegetable salads. A specialty is its *paella* (served on Sun and Tues), and the economical *pibil* tacos are outstanding. This cafe is very clean and offers sidewalk dining.

21 de Marzo 204 (across from the plaza). ✆ **314/332-0302.** Main courses $3–$12. No credit cards. Daily 7am–10:30pm.

LAS BRISAS

The Hotel La Posada (see "Where to Stay," above) offers breakfast to nonguests at its beachside restaurant; it's also a great place to mingle with other tourists and enjoy the sunset and cocktails.

Willy's ★★★ *Finds* SEAFOOD/INTERNATIONAL You're in for a treat at Willy's, one of Manzanillo's most popular restaurants. It's homey, casual, and small, with perhaps 13 tables inside and 10 more on the narrow balcony over the bay. The exquisite cuisine belies the atmosphere, with starters that include escargot and salmon carpaccio. Among the grilled specialties are shrimp imperial wrapped in bacon, red snapper tarragon, dorado basil, sea bass with mango and ginger, and tender fresh lobsters (four to a serving). Live guitar jazz plays after 8pm. If you double back left at the Las Brisas crossroads, you'll find Willy's on the right, down a short side street that leads to the ocean.

Las Brisas crossroads. ✆ **314/333-1794.** Reservations required. Main courses $8–$17. MC, V. Daily 7pm–midnight.

SANTIAGO ROAD

The restaurants below are on the Costera Madrid between downtown and the Santiago Peninsula, including the Salahua area.

Benedetti's Pizza PIZZA There are several branches in town, so you'll probably find a Benedetti's not far from where you are staying. The variety is extensive; add some *chimichurri* sauce to enhance the flavor. Benedetti's specializes in seafood pizzas, such as smoked oyster and anchovy. You can also select from pastas, sandwiches, burgers, fajitas, salads, Mexican soups, cheesecake, and apple pie. This branch is on the Costera Madrid, on the left, just after the Las Brisas turn across from the Coca-Cola plant.

Av. del Mar 1, Crucero Las Brisas. ✆ **314/334-0141.** Pizza $9–$12; main courses $2–$5.55. AE, MC, V. Daily 1–11:30pm.

Bigotes III *Finds* SEAFOOD Locals flock to this large, breezy restaurant (the name translates as "Mustaches") by the water for the good food and festive atmosphere. Strolling singers serenade diners, who dig into large portions of grilled seafood.

Puesta del Sol 3. ✆ **314/333-1236.** Main courses $9.50–$23. MC, V. Daily noon–10pm. From downtown, follow the Costera Madrid past the Las Brisas turnoff; the restaurant is behind the Penas Coloradas Social Club, across from the beach.

Manolo's Norteño Campestre INTERNATIONAL/STEAK/SEAFOOD Owners Manuel and Juanita López and family offer excellent dining in a tropical garden setting. They cater to American tastes: Dinners include a "safe" salad. Among the popular entrees are filet of fish Manolo (on a bed of spinach with melted cheese, Florentine-style), and frog legs in brandy batter. Most people can't leave without being tempted by the fresh coconut or homemade pecan pie.

Km 11.5, Costera Miguel de la Madrid. ✆ **314/333-0475.** Main courses $5–$20. AE, MC, V. Mon–Sat 5pm–midnight. From downtown, follow the Costera Madrid; Manolo's is on the right, about 3 blocks before the turn to Las Hadas.

SANTIAGO PENINSULA

Legazpi ★★ INTERNATIONAL This is a top choice in Manzanillo for sheer elegance, gracious service, and outstanding food. The candlelit tables are set with silver and flowers. Enormous bell-shaped windows on two sides show off the sparkling bay below. The sophisticated menu includes prosciutto with melon marinated in port wine, crayfish bisque, broiled salmon, roast duck, lobster, veal, and flaming desserts from crepes to Irish coffee.

In the Brisas Las Hadas hotel, Santiago Peninsula. ✆ **314/334-0000.** Main courses $8.50–$16. AE, MC, V. High season daily 7–11:30pm. Closed low season.

5 Manzanillo After Dark

Nightlife in Manzanillo is much more exuberant than you might expect, but then Manzanillo is not only a resort town—it's a thriving commercial center. Clubs and bars tend to change from year to year, so check with your concierge for current hot spots. Some area clubs have a dress code prohibiting shorts or sandals, principally applying to men.

Perennial favorites include **Carlos 'n' Charlie's,** Av. Audiencia Cocoteros s/n (✆ **314/334-1272**), always a good choice for food and fun. In the evening during high season, there may be a minimum or cover if you come just to drink and dance, but the cover includes three drinks. **El Bar de Félix,** between Salahua and Las Brisas by the Avis rental-car office (✆ **314/334-1444**), is open Tuesday through Sunday from 2pm to midnight, and has an $8 minimum consumption charge. Music ranges from salsa and ranchero to rock and house—it's the most consistently lively place in town. **Vog Disco** (✆ **314/333-1875**), Km 9.2 Bulevar Costero Miguel de la Madrid, features alternative music in a cavernous setting; it's Manzanillo's current late-night hot spot, open until 5am, but only on Friday and Saturday. Cover charge for women is $10, for men $15. Also very popular—with a built-in crowd—is the nightclub at the **Club Maeva Hotel & Resort** (✆ **800/523-8450**), on the inland side of the main highway, north of the Santiago Peninsula. It's open Tuesday, Thursday, and Saturday from 10pm to 3am. Couples are given preferential entrance. Nonguests are welcome but must pay an entrance fee, after which all drinks are included. The fee varies depending on the night of the week and the time of year.

6

Settling into Guadalajara

Guadalajara is the second-largest city in Mexico (with 3.5 million people, it's a very distant second to Mexico City), but because it's the homeland of mariachi music, the *jarabe tapatío* (the Mexican hat dance), and tequila, many consider it the most Mexican of cities. Despite its size, Guadalajara is easy to navigate, and the people are friendly and helpful. And unlike in Mexico City, visitors can enjoy big-city pleasures without big-city hassles.

Guadalajara is the capital of the state of Jalisco and on occasion in Mexico's stormy history has functioned as the nation's capital. The historic center of Guadalajara, especially the area around the cathedral, is a wonderful place to wander among colonial plazas, fountains, churches, and convents. On the relatively new Plaza Tapatía, you can enjoy a pleasant walk from the cathedral all the way to the impressive Hospicio Cabañas. With its shopping, restaurants, cultural life, history, architecture, and mild climate, Guadalajara is a great side trip into the interior from Puerto Vallarta or Manzanillo.

The handicrafts and decorative arts here are perhaps the best in Mexico. Shoppers can browse through the sophisticated shops of **Tlaquepaque,** which offer an immense variety of merchandise. Or they can visit **Tonalá,** a bargain-hunter's paradise with hundreds of workshops.

While in Guadalajara, you will undoubtedly come across the word *tapatío* (or *tapatía*). In the early days, people from the area were known to trade in threes, called *tapatíos.* Gradually, the locals came to be called *tapatíos,* too, and the word now signifies Guadalajaran when referring to a thing, a person, or a manner of doing something.

1 Guadalajara Essentials

GETTING THERE

BY PLANE Guadalajara's international airport is a 25- to 45-minute ride from the city. Taxi tickets to Guadalajara, priced by zone, are for sale in front of the airport. Taxis are the only transport from town to the airport ($12–$14).

Major Airlines See chapter 1 for a list of toll-free numbers for international airlines serving Mexico. Numbers in Guadalajara are: **AeroMar** (✆ 33/3615-8509), **Aeromexico** (✆ 800/021-4010), **American** (✆ 01-800/904-6000), **Continental** (✆ 01-800/900-5000), **Delta** (✆ 33/3630-3530), **Mexicana** (✆ 01-800/502-2000), and **United** (✆ 33/3616-9489).

Of the smaller airlines, **Aviacsa** (✆ 33/3616-9706) has international flights from Los Angeles, Las Vegas, and Houston. **Aerocalifornia** (✆ 33/3616-2525) serves Guadalajara from Tijuana, Mexico City, Los Mochis, La Paz, and Puebla. **Azteca** (✆ 33/3630-4615) is a new airline with service to and from several cities in Mexico and along the border. **Allegro** (✆ 877/443-7585 in the U.S., or 33/3647-7799) operates flights to and from Oakland and Las Vegas.

BY CAR Guadalajara is at the hub of several four-lane toll roads (called *cuotas* or *autopistas*), which can cut travel time considerably but are expensive. From Nogales on the **U.S. border,** follow Highway 15 south (21 hr.). From **Tepic,** a quicker route is toll road 15D (5 hr., $30). From **Puerto Vallarta,** go north on Highway 200 to Compostela; toll road 68D heads east to join the Tepic toll road. Total time is 5½ hours, and the tolls add up to $25. From **Barra de Navidad,** on the coast southeast of Puerto Vallarta, take Highway 80 northeast (4½ hr.). From **Manzanillo,** you might also take this road, but toll road 54D through Colima to Guadalajara (3½ hr., $22) is faster. From **Mexico City,** take toll road 15D (7 hr., $43).

BY BUS Two bus stations serve Guadalajara. The old one, near downtown, has buses to Lake Chapala and other nearby areas; the new one, 10km (6 miles) southeast of downtown, handles buses to more distant destinations.

The Old Bus Station For destinations within 96km (60 miles) of Guadalajara, including Lake Chapala, Ajijic, Jocotepec, Mazamitla, and San Juan Cosalá, go to the old bus terminal, on Niños Héroes off Calzada Independencia Sur. If your destination is the Lake Chapala region, look for **Transportes Guadalajara-Chapala,** which operates frequent bus and *combi* (minivan) service to Chapala beginning at 6am.

The New Bus Station **The Central Camionera** is a 35-minute ride from downtown. Taxi fare for the trip is about $9. This bus station resembles an international airport, with seven terminals connected by a covered walkway. Each building contains different bus lines, offering first- and second-class service for different destinations, so it can

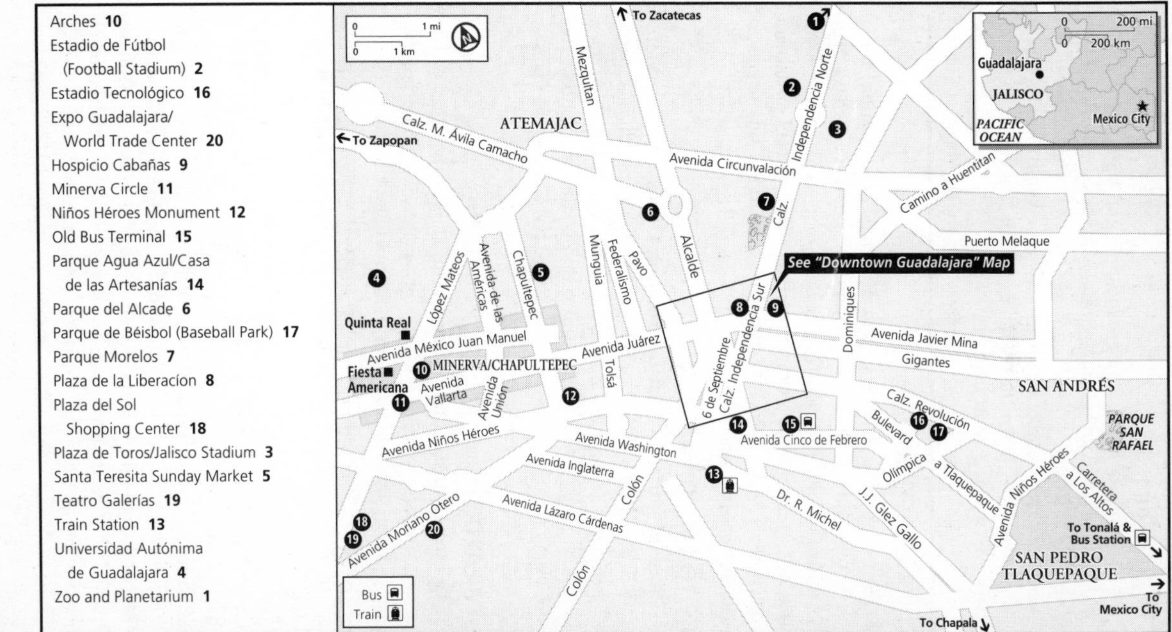
Arches 10
Estadio de Fútbol (Football Stadium) 2
Estadio Tecnológico 16
Expo Guadalajara/ World Trade Center 20
Hospicio Cabañas 9
Minerva Circle 11
Niños Héroes Monument 12
Old Bus Terminal 15
Parque Agua Azul/Casa de las Artesanías 14
Parque del Alcade 6
Parque de Béisbol (Baseball Park) 17
Parque Morelos 7
Plaza de la Liberacíon 8
Plaza del Sol Shopping Center 18
Plaza de Toros/Jalisco Stadium 3
Santa Teresita Sunday Market 5
Teatro Galerías 19
Train Station 13
Universidad Autónima de Guadalajara 4
Zoo and Planetarium 1
0 1 mi
0 1 km
To Zacatecas
To Zapopan
ATEMAJAC
Calz. M. Ávila Camacho
Mezqultan
Calz. Independencia Norte
Avenida Circunvalación
Camino a Huentitan
Puerto Melaque
See "Downtown Guadalajara" Map
López Mateos
Avenida de las Américas
Chapultepec
Munguia
Federalismo
Pavo
Alcalde
Calz. Independencia Sur
6 de Septiembre
Dominiques
Avenida Javier Mina
Gigantes
SAN ANDRÉS
Quinta Real
Avenida México Juan Manuel
Avenida Juárez
MINERVA/CHAPULTEPEC
Fiesta Americana
Avenida Vallarta
Avenida Unión
Tolsá
Avenida Niños Héroes
Avenida Washington
Avenida Cinco de Febrero
Calz. Revolución
Bulevard
Olímpica
a Tlaquepaque
Avenida Niños Héroes
Carretera a Los Altos
PARQUE SAN RAFAEL
Avenida Inglaterra
Colón
Dr. R. Michel
J.J. Glez Gallo
Avenida Lázaro Cárdenas
Avenida Moriano Otero
To Tonalá & Bus Station
SAN PEDRO TLAQUEPAQUE
To Mexico City
To Chapala
Bus
Train
0 200 mi
0 200 km
Guadalajara
JALISCO
PACIFIC OCEAN
Mexico City

Impressions

The men [of Guadalajara] are handsome and cling to their attractive charro outfits and extremely large sombreros. At one time the brims of their hats were so wide that they were declared a public nuisance. Any man caught wearing a sombrero with a brim that extended much beyond his shoulders was arrested and fined.

—Burton Holmes, Mexico (1939)

be a little confusing. The best place to get bus information, make reservations, and buy tickets is downtown at the **Agencia Plaza Tapatía,** Calzada Independencia 254, a bus-ticket agency under Plaza Tapatía. It works with all six main bus lines that connect Guadalajara to the rest of Mexico. Many travel agencies also sell bus tickets to important destinations.

VISITOR INFORMATION

The **State of Jalisco Tourist Information Office** is at Calle Morelos 102 (© **33/3668-1600** or 33/3668-1601) in the Plaza Tapatía, at Paseo Degollado and Paraje del Rincón del Diablo. It's open Monday through Friday from 9am to 8pm; Saturday, Sunday, and festival days from 9am to 1pm. The office has a supply of maps as well as a monthly calendar of cultural events in the city.

CITY LAYOUT

The **Centro Histórico (city center),** with all its attractions, will be of great interest to the visitor. On the west side is the fashionable hotel and restaurant district, with boutiques and shopping centers; to the northwest is **Zapopan,** home of Guadalajara's patron saint; and to the southeast are the crafts towns of **Tlaquepaque** and **Tonalá.**

The main artery for traffic from downtown to the west side is **Avenida Vallarta.** It starts downtown as **Juárez.** The main arteries for returning to downtown are **Mexico** (called Juan Manuel downtown) and **Hidalgo,** both north of Vallarta. Vallarta heads due west, where it intersects another major artery, **Avenida Adolfo López Mateos,** at **Minerva Circle** (*Fuente Minerva* or simply *La Minerva*). Minerva Circle, a 15-minute drive from downtown, is the central point of reference for the west side. To go to Zapopan from downtown, take Avenida Avila Camacho, which you can pick up on Alcalde; it takes 20 minutes by car. To Tlaquepaque and Tonalá, take Calzada

Revolución. Tlaquepaque is 8km (5 miles) from downtown and takes 15 to 20 minutes by car; Tonalá is 5 minutes farther. Another major thoroughfare, Calzada Lázaro Cárdenas, connects the west-side hotel district to Tlaquepaque and Tonalá, bypassing downtown; it cuts travel time considerably.

GUADALAJARA NEIGHBORHOODS IN BRIEF

Centro Histórico The heart of the city contains the five main plazas, the cathedral, and several museums and public buildings. Two of those buildings hold spectacular murals by Orozco, in my opinion the best of the Mexican muralists. Theaters, restaurants, shops, and clubs dot the area, which also holds the largest covered market in Latin America. All of this is in a space roughly 12 blocks by 12 blocks, an easy area for a good walker to explore on foot. On the plazas and pedestrian-only streets, walking can be quite pleasant.

Parque Agua Azul This is a large inner-city green space 20 blocks south of the Centro Histórico. It has a children's area and miniature train. Nearby you'll find the state-run crafts shop (worth the short trip), theaters, and the anthropology museum.

Chapultepec/Minerva Circle/Plaza del Sol These areas constitute the west side of the city. Chapultepec is the neighborhood between downtown and Minerva Circle. Surrounding Minerva are several malls. Southwest from Minerva Circle along Avenida López Mateos is the Plaza del Sol area. The west side holds most of the fine dining spots, luxury hotels, boutiques, and galleries, as well as the American, British, and Canadian consulates.

Zapopan Founded in 1542, Zapopan is a suburb of Guadalajara. It's noted for its 18th-century basilica, the home of Guadalajara's patron saint, the Virgin of Zapopan. Enormous throngs of people honor her every October 12. Zapopan's main square and basilica are worth seeing. Next to the basilica is a small museum about the life and customs of the Huichol Indians, who live in a remote region of the state. Proceeds of the museum shop go to aid the Indians.

Tlaquepaque This was a village of artisans (especially potters) that grew into a market center. In the last 30 years, it has attracted designers from all over Mexico. Every major form of art and craft is for sale here: furniture, pottery, glass, jewelry, woodcarvings, leather goods, sculptures, and paintings. The shops are sophisticated, yet Tlaquepaque's center retains a small-town feel that makes door-to-door browsing enjoyable and relaxing.

Tonalá This has remained a town of artisans. Plenty of stores sell mostly local products from the town's more than 400 workshops. You'll see wrought iron, ceramics, blown glass, and papier-mâché. A busy street market operates each Thursday and Sunday.

GETTING AROUND

BY TAXI Taxis are the best and easiest way to get around town. Almost all of them have meters, and though drivers are reluctant to use them, you can insist that they do. There are three rates: for day, night, and suburbia. There is also a standard cab fare structure used by drivers who work the large hotels. To get an idea, check with the hotel staff about the specific rate for your destination. On my last visit the rates were the following: downtown to the west side, $5 to $7; downtown or west side to Tlaquepaque, $6 to $9; to new bus station, $9; to airport, $12 to $14.

BY CAR Keep in mind the several main arteries (see "City Layout," above). The **Periférico** is a loop around the city that connects with most other highways into town. Traffic on the two-lane Periférico is slow and filled with trucks. Several important freeway-style thoroughfares crisscross the city. **González Gallo** leads south from the town center and connects with the road to Lake Chapala. **Avenida Vallarta** continues past La Minerva and eventually feeds onto **Highway 15,** bound for Tequila and on to Puerto Vallarta.

BY BUS & *COLECTIVO* The electric bus is quite handy for travel between downtown and the west side. It bears the sign PAR VIAL and runs east along Hidalgo and west along the next street to the north, Calle Independencia (not Calzada Independencia). Hidalgo passes along the north side of the cathedral. The Par Vial goes as far east as Mercado Libertad and as far west as Minerva Circle.

Six varieties of city buses run along many of the same routes but offer different grades of service. The best are the **Turquesa buses,** or *autobuses de lujo,* which are easy to distinguish from the normal buses. They are air-conditioned, have comfortable seats, and carry only as many passengers as there are seats; they are worth the price (about 60¢ for most destinations). The handiest route is the **706 tur,** which runs from the Centro Histórico southeast to Tlaquepaque, the *central camionera* (the new bus station), and Tonalá. For more information on Tlaquepaque and Tonalá, see "Shopping," in chapter 7. The same bus runs in the reverse direction, northwest to Zapopan. You can catch this bus on Avenida 16 de Septiembre.

Many buses run north-south along the Calzada Independencia (not Calle Independencia), but the **san juan de dios–estacion 174** bus goes between the points you are likely to want—San Juan de Dios church, next to the Mercado Libertad, and the railroad station *(estación)* past Parque Agua Azul. Fares are generally 40¢; exact change is not necessary. The city also has a light rail system, **Tren Ligero,** but it doesn't serve areas that are of interest to visitors.

FAST FACTS: Guadalajara

American Express The local office is at Av. Vallarta 2440, Plaza los Arcos (✆ **33/3615-8910**); it's open Monday through Friday from 9am to 6pm, Saturday from 9am to noon.

Area Code The telephone area code is **33.**

Books/Newspapers/Magazines **Gonvil,** a popular bookstore chain, has a branch across from Plaza de los Hombres Ilustres on Avenida Hidalgo, and another a few blocks south at Avenida 16 de Septiembre 118 (Alcalde becomes 16 de Septiembre south of the cathedral). It carries few English selections. **Sanborn's,** at the corner of Juárez and 16 de Septiembre, does a good job of keeping English-language periodicals in stock, but most are specialty magazines. Many newsstands sell the two English local papers, the *Guadalajara Reporter* and the *Guadalajara Weekly.* For the widest selection of English-language books, try **Sandi Bookstore,** Av. Tepeyac 178 (✆ **33/3121-0863**), in the Chapalita neighborhood on the west side.

Business Hours Store hours are Monday through Saturday from 10am to 2pm and 4 to 8pm.

Climate & Dress Guadalajara is mild year-round, with the occasional freak cold spell. Generally, November through March you'll need a sweater in the evening. The warmest months, April and May, are hot and dry. June through September, the city gets afternoon and evening showers that keep the temperature a bit cooler. Dress in Guadalajara is conservative; attention-getting sportswear (short shorts, halters, and the like) is out of place.

Consulates The largest **American consular offices** in the world are here, at Progreso 175 (✆ **33/3825-2998** or 33/3825-2700). Other consulates include the **Canadian consulate,** Hotel Fiesta Americana, Local 31 (✆ **33/3615-6215**); the **British consulate,** Eulogio Parra 2539, Oficina 12 (✆ **33/3616-0629**); and the

Australian consulate, López Cotilla 2030 (✆ **33/3615-7418**). These offices all keep roughly the same hours: Monday through Friday from 8am to 4pm.

Currency Exchange The best rates are found 3 blocks south of the cathedral on López Cotilla, between Corona and Degollado. There are more than 20 *casas de cambio* on these 2 blocks. Almost all post their rates, which are better than the banks', without the long lines.

Elevation Guadalajara sits at 1,700m (5,576 ft.).

Emergencies The emergency phone number is ✆ **080.**

Hospitals For medical emergencies, visit the **Hospital México-Americano,** Cólomos 2110 (✆ **33/3642-7152**).

Internet Access Ask at your hotel for the closest Internet access. Most of the big hotels have business centers that you can use. If you're downtown, **C.C.C.P.** is an Internet cafe at Avenida Alcalde 159-34, just north of the cathedral in a small shopping center called Plaza Alegria. Its hours are Monday through Saturday from 9am to 9pm.

Language Classes Foreigners can study Spanish at the **Foreign Student Study Center,** University of Guadalajara, Calle Tomás V. Gómez 125, 44100 Guadalajara, Jal. (✆ **33/3616-4399**). **IMAC** is a private Spanish school at Donato Guerra 180 in the Centro Histórico (✆ **33/3613-1080**).

Luggage Storage/Lockers You can store luggage in the main bus station, the Central Camionera, and at the Guadalajara airport.

Police Tourists should first try to contact the Jalisco tourist information office in Plaza Tapatía (✆ **33/3658-1600**). If you can't reach the office, call the municipal police at ✆ **33/3617-6060.**

Post Office The *correo* is at the corner of Carranza and calle Independencia, about 4 blocks northeast of the cathedral. Standing in the plaza behind the cathedral, facing the Degollado Theater, walk to the left and turn left on Carranza; walk past the Hotel Mendoza, cross Calle Independencia, and look for the post office on the left. It's open Monday through Thursday from 9am to 5pm, Saturday from 10am to 2pm.

Safety Guadalajara doesn't have the violent crime that Mexico City does. Crimes against tourists and foreign students are infrequent and most often take the form of pickpocketing and purse snatching. Criminals usually work in teams and target travelers in busy places, such as outdoor restaurants: One will create a distraction while the other slips off with whatever the tourist has set down. Purse-snatchers usually target unaccompanied women at night and rarely in places with crowds. The same is true of necklace snatching (the assailant grabs a necklace, especially if it has a gold chain, and pulls hard, hoping it will break). Be especially alert if someone spills something on you—this is a common trick.

2 Where to Stay

Life has been good to Guadalajara's *hoteleros,* and prices have risen accordingly. Rates shown are the standard rack rates and include the 17% tax. In slow periods, look for discounts; the big hotels often give business discounts.

Almost all of the luxury hotels in Guadalajara are on the west side, which has the majority of the shopping malls, boutiques, fashionable restaurants, and clubs. There is also a lot to do in the Centro Histórico, making it a good place to stay. Finally, Tlaquepaque is a comfortable suburb and is perfect for shoppers; the only drawback is that almost everything shuts down by 7 or 8pm. Chain hotels not included below are the Hilton, Camino Real, Howard Johnson, and Crowne Plaza.

VERY EXPENSIVE

Fiesta Americana ★★ A sharp 22-story luxury hotel, similar to the Presidente Inter-Continental but less expensive and with fewer amenities, the Fiesta Americana caters mainly to business travelers. The location is excellent—in front of Minerva Circle, in western Guadalajara—and service is great. Request floors 4 through 10, which have been remodeled. Rooms are large and carpeted, with two doubles or one king and a soundproof door. The large, well-equipped bathrooms hold shower/tub combinations. The furniture is modern and understated.

Aurelio Aceves 225, Glorieta Minerva, 44100 Guadalajara, Jal. ✆ **800/FIESTA-1** in the U.S. and Canada, or 33/3825-3434. Fax 33/3630-3725. www.fiestaamericana.com.mx. 391 units. $210–$244 double, $260 Fiesta Club double; $281–$624 suite. AE, DC, MC, V. Free secured parking. **Amenities:** Restaurant; lobby bar; heated medium-sized pool; golf privileges at local club; 2 lighted tennis courts; exercise room; children's activities (Fiesta kids' program on Sun); concierge; tour desk; business center; executive business services; salon; 24-hr. room service; massage; babysitting; same-day laundry and dry cleaning; nonsmoking rooms; executive-level rooms. 1 room is equipped for guests with disabilities. *In room:* A/C, TV with pay movies, dataport, minibar, coffeemaker, hair dryer.

Hotel Presidente InterContinental ★★★ Housed in a 14-story glass building with an atrium lobby, this hotel offers the most comprehensive list of services and amenities in Guadalajara. There is little turnover in staff, and the concierge has proven more capable and knowledgeable than any other in the city. The recently remodeled rooms are comfortable and quiet, with modern furnishings that include a desk and a small table with two chairs. Club rooms have discreet check-in and are on limited-access hallways; rates include continental breakfast, newspaper, and evening cocktails. The extra privacy and services are good for Mexican soap opera stars or repeat guests who like having their preferences known in advance. If you're neither of these, opt for one of the other rooms. The lobby bar is popular; during the season, bullfighters relax here after the *corrida.* The hotel sits across from the Plaza del Sol shopping center in western Guadalajara.

Av. López Mateos Sur y Moctezuma, 45050 Guadalajara, Jal. ✆ **800/327-0200** in the U.S. and Canada, or 33/3678-1234. Fax 33/3678-1222. www.interconti.com. 409 units. $240–315 double, $320 club double; $395 suite. Weekend packages available. AE, DC, MC, V. Valet or self-parking $4. **Amenities:** 2 restaurants; lobby bar; outdoor heated pool; golf at nearby clubs; 24-hr. health club with saunas, steam rooms, and whirlpools; concierge; tour desk; car rental; large 24-hr. business center; executive business services; salon; 24-hr. room service; massage; babysitting; same-day laundry and dry cleaning; nonsmoking rooms; executive-level rooms. *In room:* A/C, TV with pay movies, dataport, minibar, hair dryer, iron, safe.

Quinta Real ★★★ This chain specializes in building properties that are suggestive of Mexico's heritage, in contrast to the comfortable but generic luxury hotel. No glass skyscraper here—two four-story buildings made of stone, wood, plaster, and tile occupy lush grounds. Rooms vary quite a bit: Eight have brick cupolas, some have balconies, and four are equipped with a whirlpool tub in the bathroom. All are large, with a split-level layout and antique decorative touches. And all come with large, fully equipped bathrooms with tub/shower combinations and excellent water pressure. You can choose between two doubles or one king-size bed. The hotel is 2 blocks from Minerva Circle in western Guadalajara. Ask for a room that doesn't face López Mateos.

Av. México 2727 (at López Mateos), 44680 Guadalajara, Jal. ✆ **800/445-4565** in the U.S. and Canada, or 33/3669-0600. Fax 33/36690601. www.quintareal.com. 75 suites. $310 master suite, $330 grand-class suite. AE, DC, MC, V. Free secured parking.

Amenities: Restaurant; bar; small outdoor heated pool; golf at local club; access to nearby health club; concierge; tour desk; car rental; business center; executive business services; room service until midnight; babysitting; same-day laundry and dry cleaning; nonsmoking rooms. *In room:* A/C, TV, dataport, minibar, hair dryer, iron, safe.

Villa Ganz ★★ This small, stylish hotel on the near west side of the city is one of the most comfortable places to stay in Guadalajara. Rooms are big, comfortable, and decorated with flair. Each holds a basket of fruit and a bottle of wine on check-in. Bathrooms are large and well lit—some have tubs, others just showers. Bed choices include a king, a queen, or two twins. Rooms facing the garden are the quietest, but those facing the street are set back from the traffic and have double-glazed windows. The common rooms and rear garden are agreeable places to relax. Service is personal and helpful. Guests can contract with a guide or taxi driver at the hotel. In-room dining can be arranged with one of three nearby restaurants. Villa Ganz is a member of the Boutique Hotels of Mexico.

López Cotilla 1739, 44140 Guadalajara, Jal. ✆ **877/278-8018** in the U.S., 866/818-8342 in Canada, or 33/3120-1416. www.villaganz.com. 10 suites. $210–$235 double. Rates include continental breakfast. AE, MC, V. Free secured parking. Children under 12 not accepted. **Amenities:** Golf and tennis at local club; concierge; tour desk; airport transfer; room service until 11pm; same-day laundry and dry cleaning; nonsmoking rooms. *In room:* A/C, TV, dataport, hair dryer, safe.

EXPENSIVE

Holiday Inn Hotel and Suites Centro Histórico ★ This six-story hotel has the most comfortable lodging in the downtown area. Its location, a few blocks from the main square, is good, too. Standard rooms are carpeted and decorated in Mexican architectural colors. The furniture is modern Mexican with a few wrought-iron pieces—the overall effect is cheerful. The size and lighting are good; bathrooms are medium-size and well equipped, with ample counter space. For quiet, ask for a room off the street. The suites are larger, but otherwise not worth the extra cost. Room rates include transportation to (but not from) the airport.

Av. Juárez 211, 44100 Guadalajara. Jal. ✆ **800/HOLIDAY** in the U.S. or Canada, 01-800/009-9900 in Mexico, or 33/3613-1763. www.holiday-inn.com. 90 units. $175 double; $195 suite. Ask about promotional rates. AE, MC, V. Free secured parking. **Amenities:** Restaurant and bar; fitness room; business center; room service until 10:30pm; same-day laundry and dry cleaning; nonsmoking rooms. *In room:* A/C, TV, dataport, minibar, coffeemaker, hair dryer, iron.

Hotel de Mendoza ★ On a quiet street next to the Degollado Theater and Plaza Tapatía, 2 blocks from the cathedral, the Mendoza has the best location of any downtown hotel. The decor would best be described as an attempt at old Spanish, with wood paneling and old-world accents. Standard rooms are medium-size and comfortable. Bed choices are one queen, two full, or two queens. Bathrooms are medium-size, with ample counter space and good lighting. Suites have an additional sitting area and larger bathrooms. Rooms face the street, an interior courtyard, or the pool. ***One note:*** The bath towels are the narrowest I've ever seen—obviously the brainchild of a demented cost-cutting expert. If the hotel hasn't changed these, ask for a couple extra after you check in.

Carranza 16, 44100 Guadalajara, Jal. ✆ **800/221-6509** in the U.S., or 33/3613-4646. Fax 33/3613-7310. www.demendoza.com.mx. 104 units. $102 double; $122 suite. Discounts sometimes available. AE, MC, V. Secured parking $4. **Amenities:** Restaurant; bar; small pool; fitness room; Jacuzzi; tour desk; room service until 10:30pm; same-day laundry and dry cleaning; nonsmoking rooms. *In room:* A/C, TV, dataport.

MODERATE

El Aposento Hotel ★ *Value* This small hotel in a colonial house in the Centro Histórico has handsomely furnished rooms decorated in muted tones. In price, comfort, and location, it is roughly the equal of the other downtown bargain in this category—the Hotel Cervantes—but rooms here are larger and have more character (but maybe not as much light). Add the full breakfast, and you have a winner. To avoid street noise, ask for a room facing away from the street (especially Madero). Rooms come with a king or two doubles. Most bathrooms are large; half come with a shower/tub combination.

Francisco Madero 545, 44100 Guadalajara, Jal. ✆/fax **33/3614-1612.** www.elaposento.com. 28 units. $65 double. Rates include full breakfast. AE, MC, V. Free sheltered parking. **Amenities:** Tour info; massage; nonsmoking rooms. *In room:* A/C, TV.

Hotel Cervantes ★ *Value* This six-story downtown hotel offers modern amenities at a great price. The rooms are attractive and medium-size. They have wall-to-wall carpeting and tile bathrooms with ample sink areas and shower/tub combinations. The lower price is for one double bed; the higher price, for a king or two doubles. This is not a particularly noisy hotel, but if you require absolute quiet, request an interior room. The Cervantes is 6 blocks south and 3 blocks west of the cathedral.

Prisciliano Sánchez 442, Col. Centro Histórico, 44100 Guadalajara, Jal. ✆/fax **33/3613-6686.** 100 units. $65–$75 double. AE, MC, V. Free secured parking. **Amenities:** Restaurant; lobby bar; small outdoor heated pool; tour desk; room service until 10pm; babysitting; same-day laundry and dry cleaning. *In room:* A/C, TV.

La Villa del Ensueño ★ This B&B in central Tlaquepaque is a lovely alternative to big-city hotels. A modern interpretation of traditional Mexican architecture, it is a delight to the eye—small courtyards and beautiful gardens bordered by old stucco walls, which have been painted in muted shades of orange oxide or covered in carefully trimmed ivy, with an occasional wrought-iron balcony or stone staircase. The rooms are individually decorated and have more character than most hotel lodgings. All contain ceiling fans. Doubles have either two twin or two double beds. Guests receive a complimentary cocktail on arrival. The hotel is about 8 blocks from the main plaza.

Florida 305, 45500 Tlaquepaque, Jal. ✆ **800/220-8689** in the U.S., or 33/3635-8792. Fax 818/597-0637 in the U.S. www.mexonline.com/ensueno.htm. 18 units. $95 double; $105 deluxe double; $117 2-bedroom unit; $140 suite. Rates include full breakfast, light laundry service. AE, MC, V. Free secured parking. **Amenities:** Bar; indoor and small outdoor pool.

Quinta Don José ★ *Value* Good value, great location, friendly English-speaking owners—there are a lot of reasons to like this small establishment just 2 blocks from Tlaquepaque's main square. Rooms run the gauntlet from medium-size to extra large. They are comfortable, attractive, and quiet, with some nice local touches. Most of the standard and deluxe doubles have a king or two double beds and an attractive, medium-size bathroom. A couple have small private outdoor spaces. Some of the suites in back come with a full kitchen and lots of space—more than twice the size of the usual suite, with one king and one double bed. The breakfasts are good, and would you believe high-speed wireless Internet connection? Some lodgings just have a good feel to them, and this is one.

Reforma 139, 45500 Tlaquepaque, Jal. ✆ **800/537-9567** (voice mail) in the U.S. and Canada, or 33/3635-7522. Fax 33/3659-9315. www.quintadonjose.com. 11 units. $70–$88 double; $105–$140 suites. Rates include full breakfast, laundry service, Internet access. AE, MC, V. Free secured parking. **Amenities:** Bar; heated outdoor pool; tour info; in-room massage; babysitting; nonsmoking rooms. *In room:* TV.

INEXPENSIVE

Hotel San Francisco Plaza ★★ *Value* This colonial-style downtown hotel is both pleasant and a bargain. Its rooms are big and comfortable, with attractive furnishings. All have rugs or carpeting, and most have tall ceilings (except in the remodeled area behind the reception desk). The hotel is built in colonial style around four courtyards, which contain fountains and potted plants. Rooms along the Sánchez Street side are much quieter now that the management has installed double windows. Some units along the back wall of the rear patio have small bathrooms. A small plaza out front gives the hotel its name. The San Francisco Plaza is 6 blocks south and 2 blocks east of the cathedral.

Degollado 267, 44100 Guadalajara, Jal. ✆ **33/3613-8954** or 33/3613-8971. Fax 33/3613-3257. 76 units. $47 double. AE, MC, V. Free parking. **Amenities:** Restaurant; limited room service; babysitting; same-day laundry and dry cleaning; ironing service. *In room:* A/C, TV.

3 Where to Dine

Guadalajara has many excellent restaurants for fine dining and for typical local fare. Most of the fine-dining spots are on the west side. Those in the Centro Histórico are uniformly bad, excepting **La Fonda de San Miguel.** Tlaquepaque has some good choices, but they all close around 8pm. Popular eateries serving good local fare are abundant, especially in the Centro Histórico. Local dishes include *birria* (goat, lamb, or pork covered in maguey leaves and roasted). It comes in a tomato-based broth or with the broth on the side. To get it properly prepared, go to one of the many *birrierías.* There are about a half dozen in Las Nueve Esquinas neighborhood, downtown; in Tlaquepaque, try **Birriería El Sope.** Another local favorite is *torta ahogada,* a sandwich with a spicy pork filling bathed in a tomato sauce. Jalisco-style *pozole* is chicken-and-hominy soup to which you add lime juice, onion, Mexican oregano, and chiles.

For a quick meal, there are several **Sanborn's** in the city. This is a popular national chain of restaurants and coffee shops; the traditional dish is *enchiladas suizas.* It's a good idea to keep your guidebook handy when taking a taxi; many drivers are unfamiliar with even the most popular places and require an address. Make reservations in the evening, especially for restaurants on the west side.

EXPENSIVE

Chez Nené ★★★ FRENCH In a small and pleasant open-air dining room in a converted house, you can enjoy a quiet and leisurely meal of delicious French food. After doing just this, I had to meet the owner to see who was behind such work. He turned out to be a French expatriate (whose Mexican wife, Nené, is the restaurant's namesake) with definite ideas about food and dining. What I had seen and tasted confirmed everything he said. Shorn of all fads and pretense, his cooking aims at the essential in a dish. Freshness and quality of ingredients are what matters for him, and everything (except stews and such) is cooked to order. The daily menu is on a chalkboard and depends on what the owner finds that morning at the market. There are always at least a dozen main courses. The waiter answered every question I put to him and gave excellent service.

Juan Polomar y Arias 426 (continuación Rafael Sauzio), west side. ✆ **33/3673-4564.** Reservations recommended on weekends. Main courses $10–$20. AE, MC, V. Tues 4–11pm; Wed–Sat 1–5:30pm and 7:30–11:30pm; Sun 1–6pm.

MODERATE

Adobe Fonda ★★★ NUEVA COCINA This charming restaurant shares space with a large store on pedestrian-only Independencia. The surroundings are lovely. The menu is inventive and thoughtfully designed. Homemade bread and tostadas come to the table with an olive oil–based chile sauce, pico de gallo, and *requezón de epazote* (ricotta-like cheese with a Mexican herb). Among the soups are delicious *crema de cilantro* and an interesting mushroom soup with a dark beer broth. The main courses present some difficult decisions, with intriguing combinations of Mexican, Italian, and Argentine ingredients: shrimp quesadillas accompanied by *chimichurri* with *nopal* cactus; filet in creamy ancho sauce; and chicken breast in cashew and poblano chile sauce. Sample the margaritas, too.

Francisco de Miranda 27, corner of Independencia, Tlaquepaque. ✆ **33/3657-2792.** Main courses $8–$17. AE, MC, V. Daily 12:30–6:30pm.

Casa Fuerte MEXICAN/INTERNATIONAL Clothing designer Irene Pulos has turned her former showroom into this popular, charming patio restaurant. The setting is colorfully Mexicano: pastel walls and waiters sporting bold Pulos-designed vests. Imaginatively prepared dishes include shrimp in tamarind, stuffed chicken in *guajillo* sauce, fresh vegetable salads, steaks, and fajitas.

224-A Independencia, Tlaquepaque. ✆ **33/3639-6481.** Reservations recommended. Main courses $7–$14. AE, DISC, MC, V. Daily noon–8pm.

El Sacromonte ★★★ ALTA COCINA The food here is so exquisite that I try to dine here every time I'm in Guadalajara. El Sacromonte emphasizes artful presentation and design: Order "Queen Isabel's crown," and you'll be served a dish of shrimp woven together in the shape of a crown and covered in divine lobster-and-orange sauce. Or try quesadillas with rose petals in a deep-colored strawberry sauce. For soup, think about *el viejo progreso* for its unlikely combination of flavors (blue cheese and chipotle chile). The menu features amusing descriptions in verse that are very Latin, to say the least. The main dining area is a shaded, open-air patio with well-separated tables. The restaurant isn't far from the downtown area, on an eastbound street just 2 blocks north of Avenida Chapultepec.

Pedro Moreno 1398, west side. ✆ **33/3825-5447** or 33/3827-0663. Reservations recommended. Main courses $9–$17. MC, V. Mon–Sat 1:30pm–midnight.

Hostería del Angel ★★ TAPAS/SPANISH-ITALIAN DELI Sip wine and munch on a few tapas in this comfortable and casual restaurant and wine bar just a few blocks from the basilica in Zapopan. The chef-owner cooked for years in Spain and Italy, where he became fascinated with the making of cheeses and deli meats such as prosciutto and Spanish *jamón serrano.* He serves a variety of tapas, and his baguette sandwiches are very popular with the locals. The menu doesn't do a good job of explaining the dishes, so don't hesitate to ask the waitperson for explanations. The house specialty is the *rotolata*—vegetables and cold cuts surrounded by a thin layer of crispy cheese. Live music plays from 9 to 11pm Tuesday through Saturday. The restaurant is half a block off the pedestrian-only calzada, which leads to the plaza in front of the basilica.

5 de Mayo 295, Zapopan, west side. ✆/fax **33/3656-9516.** Reservations recommended. Menu items $4–$7. MC, V. Tues–Sat 9am–midnight; Sun 9am–8pm.

I Latina FUSION Warehouse chic with a porcine motif (the owner tells me that the pig is a symbol of abundance in Thailand) is the setting here. Naturally, the well-prepared menu must exhibit sophistication, which it does with carpaccio here, portobellos there—you probably get the picture. I had a stir-fry of chicken flavored with ginger, and a salad with greens, fried rice noodles, and citrus-flavored dressing. I also enjoyed people-watching. The furniture—metal and plastic—is completely in character yet comfortable. There's live music Thursday from 9 to 11pm and Sunday afternoon. Go early if you want to avoid the rush, and make reservations—this restaurant is *popularísimo.*

Av. Inglaterra, west side. ✆ **33/3647-7774.** Reservations recommended. Main courses $7–$15. MC, V. Wed–Sat 7:30pm–1am; Sun 2–6pm.

La Destilería ★★ MEXICAN You know that with a name like "The Distillery," tequila will somehow be involved. Although this museum-restaurant abounds with artifacts, photos, and curios depicting every stage of the tequila-making process, the food is what really pulls in the *tapatíos.* This place is almost sure to please everyone. Specialties include *molcajete de la casa*—steaming fajitas, *rajas* (chile strips), cheese, onion, and avocado in a large, sizzling *molcajete* (three-legged stone mortar). The steak dish *medallones a la poblana* is memorable, as is the delicately flavored fish in parsley sauce. You can order salads here without hesitation (all greens are washed in antimicrobial solution), and the dessert menu includes such favorites as *pastel de tres leches.* And, with its vast selection of tequilas, it's the perfect place to do a little tasting. La Destilería is 5 blocks northwest of Fuente Minerva.

Av. Mexico 2916 (corner of Nelson), Fraccionamiento (division). Terranova, west side. ✆ **33/3640-3440** or 33/3640-3110. Reservations recommended. Main courses $9–$14. AE, MC, V. Mon–Sat 1pm–midnight; Sun 1–6pm.

La Fonda de San Miguel ★★ *Moments* MEXICAN My favorite way to enjoy a good meal in Mexico is to have it in an elegant colonial courtyard. I love the contrast between the bright, noisy street and the cool, serene courtyard. This restaurant is in the former convent of Santa Teresa de Jesús. (You can check out the shops and galleries as you enter.) While you enjoy the stone arches and gurgling fountain, little crisp tacos, pumpkin bread, and mildly spiced butter awaken the appetite. For main courses, try *chiles en nogada* (a combination of spicy and sweet) if it's in season, or perhaps a traditional *mole poblano.* The restaurant is 4 blocks west and 1 block south of the cathedral, between Pedro Moreno and Morelos.

Donato Guerra 25, downtown. ✆ **33/3613-0809.** Reservations recommended on weekends. Breakfast $5; main courses $9–$16. AE, MC, V. Sun–Mon 9am–6pm; Tues–Sat 9am–midnight.

La Trattoria Pomodoro Ristorante ★ ITALIAN Good food, good service, and moderate prices make this restaurant perennially popular. The price of pastas and main courses includes a visit to the well-stocked salad bar. Recommendable menu items include the combination pasta plate (lasagna, fettuccini Alfredo, and spaghetti), shrimp linguini, and chicken parmigiana. The Italian owner likes to stock lots of wines from the motherland. The dining room is attractive and casual, with comfortable furniture and separate seating for smokers and nonsmokers. Reservations are not accepted during holidays.

Niños Héroes 3051, west side. ✆ **33/3122-1817.** Reservations recommended. Pasta $7–$9; main courses $8–$10. AE, MC, V. Daily 1pm–midnight. Free parking.

Mariscos Progreso SEAFOOD On a large, open patio shaded by trees and tile roofs, waiters navigate among the tables carrying large platters of delicious seafood. Mexicans do a wonderful job with seafood, and this popular restaurant does the tradition proud.

Grilling over charcoal is the specialty here, but the kitchen's repertoire includes all the Mexican standards. For a sampling of grilled favorites, try the *parrillada* for two. Sometimes there's quite a bit of *ambiente,* with mariachis adding to the commotion. At other times, the crowd thins and one can rest peacefully from the exertions of shopping with a cold drink. It's half a block from the Parián.

Progreso 80, Tlaquepaque. ✆ **33/3657-4995.** Reservations not accepted. Main courses $7–$14. AE, MC, V. Daily 11am–7pm.

INEXPENSIVE

Café Madrid MEXICAN This little coffee shop is like many coffee shops used to be—a social institution where people come in, greet each other and the staff by name, and chat over breakfast or coffee and cigarettes. Change comes slowly here. For example, despite the fact that it's an informal place, the waiters wear white jackets with black bow ties, as they did 20 years ago. The coffee and Mexican breakfasts are good, as is the standard Mexican fare served in the afternoon. The front room opens to the street, with a small lunch counter and another room in the back.

Juárez 264, downtown. ✆ **33/3614-9504.** Breakfast $2–$4; main courses $3–$6. No credit cards. Daily 7:30am–10:30pm. From the Plaza de Armas, walk 1 block on Corona to Juárez and turn right; the cafe is on the right.

La Chata Restaurant REGIONAL/MEXICAN This popular downtown spot offers good standards at reasonable prices. Aromas waft into the street from the kitchen in front, where women with their heads wrapped in bandanas busily stir, chop, and fry. Past this is a large dining area. Local dishes include *pozole* (chicken, pork, and hominy in a broth to which you add onions, radishes, chile, and oregano) and *torta ahogada* (a spicy pork sandwich bathed in sauce). If you're very hungry, the sampler platter of *antojitos* for four people will fill the bill. Or try the *plato combinado* (mole, chile relleno, rice and beans).

Corona 126 (between Juárez and López Cotilla), downtown. ✆ **33/3613-0588.** Reservations not accepted. Breakfast $3–$5; main courses $4–$7. AE, DC, MC, V. Daily 8am–11:30pm. From the Plaza de Armas, walk 1½ blocks south on Corona; La Chata is on the right.

Los Itacates Restaurant ★★ *Value* MEXICAN This is the Mexican equivalent of down-home cooking—nothing exotic or unheard-of, just well-prepared traditional food. This place, popular with office workers, is packed during the afternoon dinner hour (2–4pm), but at other times it's easy to find a table. The atmosphere is bright and colorful. You can dine outdoors at shaded sidewalk tables or in one of the three interior rooms. Specialties include *pozole, lomo adobado* (baked pork in dark chile sauce), and chiles rellenos. *Pollo Itacates* is a quarter of a chicken, two cheese enchiladas, potatoes, and rice. Los Itacates is 5 blocks north of Avenida Vallarta. Chapultepec Norte 110, west side. ✆ **33/3825-1106** or 33/3825-9551. Reservations recommended on weekends and holidays. Breakfast buffet $4; tacos 50¢; main courses $3–$7. MC, V. Mon–Sat 8am–11pm; Sun 8am–7pm.

7

Exploring Guadalajara & Beyond

Guadalajara is one of the most Mexican of Mexico's cities. Spend a few days exploring its historic downtown area, with all its cultural and architectural highlights, parks, and attractions, and even the most hard-core resort tourist will realize there is much more to Mexico than sandy beaches and souvenir shops.

1 What to See & Do in Guadalajara

SPECIAL EVENTS IN GUADALAJARA

There's always something going on from September to December. In September, when Mexicans celebrate independence from Spain, Guadalajara goes all out, with a full month of festivities. The celebrations kick off with the **Encuentro Internacional del Mariachi,** in which mariachi bands from around the world play before knowledgeable audiences and rehearse with other mariachis. Bands come from as far as Japan and Russia, and the event takes on a curious postmodern hue. There are concerts in several venues. In the Degollado Theater, you can hear orchestral arrangements of classic mariachi songs with solos by famous mariachis. You might be acquainted with many of the classics without even knowing it. The culmination is a parade of thousands of mariachis and *charros* (Mexican cowboys) through downtown. Catch it if you're there during the first 10 days of September.

On **September 15,** a massive crowd assembles in front of the Governor's Palace to await the traditional *grito* (shout for independence) at 11pm. The *grito* commemorates Father Miguel Hidalgo de Costilla's cry for independence in 1810. The celebration features live music on a street stage, spontaneous dancing, fireworks, and shouts of "*¡Viva México!*" and "*¡Viva Hidalgo!*" The next day is the official Independence Day, with a traditional parade; the plazas downtown resemble a country fair and market, with booths, games of chance, stuffed-animal prizes, cotton candy, and candied apples. Live entertainment stretches well into the night.

Downtown Guadalajara

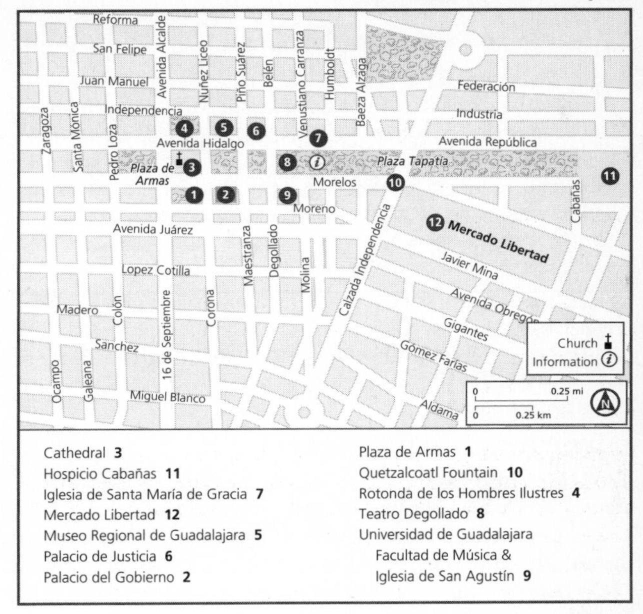

On **October 12,** a **procession** honoring Our Lady of Zapopan celebrates the feast day of the Virgin of Zapopan. Around dawn, her small, dark figure begins the 5-hour ride from the Cathedral of Guadalajara to the suburban Basilica of the Virgin of Zapopan (see "Other Attractions," below). The original icon dates from the mid-1500s; the procession began 200 years later. Today, crowds spend the night along the route and vie for position as the Virgin approaches. She travels in a gleaming new car (virginal in that it must never have had the ignition turned on), which her caretakers pull through the streets. During the previous months, the figure visits churches all over the city. You will likely see neighborhoods decorated with paper streamers and banners honoring the Virgin's visit.

The celebration has grown into a month-long event, **Fiestas de Octubre,** which kicks off with an enormous parade, usually on the first Sunday or Saturday of the month. Festivities include performing arts, rodeos *(charreadas),* bullfights, art exhibits, regional dancing, a food fair, and a Day of Nations incorporating all the consulates in Guadalajara. By the time this is over, you enter the

Fun Fact A Famous Native Son

José Clemente Orozco (1883–1949), my favorite Mexican muralist, was a native son of Guadalajara and remains a presence today. Orozco is known for his dramatic use of proportion and perspective. Three of his murals appear at the **Palacio del Gobierno;** he is also represented at the **Museo de las Artes de la Universidad de Guadalajara.** The **Instituto Cultural Cabañas** displays smaller works by the master as well as murals executed by Orozco in 1937, at the height of his powers.

holiday season of November and December, with Revolution Day (Nov 20), the Virgin of Guadalupe's saint's day (Dec 12), and several other celebrations.

DOWNTOWN GUADALAJARA

The most easily recognized building in the city is the **cathedral** ★, around which four open plazas make the shape of a Latin cross. Later, a long swath of land was cleared to extend the open area from the cathedral east to the Hospicio Cabañas, creating **Plaza Tapatía.**

Construction on the cathedral started in 1561 and continued into the 18th century. Over such a long time, it was inevitable that remodeling would take place before the building was ever completed. The result is an unusual facade that is an amalgam of several architectural styles, including baroque, neoclassical, and Gothic. An 1818 earthquake destroyed the original large towers; their replacements were built in the 1850s, inspired by designs on the bishop's dinner china. The blue and yellow that you see are Guadalajara's colors. The interior is open, airy, and majestic. Items of interest include a painting in the sacristy ascribed to the renowned 17th-century Spanish artist Bartolomé Estaban Murillo (1617–82).

To the cathedral's left is the **Plaza de Armas,** the oldest and loveliest of the plazas. A cast-iron Art Nouveau bandstand is its dominant feature. Made in France, it was a gift to the city from the dictator Porfirio Díaz in the 1890s. The female figures on the bandstand exhibited too little clothing for conservative Guadalajarans, who clothed them. The dictator, recognizing when it's best to let the people have their way, said nothing.

Facing the plaza is the **Palacio del Gobierno** ★★. This handsome palace, built in 1774, blends Spanish and Moorish elements. Inside the central courtyard, above the staircase to the right, is a spectacular mural of Hidalgo by the modern Mexican master José Clemente Orozco. The Father of Independence appears high overhead, bearing directly down on the viewer and looking as implacable as a force of nature. On one of the adjacent walls Orozco painted *The Carnival of Ideologies,* a dark satire on the prevailing fanaticisms of his day. Another of his murals is inside the second-floor chamber of representatives, depicting Hidalgo again, this time in a more conventional posture, writing the proclamation to end slavery in Mexico. The palacio is open daily from 10am to 8pm.

In the plaza on the opposite side of the cathedral from the Plaza de Armas is the **Rotonda de los Hombres Ilustres.** Sixteen white columns, each supporting a bronze statue, stand as monuments to Guadalajara's and Jalisco's distinguished sons.

Facing the east side of the rotunda is the **Museo Regional de Guadalajara,** Liceo 60 (**© 33/3614-9957**). Originally a convent, it was built in 1701 in the churrigueresque (Mexican baroque) style and contains some of the region's important archaeological finds, fossils, historic objects, and art. Among the highlights are a giant reconstructed mammoth's skeleton and a meteorite weighing 1,715 pounds, discovered in Zacatecas in 1792. On the first floor, there's a fascinating exhibit of pre-Hispanic pottery, and some exquisite pottery and clay figures recently unearthed near Tequila during the construction of the toll road. On the second floor is a small ethnography exhibit of the contemporary dress of the state's indigenous peoples, including the Coras, Huicholes, Mexicaneros, Nahuas, and Tepehuanes. It's open Tuesday through Sunday from 9am to 5:45pm. Admission is $2.50 for adults, $1 for children.

Behind the Cathedral is the Plaza de la Liberación, with the **Teatro Degollado** (deh-goh-*yah*-doh) on the opposite side. This neoclassical 19th-century opera house was named for Santos Degollado, a local patriot who fought with Juárez against Maximilian and the French. Apollo and the nine muses decorate the theater's pediment, and the interior is famous for both the acoustics and the rich decoration. It hosts a variety of performances during the year, including the Ballet Folclórico on Sunday at 10am. It's open Monday through Friday from 10am to 2pm and during performances (see "Guadalajara After Dark," later in this chapter, for more information).

To the right of the theater, across the street, is the sweet little **church of Santa María de Gracia,** built in 1573 as part of a convent for Dominican nuns. On the opposite side of the Teatro Degollado is the **church of San Agustín.** The former convent is now the **University of Guadalajara School of Music.**

Behind the Teatro Degollado begins the Plaza Tapatía, which leads to the Instituto Cabañas. It passes between a couple of low, modern office buildings. The Tourism Information Office is in a building on the right-hand side.

Beyond these office buildings, the plaza opens into a large expanse, now framed by department stores and offices and dominated by the abstract modern **Quetzalcoatl Fountain.** This fluid steel structure represents the mythical plumed serpent Quetzalcoatl, who figured so prominently in pre-Hispanic religion and culture, and exerts a presence even today.

At the far end of the plaza is the Hospicio Cabañas, formerly an orphanage and known today as the **Instituto Cultural Cabañas** ★★, Cabañas 8 (✆ **33/3617-4322**). This vast structure is impressive for both its size (more than 23 courtyards) and its grandiose architecture, especially the cupola. Created by the famous Mexican architect Manuel Tolsá, it housed homeless children from 1829 to 1980. Today, it's a thriving cultural center offering art shows and classes. The interior walls and ceiling of the main building display murals painted by Orozco in 1937. His *Man of Fire,* in the dome, is said to represent the spirit of humanity projecting itself toward the infinite. Other rooms hold additional Orozco works, as well as excellent contemporary art and temporary exhibits.

Just south of the Hospicio Cabañas (to the left as you exit) is the **Mercado Libertad** ★, Guadalajara's gigantic covered central market, the largest in Latin America. This site has been a market plaza since the 1500s; the present buildings date from the early 1950s (see "Shopping," below).

OTHER ATTRACTIONS

At **Parque Agua Azul (Blue Water Park),** plants, trees, shrubbery, statues, and fountains create a perfect refuge from the bustling city. Many people come here to exercise early in the morning. The park is open daily from 7am to 6pm. Admission is $1 for adults, 50¢ for children.

Across Independencia from the park, cater-cornered from a small flower market, is the **Museo de Arqueología del Occidente de México,** Calzada Independencia at Avenida del Campesino. It houses a fine collection of pre-Hispanic pottery from Jalisco,

Nayarit, and Colima. The museum is open Tuesday through Sunday from 10am to 2pm and 4 to 7pm. There's a small admission charge.

The state-run **Casa de las Artesanías** (© **33/3619-4664**) is at the Instituto de la Artesanía Jalisciense, just past the park entrance at Calzada Independencia and González Gallo (for details, see "Shopping," below).

Also near the park is Guadalajara's rodeo arena, **Lienzo Charro de Jalisco** (© **33/3619-0315**). Mexican cowboys, known as *charros,* are famous for their riding and lasso work, and the arena in Guadalajara is considered the big time. There are shows and competitions every Sunday at noon. The arena is at Avenida Dr. R. Michel 577, between González Gallo and Las Palomas.

The Basilica of the Virgin of Zapopan ★ A wide promenade several blocks long leads to a large, open plaza and the basilica. This is the religious center of Guadalajara. On the Virgin's feast day (see "Special Events in Guadalajara," above) the plaza fills with thousands of *tapatíos.* The 18th-century church is a lovely (and somewhat anachronistic) combination of baroque and plateresque styles. The cult of the Virgin of Zapopan practically began with the foundation of Guadalajara itself. She is much revered and the object of many pilgrimages. In front of the church are several stands selling religious figures and paraphernalia. On one side of the church is a lovely museum and store dedicated to the betterment of the Huichol Indians. It is well worth a visit.

Main Plaza, Zapopan (10km/6 miles northwest of downtown). No phone. Free admission. Daily 7am–7pm; museum daily 10am–7pm.

Museo de las Artes de la Universidad de Guadalajara This museum books many important traveling exhibitions. An early show featured contemporary artists from all over the Americas. Several rooms house the university's permanent collection, consisting mainly of works by Mexican and Jaliscan artists. There are also some bold Orozco murals: On one wall of the auditorium and the cupola above are *Man, Creator and Rebel* and *The People and Their False Leaders.* The museum is a short ride west of downtown, across from the University of Guadalajara.

Juárez 975. © **33/3625-7553.** Admission $2. Tues–Sat 10am–8pm; Sun and holidays noon–8pm.

Museo de la Ciudad This fine museum, which opened in 1992 in a former convent, chronicles Guadalajara's fascinating past. The eight rooms, beginning on the right and proceeding in chronological order, cover the period from just before the city's founding to the present. Unusual artifacts, including rare Spanish armaments and equestrian paraphernalia, give a sense of what day-to-day life was like. As you browse, dust off your Spanish and read the explanations, which give details of interest.

Independencia 684 (at M. Barcena). ✆ **33/3658-2531.** Free admission. Tues–Sun 10am–5pm.

2 Shopping

Many visitors to Guadalajara come specifically for the shopping in Tlaquepaque and Tonalá (see below). If you have little free time, try the government-run **Instituto de la Artesanía Jalisciense** ★, González Gallo 20 at Calzada Independencia (✆ **33/3619-4664**), in Parque Agua Azul, just south of downtown. This place is perfect for one-stop shopping, with two floors of pottery, silver jewelry, dance masks, glassware, leather goods, and regional clothing from around the state and the country. As you enter, on the right are museum displays showing crafts and regional costumes from the state of Jalisco. The craft store is open Monday through Friday from 10am to 6pm, Saturday from 10am to 5pm, Sunday from 10am to 3pm.

Guadalajara is known for its shoe industry; if you're in the market for a pair, try the **Galería del Calzado,** a shopping center made up exclusively of shoe stores. It's on the west side, about 6 blocks from Minerva Circle, at avenidas Mexico and Yaquis.

Mariachis and *charros* come to Guadalajara from all over Mexico to buy their highly worked belts and boots, wide-brimmed sombreros, and embroidered shirts. Several tailor shops and stores specialize in these outfits. One is **El Charro,** which has a store in the Plaza del Sol shopping center, across the street from the Hotel Presidente Inter-Continental, and one downtown on Juárez.

To view a good slice of what constitutes the material world for most Mexicans, try the mammoth **Mercado Libertad** ★ downtown. Besides food and produce, you'll see crafts, household goods, clothing, magic preparations, and more. Although it opens at 7am, the market isn't in full swing until around 10am. Come prepared to haggle.

SHOPPING IN TLAQUEPAQUE & TONALA

Almost everyone who comes to Guadalajara for the shopping has Tlaquepaque (tlah-keh-*pah*-keh) and Tonalá in mind. These two suburbs are traditional handicraft centers that produce and sell a wide variety of *artesanía.*

TLAQUEPAQUE

Located about 20 minutes from downtown, **Tlaquepaque** ★★★ has the best shopping for handicrafts and decorative arts in all of Mexico. Over the years, it has become a fashionable place, attracting talented designers in a variety of fields. Even though it's a suburb of a large city, it has a cozy, small-town feel; it's a pleasure simply to stroll through the central streets from shop to shop. No one hassles you; no one does the hard sell. There are some excellent places to eat (see "Where to Dine," in chapter 6), or you can grab some simple fare at **El Parián,** a building in the middle of town that houses a number of small eateries.

A taxi from downtown Guadalajara costs $6 (depending on where you are on the west side, it can be $7 to $9), or you can take one of the deluxe **Turquesa buses** that make a fairly quick run from downtown to Tlaquepaque and Tonalá (see "Getting Around," in chapter 6).

The **Tlaquepaque Tourism Office,** Juárez 238 (✆ **33/3635-1220,** ext. 104 or 113), has a helpful, English-speaking staff. It's open Monday through Friday from 9am to 3pm. Most stores in Tlaquepaque close between 2 and 4pm and stay open until 7 or 8pm. Most are closed or have reduced hours on Sunday.

If you are interested in pottery and ceramics, two museums are worth a visit. The **Regional Ceramics Museum,** Independencia 237 (✆ **33/3635-5404**), displays several aspects of traditional Jalisco pottery as produced in Tlaquepaque and Tonalá. The high-quality examples date back several generations. Note the crosshatch design known as *petatillo* on some of the pieces; it's one of the region's oldest traditional motifs and is, like so many other motifs, a real pain to produce. Look for the wonderful old kitchen and dining room, complete with pots, utensils, and dishes. The museum is open Tuesday through Saturday from 10am to 4pm, Sunday from 10am to 1pm; admission is free. The **Museo Pantaleón Panduro** ★★★, P. Sánchez 191 (✆ **33/3635-1089,** ext. 17), is named after a famous local 19th-century artisan. It displays prize-winning pieces from the national ceramics contest held each year in Tlaquepaque, many of which exhibit astounding virtuosity. Categories include miniatures, traditional designs, and original designs. It's open Tuesday through Sunday from 10am to 6pm; admission is free. If you still haven't had your fill, the Museo Nacional de Cerámica is in Tonalá (see below).

A number of workshops permit visitors to watch artisans at work. A popular workshop is **La Rosa de Cristal,** Contreras Medillín 173, a glassblowing factory. It's open Monday through Saturday from 10am to 7pm. If you're interested in a particular craft, talk to the city tourism office; the staff can help locate workshops that are open to the public.

The following list of Tlaquepaque shops will give you an idea of what to expect. This is just a small fraction of what you'll find; the best approach might be to just follow your nose. The main shopping is along **Independencia,** a pedestrian-only street that starts at El Parián. You can go door-to-door visiting the shops until the street ends, then work your way back on **Calle Juárez,** the next street over, north of Independencia.

Agustín Parra So you bought an old hacienda and are trying to restore its chapel—where do you go to find traditional baroque sculpture, religious art, gold-leafed objects, and even entire *retablos*? Parra is famous for exactly this kind of work, and the store is lovely. It's open Monday through Saturday from 10am to 7pm. Independencia 158. ✆ **33/3657-8530.**

Bazar Hecht One of the village's longtime favorites. Here you'll find wood objects, handmade furniture, and a few antiques. It's open Monday through Saturday from 10am to 2:30pm and 3:30 to 7pm. Juárez 162. ✆ **33/3657-0316.**

Casa Canela One of the most elegant stores in Tlaquepaque, this is a feast for the eyes. Browse through rooms full of furniture and decorative objects. It's open Monday through Friday from 10am to 2pm and 3 to 7pm, Saturday from 10am to 6pm, and Sunday from 11am to 3pm. Independencia 258, near Calle Cruz Verde. ✆ **33/3635-3717.**

Tips Packing It In

If you need your purchases packed safely so that you can check them as extra baggage, or if you want them shipped, talk to **Margaret del Rio.** She is an American who runs a large packing and shipping company at Juárez 347, Tlaquepaque (✆ **33/3657-5652**). Paying the excess baggage fee usually is cheaper than shipping but less convenient.

Sergio Bustamante Sergio Bustamante's imaginative, original bronze, ceramic, and papier-mâché sculptures are among the most sought-after in Mexico—as well as the most copied. He also designs silver jewelry. This exquisite gallery showcases his work. It's open Monday through Saturday from 10am to 7pm, Sunday from 11am to 4pm. Independencia 236 at Cruz Verde. ✆ **33/3639-5519.**

Tete Arte y Diseño Architectural decorative objects mix with pottery, antiques, glassware, and paintings at this shop. It's open Monday through Saturday from 10am to 7pm. Juárez 173. ✆ **33/3635-7347.**

Tierra Tlaquepaque Here you'll find unusual, rustic, and finely finished pottery, as well as wood sculptures, table textiles, and decorative objects. Open Monday through Saturday from 10am to 7pm, Sunday from 11am to 5pm. Independencia 156. ✆ **33/3635-9770.**

TONALÁ: A TRADITION OF POTTERY MAKING

Tonalá ★★ is a pleasant, modest town not far from Tlaquepaque. The streets were paved only recently, and there aren't any fancy shops: You will find Tonalá easier on the wallet than Tlaquepaque. The village has been a center of pottery making since pre-Hispanic times; half of the more than 400 workshops here produce a wide variety of high- and low-temperature pottery. Other local artists work with forged iron, cantera stone, brass and copper, marble, miniatures, papier-mâché, textiles, blown glass, and gesso. This is a good place to look for custom work in any of these materials; you can locate a large pool of craftspeople by asking around a little.

Market days are Thursday and Sunday. Expect large crowds, and blocks and blocks of stalls displaying locally made pottery and glassware, as well as cheap manufactured goods, food, and all kinds of bric-a-brac. "Herb men" sell a rainbow selection of dried medicinal herbs from wheelbarrows; magicians entertain crowds with sleight-of-hand; and craftspeople spread their colorful wares on the plaza's sidewalks. I prefer to visit Tonalá on non-market days, when it's much easier to get around and see the glass and pottery stores. This is the place for buying sets of margarita glasses, the widely seen blue-rimmed rustic glassware, as well as the pottery typically associated with Mexico and finely painted *petatillo* ware.

The **Tonalá Tourism Office** (✆ **33/3683-1740;** fax 33/3683-0590) is in the Artesanos building, set back from the road at Atonaltecas 140 Sur (the main street leading into Tonalá) at Matamoros. Hours are Monday through Friday from 9am to 3pm, Saturday from 9am to 1pm. The office offers free walking tours on Monday, Tuesday, Wednesday, and Friday at 9am and 2pm, and Saturday at 9am and 1pm. They include visits to artisans' workshops (where you'll see ceramics, stoneware, blown glass, papier-mâché, and the like). Tours last 3 to 4 hours and require a minimum of five people. Visitors can request an English-speaking guide. Also in Tonalá, cater-cornered from the church, you'll see a small tourism information kiosk that's staffed on market days and provides maps and useful information.

Tonalá is also the home of the **Museo Nacional de Cerámica,** Constitución 104, between Hidalgo and Morelos (✆ **33/3683-0494**). The museum occupies a two-story mansion and displays work from Jalisco and all over the country. There's a large shop in the front on the right as you enter. The museum is open Tuesday through Friday from 10am to 5pm, and Saturday and Sunday from 10am to 2pm. Admission is free; the fee for using a video or still camera is $8.50 per camera.

3 Guadalajara After Dark

FOLKLORIC BALLET

Ballet Folclórico de la Universidad de Guadalajara ★★ This dance company, acclaimed as the finest of its kind in Mexico, performs traditional dances from Jalisco and other parts of the country. For more than a decade, it has been performing at the Degollado Theater. Performances are on Sunday at 10am. Teatro Degollado, Plaza Tapatía. ✆ **33/3614-4773** or 33/3613-1115. Tickets $3–$17. Ticket office daily 10am–1pm and 4–7pm.

MARIACHIS

You can't go far in Guadalajara without coming across some mariachis, but seeing really talented performers takes some effort. Try La Feria, listed below, or **Casa Bariachi,** Av. Vallarta 2221 (✆ **33/3615-0029**). In Tlaquepaque, go to **El Parián,** the building on the town square where mariachis serenade diners under the archways.

THE CLUB & MUSIC SCENE

Guadalajara, as you might expect, has a lot of variety in entertainment. For the most extensive listing of clubs and performances, get your hands on a copy of *Ocio,* the weekly insert of *Público.* You'll find listings in the back, broken down by type of music.

Bar Copenhagen 77 On weekends, this snug little den with upholstered walls and wood trim is the perfect setting for catching a little modern jazz. The house band of three to five musicians plays bebop and Latin jazz on Friday and Saturday nights. Monday through Thursday it's classical guitar. You can have just drinks, or you can order from the small, well-thought-out menu; the specialty is paella. The club faces the Parque de la Revolución (along Juárez, 9 blocks west of the Plaza de Armas), on your left as you walk down López Cotilla. Marcos Castellanos 140-Z. ✆ **33/3826-7306.** No cover. Restaurant Mon–Sat 2pm–1am; music begins at 9pm.

El Cubilete *El Cubilete* (the dice cup) is a small club tucked away in an old downtown neighborhood called Las Nueve Esquinas (The Nine Corners). This up-and-coming area has a couple of other clubs that are worth checking out. The house band, Son de Cuba, plays a number of salsa and *cumbia* standards from Wednesday to Saturday, but doesn't get going until about 10:30. Gral. Río Seco 9. ✆ **33/3658-0406** or 33/3613-2096. $5 cover on weekends. Mon–Sat 2pm–1am; live salsa Wed–Sat 10:30pm–1am.

La Feria To get a good sampling of local color, try this multilevel restaurant and bar with a center stage. The afternoon and nighttime shows feature a variety of acts, including a great mariachi band, some very impressive (and expressive) singers, a *charro* who performs rope tricks, some *ballet folklórico* dancers, bawdy comedy acts, and a few games involving the audience. The owner promised a free drink to anyone who shows a Frommer's book—so hold him to it. You might want to try a *paloma,* the most popular tequila drink in Guadalajara. The menu is Mexican, with an emphasis on grilled meats. La Feria is downtown, 5 blocks south of the Plaza de Armas. Corona 291. ✆ **33/3613-7150** or 33/3613-1812. Reservations recommended. No cover. Daily noon–3am. Variety show at 3:30 and 10pm.

4 Side Trips from Guadalajara

TEQUILA: THE NAME SAYS IT ALL

Tequila is an entertaining (and intoxicating) town, well worth a day trip from Guadalajara. Several taxi drivers charge about $55 to take you to the town, get you into a tour of a distillery, take you to a restaurant, and haul you back to Guadalajara. A few of them speak English. One driver is José Gabriel Gómez (✆ **33/3649-0791** at home; jgabriel-taxi@hotmail.com), who has a new car and drives carefully. Call him in the evening. Tour companies also arrange bus trips to Tequila; see a travel agency in Guadalajara.

Tequila has many distilleries, including the famous brands **Sauza** and **José Cuervo.** All the distilleries—the big, modern ones and the small, more traditional ones—offer tours. If you're on your own, a good place to hook up with a tour is at the little booth outside the city hall on the main square. Two young women who speak English run tours to any of the local factories. The tour costs only $5 and lasts about 2 hours. All tours show how tequila is made, what traditions the process follows, and what differences exist between tequilas; they end, of course, with a tasting. Avenida Vallarta runs straight to the highway to Tequila, which is about an hour outside of Guadalajara.

Another approach is to take the **Tequila Express** ★★ to the town of Amatitán, home of the Herradura distillery. It leaves from the train station on Friday and Saturday, and sometimes on Sunday during vacation and holiday season. You need to be there by 10am. Buy your ticket ahead of time. The Guadalajara Chamber of Commerce (Cámara de Comercio), at Vallarta and Niño Obrero (✆ **33/3880-9099**), organizes this trip. Buy tickets at the main office; at the small office in the Centro Histórico at Morelos 395, at Calle Colón (no phone); or through Ticketmaster (✆ **33/3818-3800**). Office hours are Monday through Friday from 9am to 2 pm and 4 to 6pm. Tickets cost $60 for adults, $35 for children 6 to 12. The tour includes an open bar with tequila tasting that begins on the train, a visit to the Hacienda San José del Refugio, a tour of a distillery, dinner, and, of course, mariachis. It returns to Guadalajara at about 8pm. Travel time is 1¾ hours each way.

Appendix: Useful Terms, Phrases & Information

1 Telephones & Mail

USING THE TELEPHONES

All phone numbers listed in this book have a total of 10 digits—a two- or three-digit area code plus the telephone number. Local numbers in Mexico City, Guadalajara, and Monterrey are eight digits; everywhere else, local numbers have seven digits.

To call long distance within Mexico, dial the national long-distance code **01** before dialing the area code and then the number. Mexico's area codes *(claves)* are listed in the front of telephone directories. Area codes are listed before all phone numbers in this book. For long-distance dialing, you will often see the term "LADA," which is the automatic long-distance service offered by Telmex, Mexico's former telephone monopoly and its largest phone company. To make a person-to-person or collect call inside Mexico, dial ✆ **020.** You can also call 020 to request the correct area codes for the number and place you are calling.

To make a long-distance call to the United States or Canada, dial ✆ **001,** then the area code and seven-digit number. For international long-distance numbers in Europe, Africa, and Asia, dial ✆ **00,** then the country code, the city code, and the number. To make a person-to-person or collect call to outside Mexico, to obtain other international dialing codes, or for further assistance, dial ✆ **090.**

For additional details on making calls in Mexico and to Mexico, see p. 58.

POSTAL GLOSSARY

Airmail **Correo Aéreo**
Customs **Aduana**
General delivery **Lista de correos**
Insurance (insured mail) **Seguro (correo asegurado)**
Mailbox **Buzón**

Money order **Giro postal**
Parcel **Paquete**
Postal service **Correos**
Post office **Oficina de correos**
Post office box (abbreviation) **Apdo. Postal**
Registered mail **Registrado**
Rubber stamp **Sello**
Special delivery, express **Entrega inmediata**
Stamp **Estampilla** or **timbre**

2 Basic Vocabulary

Most Mexicans are very patient with foreigners who try to speak their language; it helps a lot to know a few basic phrases. I've included simple phrases for expressing basic needs, followed by some common menu items.

ENGLISH-SPANISH PHRASES

English	Spanish	Pronunciation
Good day	**Buen día**	bwehn *dee*-ah
Good morning	**Buenos días**	*bweh*-nohss *dee*-ahss
How are you?	**¿Cómo está?**	*koh*-moh ehss-*tah?*
Very well	**Muy bien**	mwee byehn
Thank you	**Gracias**	*grah*-syahss
You're welcome	**De nada**	deh *nah*-dah
Good-bye	**Adiós**	ah-*dyohss*
Please	**Por favor**	pohr fah-*vohr*
Yes	**Sí**	see
No	**No**	noh
Excuse me	**Perdóneme**	pehr-*doh*-neh-meh
Give me	**Déme**	*deh*-meh
Where is . . . ?	**¿Dónde está . . . ?**	*dohn*-deh ehss-t*ah?*
the station	**la estación**	lah ehss-tah-*syohn*
a hotel	**un hotel**	oon oh-*tehl*
a gas station	**una gasolinera**	*oo*-nah gah-soh-lee-*neh*-rah
a restaurant	**un restaurante**	oon res-tow-*rahn*-teh
the toilet	**el baño**	el *bah*-nyoh
a good doctor	**un buen médico**	oon bwehn *meh*-dee-coh
the road to . . .	**el camino a/ hacia . . .**	el cah-*mee*-noh ah/ *ah*-syah

To the right	**A la derecha**	ah lah deh-*reh*-chah
To the left	**A la izquierda**	ah lah ees-*kyehr*-dah
Straight ahead	**Derecho**	deh-*reh*-choh
I would like	**Quisiera**	key-*syeh*-rah
I want	**Quiero**	*kyeh*-roh
to eat	**comer**	koh-*mehr*
a room	**una habitación**	*oo*-nah ah-bee-tah-*yohn*
Do you have . . . ?	**¿Tiene usted . . . ?**	tyeh-neh oo-*sted?*
a book	**un libro**	oon *lee*-broh
a dictionary	**un diccionario**	oon deek-syow-*nah*-ryo
How much is it?	**¿Cuánto cuesta?**	*kwahn*-toh *kwehss*-tah?
When?	**¿Cuándo?**	*kwahn*-doh?
What?	**¿Qué?**	keh?
There is (Is there . . . ?)	**(¿)Hay (. . . ?)**	eye?
What is there?	**¿Qué hay?**	keh eye?
Yesterday	**Ayer**	ah-*yer*
Today	**Hoy**	oy
Tomorrow	**Mañana**	mah-*nyah*-nah
Good	**Bueno**	*bweh*-noh
Bad	**Malo**	*mah*-loh
Better (best)	**(Lo) Mejor**	(loh) meh-*hohr*
More	**Más**	mahs
Less	**Menos**	*meh*-nohss
No smoking	**Se prohibe fumar**	seh proh-*ee*-beh foo-*mahr*
Postcard	**Tarjeta postal**	tar-*heh*-ta pohs-*tahl*
Insect repellent	**Repelente contra insectos**	reh-peh-*lehn*-te *cohn*-trah een-*sehk*-tos

MORE USEFUL PHRASES

English	Spanish	Pronunciation
Do you speak English?	**¿Habla usted inglés?**	ah-blah oo-*sted* een-*glays?*
Is there anyone here who speaks English?	**¿Hay alguien aquí qué hable inglés?**	eye *ahl*-ghee-en ah-key kay *ah*-blay een-*glays?*
I speak a little Spanish.	**Hablo un poco de español.**	*ah*-blow oon *poh*-koh day ess-pah-*nyol*

I don't understand Spanish very well	**No (lo) entiendo muy bien el español.**	noh (loh) ehn-tee-*ehn*-do myee bee-ayn el ess-pah-*nyol*
The meal is good.	**Me gusta la comida.**	meh *goo*-stah lah koh-*mee*-dah
What time is it?	**¿Qué hora es?**	keh *oh*-rah ehss?
May I see your menu?	**¿Puedo ver el menú (la carta)?**	*pueh*-do vehr el meh-*noo* (lah *car*-tah)?
The check, please.	**La cuenta, por favor.**	lah *quehn*-tah pohr fa-*vorh*
What do I owe you?	**¿Cuánto le debo?**	*kwahn*-toh leh *deh*-boh?
What did you say?	**¿Mande?** (formal) **¿Cómo?** (informal)	*mahn*-deh? *koh*-moh?
I want (to see) . . .	**Quiero (ver) . . .**	*kyeh*-roh vehr
a room	**un cuarto** or **una habitación**	oon *kwar*-toh, *oo*-nah ah-bee-tah*syohn*
for two persons	**para dos personas**	*pah*-rah dohss pehr-*soh*-nahs
with (without) bathroom	**con (sin) baño.**	kohn (seen) *bah*-nyoh
We are staying here only	**Nos quedamos aquí solamente**	nohs keh-*dah*-mohss ah-*kee* soh-lah-*mehn*-teh
one night	**una noche**	*oo*-nah *noh*-cheh
one week	**una semana**	*oo*-nah seh-*mah*-nah
We are leaving tomorrow	**Partimos (Salimos) mañana**	pahr-*tee*-mohss (sah-*lee*-mohss) mah-*nya*-nah
Do you accept . . . ?	**¿Acepta usted . . . ?**	ah-*sehp*-tah oo-*sted*
. . . traveler's checks?	**. . . cheques de viajero?**	*cheh*-kehss deh byah-*heh*-roh?

Is there a laundromat?	**¿Hay una lavandería?**	eye *oo*-nah lah-*vahn*-deh-*ree*-ah
. . . near here?	**. . . cerca de aquí?**	*sehr*-kah deh ah-*kee*
Please send these clothes to the laundry	**Hágame el favor de mandar esta ropa a la lavandería.**	*ah*-gah-meh el fah-*vohr* deh mahn-*dahr* *ehss*-tah *roh*-pah a lah lah-*vahn*-deh-*ree*-ah

NUMBERS

1 **uno** (*ooh*-noh)
2 **dos** (dohs)
3 **tres** (trayss)
4 **cuatro** (*kwah*-troh)
5 **cinco** (*seen*-koh)
6 **seis** (sayss)
7 **siete** (*syeh*-tay)
8 **ocho** (*oh*-choh)
9 **nueve** (*nway*-bay)
10 **diez** (dee-ess)
11 **once** (*ohn*-say)
12 **doce** (*doh*-say)
13 **trece** (*tray*-say)
14 **catorce** (kah-*tor*-say)
15 **quince** (*keen*-say)
16 **dieciseis** (de-*ess*-ee-sayss)
17 **diecisiete** (de-*ess*-ee-*syeh*-tay)
18 **dieciocho** (dee-*ess*-ee-*oh*-choh)
19 **diecinueve** (dee-*ess*-ee-*nway*-bay)
20 **veinte** (*bayn*-tay)
30 **treinta** (*trayn*-tah)
40 **cuarenta** (kwah-*ren*-tah)
50 **cincuenta** (seen-*kwen*-tah)
60 **sesenta** (say-*sen*-tah)
70 **setenta** (say-*ten*-tah)
80 **ochenta** (oh-*chen*-tah)
90 **noventa** (noh-*ben*-tah)
100 **cien** (see-en)
200 **doscientos** (*dos*-se-en-tos)
500 **quinientos** (*keen*-ee-ehn-tos)
1000 **mil** (meal)

TRANSPORTATION TERMS

English	Spanish	Pronunciation
Airport	**Aeropuerto**	ah-eh-roh-*pwehr*-toh
Flight	**Vuelo**	*bweh*-loh
Rental car	**Arrendadora de autos**	ah-rehn-da-doh-rah deh ow-tohs
Bus	**Autobús**	ow-toh-*boos*
Bus or truck	**Camión**	ka-*myohn*
Lane	**Carril**	kah-*reel*
Nonstop	**Directo**	dee-*rehk*-toh
Baggage (claim area)	**Equipajes**	eh-kee-*pah*-hehss
Intercity	**Foraneo**	foh-rah-*neh*-oh
Luggage storage area	**Guarda equipaje**	gwar-dah eh-kee-*pah*-heh

Arrival gates	**Llegadas**	yeh-*gah*-dahss
Originates at this station	**Local**	loh-*kahl*
Originates elsewhere	**De paso**	deh *pah*-soh
Stops if seats available	**Para si hay lugares**	*pah*-rah see eye loo-*gah*-rehs
First class	**Primera**	pree-*meh*-rah
Second class	**Segunda**	seh-*goon*-dah
Nonstop	**Sin escala**	seen ess-*kah*-lah
Baggage claim area	**Recibo de equipajes**	reh-see-boh deh eh-kee-*pah*-hehss
Waiting room	**Sala de espera**	*sah*-lah deh ehss-*peh*-rah
Toilets	**Sanitarios**	sah-nee-*tah*-ryohss
Ticket window	**Taquilla**	tah-*kee*-yah

3 Menu Glossary

Botana An appetizer.

Buñuelos Round, thin, deep-fried crispy fritters dipped in sugar.

Carnitas Pork deep-cooked (not fried) in lard, and then simmered and served with corn tortillas for tacos.

Ceviche Fresh raw seafood marinated in fresh lime juice and garnished with chopped tomatoes, onions, chiles, and sometimes cilantro.

Chiles en nogada Poblano peppers stuffed with a mixture of ground pork and beef, spices, fruits, raisins, and almonds. Can be served either warm—fried in a light batter—or cold, sans the batter. Either way it is then covered in walnut-and-cream sauce.

Chiles rellenos Usually poblano peppers stuffed with cheese or spicy ground meat with raisins, rolled in a batter, and fried.

Churro Tube-shaped, breadlike fritter, dipped in sugar and sometimes filled with *cajeta* (milk-based caramel) or chocolate.

Enchilada A tortilla dipped in sauce, usually filled with chicken or white cheese, and sometimes topped with *mole* (*enchiladas rojas* or *de mole*), or with tomato sauce and sour cream (*enchiladas suizas*—Swiss enchiladas), or covered in a green sauce *(enchiladas verdes),* or topped with onions, sour cream, and guacamole *(enchiladas potosinas).*

Frijoles refritos Pinto beans mashed and cooked with lard.

Gorditas Thick, fried corn tortillas, slit and stuffed with choice of cheese, beans, beef, chicken, with or without lettuce, tomato, and onion garnish.

Huevos mexicanos Scrambled eggs with chopped onions, hot green peppers, and tomatoes.

Manchamantel Translated, means "tablecloth stainer." A stew of chicken or pork with chiles, tomatoes, pineapple, bananas, and jícama.

Masa Ground corn soaked in lime; the basis for tamales, corn tortillas, and soups.

Pan dulce Lightly sweetened bread in many configurations, usually served at breakfast or bought in any bakery.

Papadzules Tortillas stuffed with hard-boiled eggs and seeds (pumpkin or sunflower) in a tomato sauce.

Pibil Pit-baked pork or chicken in a sauce of tomato, onion, mild red pepper, cilantro, and vinegar.

Pipián A sauce made with ground pumpkin seeds, nuts, and mild peppers.

Quesadilla Corn or flour tortillas stuffed with melted white cheese and lightly fried.

Salsa verde An uncooked sauce using the green tomatillo and puréed with spicy or mild hot peppers, onions, garlic, and cilantro; on tables countrywide.

Sopa de tortilla A traditional chicken broth–based soup, seasoned with chiles, tomatoes, onion, and garlic, served with crispy fried strips of corn tortillas.

Sopa tlalpeña (or *caldo tlapeño*) A hearty soup made with chunks of chicken, chopped carrots, zucchini, corn, onions, garlic, and cilantro.

Sopa tlaxcalteca A hearty tomato-based soup filled with cooked nopal cactus, cheese, cream, and avocado, with crispy tortilla strips floating on top.

Tacos al pastor Thin slices of flavored pork roasted on a revolving cylinder dripping with onion slices and juice of fresh pineapple slices. Served in small corn tortillas, topped with chopped onion and cilantro.

Tamal Incorrectly called a tamale (*tamal* singular, *tamales* plural). A meat or sweet filling rolled with fresh *masa,* wrapped in a corn husk or banana leaf, and steamed.

Torta A sandwich, usually on *bolillo* bread, typically with sliced avocado, onions, and tomatoes, with a choice of meat and often cheese.

Zacahuil Pork leg tamal, packed in thick *masa,* wrapped in banana leaves, and pit-baked, sometimes pot-made with tomato and *masa;* a specialty of mid- to upper Veracruz.

Index

See also Accommodations, Restaurants.

General Index

Accommodations

Restaurants

FROMMER'S® MEMORABLE WALKS

Chicago
London
New York
Paris
San Francisco

FROMMER'S® WITH KIDS GUIDES

Chicago
Las Vegas
New York City
Ottawa
San Francisco
Toronto
Vancouver
Washington, D.C.

SUZY GERSHMAN'S BORN TO SHOP GUIDES

Born to Shop: France
Born to Shop: Hong Kong, Shanghai & Beijing
Born to Shop: Italy
Born to Shop: London
Born to Shop: New York
Born to Shop: Paris

FROMMER'S® IRREVERENT GUIDES

Amsterdam
Boston
Chicago
Las Vegas
London
Los Angeles
Manhattan
New Orleans
Paris
Rome
San Francisco
Seattle & Portland
Vancouver
Walt Disney World®
Washington, D.C.

FROMMER'S® BEST-LOVED DRIVING TOURS

Britain
California
Florida
France
Germany
Ireland
Italy
New England
Northern Italy
Scotland
Spain
Tuscany & Umbria

HANGING OUT™ GUIDES

Hanging Out in England
Hanging Out in Europe
Hanging Out in France
Hanging Out in Ireland
Hanging Out in Italy
Hanging Out in Spain

THE UNOFFICIAL GUIDES®

Bed & Breakfasts and Country Inns in:
  California
  Great Lakes States
  Mid-Atlantic
  New England
  Northwest
  Rockies
  Southeast
  Southwest
Best RV & Tent Campgrounds in:
  California & the West
  Florida & the Southeast
  Great Lakes States
  Mid-Atlantic
  Northeast
  Northwest & Central Plains
  Southwest & South Central Plains
  U.S.A.
Beyond Disney
Branson, Missouri
California with Kids
Central Italy
Chicago
Cruises
Disneyland®
Florida with Kids
Golf Vacations in the Eastern U.S.
Great Smoky & Blue Ridge Region
Inside Disney
Hawaii
Las Vegas
London
Maui
Mexio's Best Beach Resorts
Mid-Atlantic with Kids
Mini Las Vegas
Mini-Mickey
New England & New York with Kids
New Orleans
New York City
Paris
San Francisco
Skiing & Snowboarding in the West
Southeast with Kids
Walt Disney World®
Walt Disney World® for Grown-ups
Walt Disney World® with Kids
Washington, D.C.
World's Best Diving Vacations

SPECIAL-INTEREST TITLES

Frommer's Adventure Guide to Australia & New Zealand
Frommer's Adventure Guide to Central America
Frommer's Adventure Guide to India & Pakistan
Frommer's Adventure Guide to South America
Frommer's Adventure Guide to Southeast Asia
Frommer's Adventure Guide to Southern Africa
Frommer's Britain's Best Bed & Breakfasts and Country Inns
Frommer's Caribbean Hideaways
Frommer's Exploring America by RV
Frommer's Fly Safe, Fly Smart
Frommer's France's Best Bed & Breakfasts and Country Inns
Frommer's Gay & Lesbian Europe
Frommer's Italy's Best Bed & Breakfasts and Country Inns
Frommer's Road Atlas Britain
Frommer's Road Atlas Europe
Frommer's Road Atlas France
The New York Times' Guide to Unforgettable Weekends
Places Rated Almanac
Retirement Places Rated
Rome Past & Present